Beer Lover's Colorado

First Edition

Lee Williams

Guilford, Connecticut

All the information in this guidebook is subject to change.
We recommend that you call ahead to obtain current information
before traveling.

Copyright © 2012 Morris Book Publishing, LLC

Editor: Kevin Sirois
Project Editor: Meredith Dias
Layout Artist: Casey Shain
Text Design: Sheryl P. Kober
Maps: Alena Joy Pearce © Morris Book Publishing, LLC

ISBN 978-0-7627-8098-3

Printed in the United States of America

10 9 8 7 6 5 4 3 2 1

Contents

Introduction ix

How to Use This Guide xi

Denver 1

Breweries

Blue Moon Brewing Company
   at the Sandlot 2

Breckenridge Brewery 4

CAUTION: Brewing Company 6

Copper Kettle Brewing Company 8

Del Norte Brewing Company 10

Denver Beer Co. 11

Great Divide Brewing Company 13

Renegade Brewing Company 15

River North Brewery 17

Strange Brewing Company 18

Wit's End Brewing Company 20

Brewpubs

Bull & Bush Pub & Brewery 22

Denver ChopHouse & Brewery 24

Pint's Pub Brewery & Freehouse 25

Rock Bottom Restaurant
   & Brewery 26

Wynkoop Brewing Company 28

Beer Bars

Ale House at Amato's 30

Breckenridge Colorado Craft 30

Cheeky Monk Belgian Beer Cafe 31

Colt & Gray 31

Denver Bicycle Cafe 32

Euclid Hall Bar & Kitchen 32

Falling Rock Tap House 33

Freshcraft 34

Hops & Pie 36

Rackhouse Pub 37

Star Bar Denver 38

Vine St. Pub & Brewery 38

Wazee Supper Club 39

*Denver Area: Arvada,
Aurora, Castle Rock, Golden,
Lone Tree & Parker* 41

Breweries

AC Golden Brewing Company
   (MillerCoors) 42

Arvada Beer Company 44

Coors Brewing Company
   (MillerCoors) 45

Dry Dock Brewing Company 46

Elk Mountain Brewing 48

Golden City Brewery 50

Lone Tree Brewing Company 52

Brewpubs

Dad & Dude's Breweria 54

Rockyard American Grill & Brewing
   Company 55

Yak & Yeti Restaurant & Brewpub 56

Boulder 59

Breweries

Asher Brewing Company 60

Avery Brewing Company 62

Boulder Beer Company 64

Crystal Springs Brewing Company 66
Twisted Pine Brewing Company 68
Upslope Brewing Company 70
Brewpubs
Mountain Sun Pub & Brewery 73
Walnut Brewery 75
Beer Bars
Backcountry Pizza & Tap House 77
The West End Tavern 78

Fort Collins 81
Breweries
Anheuser-Busch, Fort Collins 82
Crooked Stave Brewing Company 84
Equinox Brewing Company 86
Fort Collins Brewery 88
Funkwerks 91
New Belgium Brewing Company 92
Odell Brewing Company 94
Pateros Creek Brewing Company 97
Brewpub
CooperSmith's Pub and Brewery 99
Beer Bars
Choice City Butcher & Deli 100
Cranknstein 100
The Mayor of Old Town 101

*Front Range: Estes Park,
Greeley, Idaho Springs,
Longmont & Loveland* 103
Breweries
Big Beaver Brewing Company 104
Crabtree Brewing Company 105

Estes Park Brewery 107
Grimm Brothers Brewhouse 109
Left Hand Brewing Company 110
Oskar Blues Brewery 113
Tommyknocker Brewery 115
Brewpubs
Pitcher's Brewery & Sports Shack 117
Pumphouse Brewery & Restaurant 118
Beer Bar
Oskar Blues Home Made Liquids
& Solids 120

*South Central: Alamosa,
Buena Vista, Colorado Springs,
Monument, Pueblo, Salida
& Woodland Park* 123
Breweries
BierWerks Brewery 124
Black Fox Brewing Company 125
Bristol Brewing Company 127
Rocky Mountain Brewery 128
Brewpubs
Amicas Pizza & Microbrewery 130
Colorado Mountain Brewery 131
Eddyline Restaurant & Brewery 132
Phantom Canyon Brewing
Company 134
Pikes Peak Brewing Co. 136
San Luis Valley Brewing Company 137
Shamrock Brewing Company 138
TRiNiTY Brewing Company 139
Beer Bar
TRiNiTY Brewing Company 141

Northwest: Aspen, Carbondale, Dillon, Eagle, Edwards, Frisco, Glenwood Springs, Grand Junction & Grand Lake 143

Breweries

Aspen Brewing Company 144

Bonfire Brewing 145

Crazy Mountain Brewing Company 147

Grand Lake Brewing Company 149

Brewpubs

Backcountry Brewery 151

Carbondale Beer Works 152

Dillon Dam Brewery 152

Glenwood Canyon Brewing Company 153

Kannah Creek Brewing Company 154

Pug Ryan's Steakhouse & Brewery 155

Rockslide Restaurant & Brewery 156

Southwest: Crested Butte, Dolores, Durango, Montrose, Ouray, Pagosa Springs, Paonia, Ridgway, Silverton & Telluride 159

Breweries

Durango Brewing Co. 160

Revolution Brewing 161

Silverton Brewing Company 163

Ska Brewing Company 164

Telluride Brewing Company 166

Brewpubs

Carver Brewing Company 168

Colorado Boy Pub & Brewery 169

Dolores River Brewery 169

Eldo Brewery and Taproom 170

Horsefly Brewing Company 171

Ouray Brewery 172

Pagosa Brewing Company 173

Smuggler Joe's Brewpub 174

Steamworks Brewing Company 174

Beer Festivals 176

BYOB: Brew Your Own Beer 183

Beer Recipes 183

In the Kitchen 196

Food Recipes 196

Beer Cocktails 202

Pub Crawls 204

Downtown Denver 204

Denver: Highland-Berkeley 207

Uptown Denver 208

South Denver 210

Boulder 212

Fort Collins 214

Appendix: Beer Lover's Pick List 218

Photo Credits 220

Index 221

About the Author

Lee Williams grew up in Bristol, England, and now resides in Denver, Colorado. In 2009 he created Hoptopia, a website, iPhone, and Android app featuring his colorful and in-depth beer reviews. Between summer 2009 and summer 2012, Hoptopia became one of the most popular beer-related sites and beer social-media brands online. (Note: Hoptopia is currently offline and is being revamped into a new project.) Lee has written for numerous beer blogs and beer festivals and sponsored one of the most popular badges (earned by tasting and checking in a wide selection of IPAs) on beer social network Untappd. Before moving to Colorado, he spent nearly a decade exploring the rich beer culture of the mid-Atlantic region. Lee lives with his longtime, beer-loving girlfriend, Stevie Caldarola.

Acknowledgments

First of all I want to say thank you to you for choosing to purchase this book. It has been an epic labor of love and to know that even a few of you will be using it to better explore the incredible beer culture in Colorado is humbling and uplifting. I hope you enjoy your beer travels around this, one of the most magnificent and beautiful places on Earth.

This challenging book would not have been possible without the infinite patience, assistance, and unending help of my designated driver, best friend and girlfriend, Stevie Caldarola. Stevie also shot many of the beautiful and insightful photographs that grace the pages of *Beer Lover's Colorado*. This book is unquestionably dedicated as much to Stevie as it is to the all of the creative and talented breweries that make beer in Colorado. So join me in raising a glass of good Colorado beer to Stevie, for without her you might not be drinking said beer.

Another person that this book definitely wouldn't exist without is my friend and fellow good-beer champion, Sean Buchan. Sean is responsible for some of the trusted designated driving during my research, and also for much of the stunning photography found within.

Other people who took time out of their busy lives to help me tell this story of modern beer culture in Colorado are Amanda Johnson at Odell Brewing Company; Jason Yester at TRiNiTY Brewing Company; Chad Yakobson at Crooked Stave Brewing Company; Andy Parker and Joe Osborne at Avery Brewing Company; Jeff and Allison Crabtree at Crabtree Brewing Company; Steve Jones at Pateros Creek Brewing Company; Lisa Zimmer at Tenth and Blake Beer Company; Jeff Cornell at AC Golden Brewing Company; Alex Violette at Upslope Brewing Company; Todd and Terry Usry and Todd Thibault at Breckenridge Brewery; Ro Guenzel, Josh Goldberg, and Emily Armstrong at Left Hand Brewing Company; Justin Lloyd at Star Bar Denver; Kevin Burke at Colt & Gray; Tony Simmons at Pagosa Brewing Company; Hanna Laney at Great Divide Brewing Company; Jeremy Gobien and Kristen Kozik at Copper Kettle Brewing Company; Anthony Paranino at Anheuser-Busch; Evan Benn at STLToday.com; Adam Nason at BeerPulse.com; Tess McFadden at Boulder Beer Company; Bryce Clark at Hatch; Jonathan Shikes at *Westword*; Jason Forgy at Freshcraft; Brittany

Dern at Oskar Blues Brewery; Chris Black at Falling Rock Tap House; Charlie Berger and Patrick Crawford at Denver Beer Co.; Kristopher Oyler at Steamworks Brewing Company; Gordon Schuck, Brad Lincoln, Andy Mitchell, and Jean Parker-Ruiz at Funkwerks; Scott Witsoe at Wit's End Brewing Company; Scott Blauweiss at Mr. B's Wine & Spirits; Shannon Westcott at Equinox Brewing Company; Leah Watson and Drew Watson at Hops & Pie; Austin Weatherford at BierWerks Brewery; Chris Wright at Pikes Peak Brewing Co.; Lacey Barron at Lone Tree Brewing Company; John McClure at Rock Bottom Restaurant & Brewery; Duncan Clauss at Aspen Brewing Company; Brian England at Eddyline Restaurant and Brewery; Bryan Simpson at New Belgium Brewing Company; Dave Welz at Ska Brewing Company; Kimberlee Ruben at Fort Collins Brewery; Aaron Heaton at Grimm Brothers Brewhouse; and countless other people. Thank you!

Introduction

It should come as no surprise that Colorado has earned the tagline "the Napa Valley of beer." Only California with more than 300 breweries, and with its 38 million people, has more breweries than Colorado. To really put things in perspective, as of the end of 2011, Colorado had a population of just over five million and more than 140 breweries. For those beer lovers not lucky enough to live in Colorado, that's 140 good reasons to visit the state.

In many ways Colorado is the quietest of America's craft beer heavyweight regions, happily thriving in the shadow of better-known beer epicenters like California and Oregon. Colorado produces more beer per capita than any other state in the nation and that cannot be wholly attributed to Coors and Anheuser-Busch having long-established and large-scale breweries based in the state.

Colorado's breweries have a history of making history. The Coors brewery in Golden is one the oldest in America and is still the largest single-site brewery in the world. Boulder Beer Company in Boulder is one of the earliest pioneering craft breweries in America, helping establish a trend that has blossomed into a global movement, and with it, big business.

Few breweries in America have done as much as New Belgium to put off-centered and previously exotic styles of beer in the hands of so many drinkers from coast to coast. New Belgium established the first legitimate sour beer program in America, inspiring countless others in its puckering wake. Colorado is a now a leader in the production of sour- and wood-aged beer.

Oskar Blues was the first craft brewery to boldy go where no craft brewery had gone before when it decided to start canning its big bold beers. Today Colorado leads the nation in canning craft beer, with three times the number of breweries distributing canned craft beer than California, its nearest rival.

Colorado has an unusually large number of regional craft breweries, businesses that early on realized the potential of selling their beer outside the state. There are more regional craft breweries in Colorado than any other state of comparable size. New Belgium, more than any other brewery in the state, optimizes this model. Few in America have not heard of New Belgium or Fat Tire. Following confidently in that brewery's expansive footsteps, the likes of Odell, Avery, Great Divide, Breckenridge, Ska, Tommyknocker, Oskar Blues, and Fort Collins soon became as well-known outside Colorado, as they were inside. This thought process and adaptive way of doing business has helped make Colorado a truly dominant, yet quietly confident player in the beer industry. Also contributing to Colorado's success is the Brewers Association, which is based in the state. Every year it hosts the Great American Beer Festival (GABF) in Denver. The GABF is the largest festival of its kind in the world. Colorado has little need to shout about its importance in the beer industry; its beers are already available far and wide, proudly speaking for the state.

As the craft beer industry matures and grows, Colorado finds itself once again leading the way forward for the industry as a whole. Several of Colorado's larger craft breweries have recently announced their intention to open large-scale breweries on the East Coast.

Few states offer visitors or its citizens the depth and breadth of homebrew-quality beer that Colorado does. It's the reason you're reading this book after all.

Welcome to Colorado, the place beer lovers like to call home.

How to Use This Guide

This book does not seek to document every single brewery in Colorado. It is instead a helpful guide to the most unique and most important breweries, brewpubs, beer bars, and beer festivals in the state.

The establishments listed in *Beer Lover's Colorado* are organized alphabetically within the following cities and regions: Denver, Denver Area, Boulder, Fort Collins, Front Range, South Central, Northwest, and Southwest.

It's important to note that the breweries in this book are production breweries, those that bottle, keg, and can most of their beer for sale and distribution to bars, restaurants, and liquor stores. Some have a taproom on-site where you can sample their product. The brewpub listings are made up of establishments that sell the majority of the beer they brew on the premises at their own restaurant and bar.

For each brewery I discuss the background, mission, and theme of the brewery and highlight the most interesting beers they produce. Every brewery listing contains a **Beer Lover's Pick,** an absolute must-try beer regardless of your specific taste for certain styles, complete with tasting notes. There are so many great styles of beer brewed in the state that it would be downright criminal for me to only highlight certain popular types. Better beer education and appreciation comes only through trying as many different kinds of beer as possible. Believe me, I know.

The brewpub listings are similarly constructed with a brief description of the food menu in addition to some words about the kinds of beers you can expect to find at each establishment. The brewpubs do not have a specific beer highlighted as a Beer Lover's Pick because their tap lists and the beers they brew tend to be more fluid and can change from week to week.

The beer bar listings highlight only the very best beer bars in Colorado. In a few instances the taproom of a brewery might be included because it also carries a selection of guest beers, making it a beer bar rather than simply a taproom selling its own beer. As in most states, the concentration of best beer bars tends to be in the largest and busiest metro areas, and Colorado is no different. Denver, Boulder, and Fort Collins are all well represented for that reason. Each beer bar listing describes the number of taps and sorts of beers you can expect to find at each spot. Where appropriate there is also a broad description of the all-important food menu for the bar.

In addition to the brewery, brewpub, and beer bar listings that make up the bulk of this guide, you'll also find chapters on:

Beer Festivals: This section features the very best and most popular beer fests in the state. Where appropriate, basic etiquette and planning for a particular festival are also discussed.

BYOB: Brew Your Own Beer: This chapter is aimed squarely at those of you who would like to re-create some of the best beers brewed in Colorado at home. These recipes were kindly provided by their respective breweries and in all but one or two instances, this is the first time they have been published anywhere. Some preexisting all-grain homebrewing knowledge is useful when tackling these recipes, but certainly not necessary. There was, after all, a time when the only way to learn to brew was by starting out all grain. All of the recipes have been carefully resized from their large commercial batches to a more manageable five-gallon batch.

In the Kitchen: The process described in this chapter is much like that in the BYOB chapter, although significantly less demanding in terms of time, equipment, and preexisitng know-how. Some of the best brewpubs and beer bars in Colorado have kindly submitted food recipes and beer cocktail recipes so that you can re-create them at home. All of the recipes incorporate Colorado craft beer. You can, of course, substitute these with the same style of beer if you cannot find the exact cited label.

Pub Crawls: In this chapter I break down some of Colorado's greatest beer-centric cities and areas into walkable (or taxi-able) tours during which you can sample some of the best beer on offer throughout the region. Outside of Denver, Boulder, Fort Collins, Colorado Springs, and Durango, breweries tend to be scattered throughout the rest of the state. Many of the more-trafficked mountain towns, ski resorts, and outdoor activity–friendly areas are home to some fantastic beer bars and in some instances more than one brewery or brewpub.

Glossary of Terms

ABV: Alcohol by volume—the percentage of alcohol in a beer. A typical domestic beer is a little less than 5 percent ABV.

Ale: Beer brewed with top fermenting yeast. Quicker to brew than lagers, and most every craft beer is a style of ale. Popular styles of ales include pale ales, amber ales, stouts, and porters.

Altbier: A German style of ale, typically brown in color, smooth, and fruity.

Barleywine: Not a wine at all but a high-ABV ale that originated in England and is typically sweet. American versions often have large amounts of hops.

Barrel of beer: Production of beer is measured in barrels. A barrel equals 31 gallons.

Beer: An alcoholic beverage brewed with malt, water, hops, and yeast.

Beer bar: A bar that focuses on carrying craft or fine imported beers.

Bitter: An English bitter is an English-style of ale, more hoppy than an English mild, but less hoppy than an IPA.

Bock: A German-style lager, typically stronger than the typical lager.

Bomber: Most beers are packaged in 12-ounce bottles. Bombers are 22-ounce bottles.

Brewpub: Typically a restaurant, but sometimes a bar, that brews its own beers on premises.

Cask ale: Also known as real ales, cask ales are naturally carbonated and are usually served with a hand pump rather than forced out with carbon dioxide or nitrogen.

Clone beer: A clone beer is a homebrew recipe based on a commericial beer.

Contract brewery: A company that does not have its own brewery and pays someone else to brew and bottle its beer.

Craft beer: High-quality, flavorful beer made by small breweries.

Double: Two meanings. Most often meant as a higher-alcohol version of a beer, most typically used in reference to a double, or imperial, IPA. Can also be used as an American translation of a Belgian dubbel, a style of Belgian ale.

ESB: Extra special bitter. A traditional malt-heavy English pub ale with low bitterness, usually served on cask.

Gastropub: A beer-centric bar or pub that exhibits the same amount of care selecting its foods as it does its beers.

Growler: A half-gallon jug of beer. Many brewpubs sell growlers of their beers to go.

Gypsy brewer: A company that does not own its own brewery, but rents space at an existing brewery to brew their beer themselves.

Hops: Hops are flowers used in beers to produce aroma, bitterness, and flavor. Nearly every beer in the world has hops.

IBU: International bittering units. Used to measure how bitter a beer is.

Imperial: A higher alcohol version of a regular-strength beer.

IPA: India Pale Ale. A popular style of ale created in England that has taken a decidedly American twist over the years. Often bitter, thanks to more hops used than in other styles of beer.

Kolsch: A light, refreshing German-style ale.

Lager: Beer brewed with bottom fermenting yeast. Takes longer and is harder to brew than ales. Popular styles of lagers include black lagers, doppelbocks, Pilsners, and Vienna lagers.

Malt: Typically barley malt, but sometimes wheat malt. Malt provides the fermentable sugar in beers. The more fermentable sugar, the higher the ABV in a beer. Without malt, a beer would be too bitter from the hops.

Microbrewery: A brewery that brews less than 15,000 barrels of beer a year.

Nanobrewery: A brewery that brews four barrels of beer per batch or less.

Nitro draft: Most beers that are served on draft using kegs pressurized with carbon dioxide. Occasionally, particularly with stouts, nitrogen is used, which helps create a creamier body.

Pilsner: A style of German or Czeckolovian lager, usually light in color. Most mass-produced beers are based on this style.

Porter: A dark ale, similar to the stout but with less roasted characters.

Pounders: 16-ounce cans.

Quad: A strong Belgian-style ale, typically sweet and high in alcohol.

Regional brewery: A brewery that brews up to 6,000,000 barrels of beer a year.

Russian imperial stout: A higher-alcohol, thicker-bodied version of regular stouts.

Saison: Also known as a Belgian or French farmhouse ale. It can be fruity, and it can also be peppery. Usually refreshing.

Seasonal: A beer that is only brewed at a certain time of year to coincide with the seasons.

Session beer: A low-alcohol beer, one that you can have several of in one long "session" of drinking.

Stout: A dark beer brewed with roasted malts.

Strong ale: A style of ale that is typically both hoppy and malty and can be aged for years.

Tap takeover: An event where a bar or pub hosts a brewery and offers several of its beers on tap.

Triple (Tripel): A Belgian-style ale, typically lighter in color than a dubbel but higher in alcohol.

Wheat beer: Beers, such as Hefeweizens and witbiers, that are brewed using wheat malt along with barley malt.

Yeast: The living organism that is in beer that causes the sugars to ferment and become alcohol.

Denver

Denver is Colorado's largest metro area and is the largest metro area in the wider Rocky Mountain region as a whole. The creative sensibility that pervades the expansive Denver area, not surprisingly, also influences and supports the wide variety of breweries, bars, and brewpubs that pepper this modern city. From small breweries with specific and bold identities to established large-scale production breweries that distribute nationally, the overall beer environment and experience in Denver is a happy and healthy one of friendly rivalry, cohabitation, and cooperation. The choice of beers brewed and served in Denver is on par with the very best beer regions and cities in the world.

Breweries

BLUE MOON BREWING COMPANY AT THE SANDLOT

2161 Blake St., Denver, CO 80205; (303) 298-1587; BlueMoonBrewingCompany.com
Founded: 1995 **Founder:** Keith Villa **Brewer:** Keith Villa **Flagship Beer:** Blue Moon
Belgian White Ale **Year-round Beers:** Blue Moon Belgian White Ale, Pale Moon
Seasonals/Special Releases: Summer Honey Wheat Ale, Harvest Pumpkin Ale, Winter
Abbey Ale, Spring Blonde Wheat Ale, Spiced Amber Ale, Grand Cru, Chardonnay Blonde,
Peanut Butter Ale **Tours:** None **Taproom:** Only open during baseball games

Blue Moon is an enigma in many regards. The beer was born in 1995 out of drive to create something new by Coors brewer Keith Villa at the SandLot brewery at Coors Field, home of the Colorado Rockies baseball team. The birthplace explains the beer's original name of Bellyslide Belgian Wit. Even though the beer sold well at the stadium, Coors was initially reluctant to free up space at its main brewery in Golden to brew larger batches in order to sell the beer in other locations. So, the beer was brewed at a brewery for hire in upstate New York, and Villa traveled around the country selling the beer on behalf of Coors himself.

Upon the national rollout of the beer, the name was changed from Bellyslide to **Blue Moon,** the name taken from the phrase, "once in a blue moon," referring to the beer's rare and immediate popularity.

The debate as to whether beers like Blue Moon are craft or not is an endless and essentially moot one. The beer exists and sells by the pallet. In 2008 it became the best-selling "craft beer" in America. A small amount of Blue Moon is still brewed at the SandLot and is poured on game days alongside a plethora of other SandLot beers. The brewery bar is only open on game days, and you need a baseball gameday ticket to get into the bar. A team of full-time brewers work at the SandLot year-round, cranking out many styles of beer that can usually only be tasted at large beer festivals and competitions like the Great American Beer Festival (GABF) and the World Beer Cup. The brewery has amassed a staggering number of medals over the years at such events.

Today the SandLot's main purpose is to come up with new Blue Moon seasonals and special release beers. Recent experiments have included a Caramel Apple Spiced ale, a Blackberry Tart ale, and a Dark Chocolate Bacon Porter.

Blue Moon Belgian White Ale

Style: Witbier

ABV: 5.4 percent

Availability: Year-round on tap, in bottles, and
in cans

For many in America Blue Moon is the gateway
beer to the wider world of craft and import
beer. The birth of the beer is storied and is an
important part of brewing history in America
and, more specifically, Colorado. The hazy, soft-
white, effervescent ale does not stray from the
traditional Belgian model, delivering a vibrant
citrus aroma and flavor, with wheat derived
smoothness. While not considered a craft beer
by many hard-core craft beer aficionados, Blue
Moon Belgian White remains an integral beer in
the story of good beer in Colorado, and enjoying a pour at a Colorado Rockies baseball game
is a right of regional passage.

BRECKENRIDGE BREWERY

471 Kalamath St., Denver, CO 80204; (800) 328-6723; BreckBrew.com;
Twitter: @breckbrew

Founded: 1990 **Founder:** Richard Squire **Brewer:** Todd Usry **Flagship Beer:** Avalanche
Amber-style Ale **Year-round Beers:** Avalanche Amber-style Ale, Lucky U IPA, Vanilla
Porter, Agave Wheat, Oatmeal Stout **Seasonals/Special Releases:** Pandora's Bock,
Autumn Ale, Christmas Ale, SummerBright Ale, Regal Double Pilsner, 471 Small Batch
Double IPA, 72 Imperial Chocolate Cream Stout, Extra ESB, Stranahan's Well-Built ESB
Tours: Sat 2, 3, 4, and 5 p.m. **Taproom:** Mon through Sat 11 a.m. to 9 p.m. Growlers and
bottled beers are available to go. The tasting room is expansive, with plenty of seating,
and serves a full menu of excellent in-house smoked barbecue.

In 1990 practiced homebrewer Richard Squire opened only the third craft brewery
in Colorado in the popular ski town of Breckenridge. The aptly named Breckenridge

Brewery was a small affair, built with locals and visiting skiers in mind. It was an overnight success, and in 1992 the brewery moved into the more competitive Denver market and opened a bottling facility in a then run-down area of downtown. A few years later, on an adjacent site, Coors Field baseball stadium opened for business, and with it the neighborhood's fortunes were forever changed for the better. Three years later Breckenridge began brewing, kegging, and bottling its beer at a full-production brewery on Kalamath Street, south of downtown. The original Denver location still exists today as Breckenridge Ball Park Pub.

Avalanche Amber is the brewery's flagship beer and is a solid rendition of the broad style. For the more involved beer geek, though, the brewery produces plenty of more interesting and complex ales and lagers.

The highlight of the the Breckenridge's year-round releases is **Oatmeal Stout.** The beer has lush notes of freshly brewed coffee and high cocoa dark chocolate. The body is dense, and the robust flavors lead the drinker to believe he or she is drinking something more along the lines of an imperial stout. At less than 5 percent ABV, though, Oatmeal Stout is a beer designed for pint-after-pint enjoyment.

Breckenridge's **471 Small Batch Double IPA** is a Colorado hophead favorite. This bold IPA is released throughout the year on tap and in 12-ounce four packs. It has a strong and biting citrus aroma, with sticky orange marmalade, peach preserve, and light green-grass notes. Flavors of blood orange, pink grapefruit, and sugared lemon complement the beer's cereal foundation.

Denver

Stranahan's Breckenridge Well Built ESB

Style: ESB

ABV: 7.8 percent

Availability: Year-round on tap and in 750-milliter bottles

In February 2012 Breckenridge released the initial batch of Well Built ESB in 750-milliliter cork-and cage-finished bottles. The beer was made in collaboration with Denver's highly regarded Stranahan's Colorado Whiskey. The base is Breckenridge Extra ESB, which is then aged for up to 3 months in freshly emptied Stranahan's whiskey barrels. The finished 7.8 percent ABV beer has aromatic notes of currant, fig, and coconut; a gripping red-wine astringency; and a fruity-dry finish. This is definitely a beer aimed at those who enjoy American whiskey and fine red wines.

CAUTION: BREWING COMPANY

12445 E. 39th Ave., Denver, CO 80239; (970) 315-2739; CautionBrewingCo.com; **Twitter:** @cautionbrewing

Founded: 2011 **Founders:** Danny Wang and Betty Wang **Brewers:** Danny Wang and Betty Wang **Flagship Beer:** Lao Wang Lager **Year-round Beers:** Lao Wang Lager, Honey Matrimony Brown Ale, Wild Blonde Ale **Seasonals/Special Releases:** Changes **Tours:** None **Taproom:** Fri 4 to 8 p.m., Sat and Sun 2 to 8 p.m.

CAUTION: Brewing Company founders Betty and Danny Wang were inspired to start a brewery following a tour of New Belgium brewery in 2009. They began researching online exactly how one goes about brewing beer and soon found themselves loading up with equipment and supplies at their local homebrew store. They named their initial homebrewing project I.E. Brewing Company. Months passed, and after some constructive feedback from friends about their largely successful first

batches of beer and their overall brewery idea, Betty and Danny decided to change the name of their brewery to the more-bold and less-confusing CAUTION: Brewing Company.

CAUTION opened for business in late 2011 in a northwest industrial corridor of metro Denver off of I-70. The couple secured a five-barrel brewhouse that Odell Brewing Company was selling. It's large enough that it should provide enough brewing capacity for several years.

Honey Matrimony Brown Ale is a 5.9 percent ABV American brown ale, brewed with local honey. The beer combines a chocolate-covered nut richness, and subtle underlying sweetness. **Toaster Bat Black Smoked Robust Porter** is that strange and often-confused style of beer, the American porter. This 8.5 percent example is engineered to have a smokey personality. The smoke arrives courtesy of smoked and peated malts, more commonly associated with scotch whiskey and German *rauchbiers*. The black beer has bitter baking chocolate and licorice notes. **Wild Blonde** is a quaffable and thoroughly sessionable 4.6 percent ABV American blonde ale brewed with organic wild rice. The sunshine-colored beer has a soft, yellow-fruit aroma and body and a clean, not-too-bitter finish.

CAUTION opened a weekend tasting room in summer 2012.

Lao Wang Lager
Style: Happoshu
ABV: 5.1 percent
Availability: Year-round on tap

The inspiration behind Lao Wang Lager is an uncommon one. The 5.1 percent ABV spiced lager is designed to pair well with a wide range of Asian dishes. In addition to unnamed "secret" spices, the beer is brewed with organic wild rice, which gives the beer an earthy flavor but light texture. Rice is a common ingredient in Japanese Happoshu lagers and is used in many mass-produced American-style Pilsners to lighten their body. Malt and hop character are intentionally restrained. Lao Wang Lager is available almost exclusively at Lao Wang Noodle House but does occasionally appear elsewhere at select locations around Denver, including Denver Bicycle Cafe.

COPPER KETTLE BREWING COMPANY

1338 S. Valentia St., Unit 100, Denver, CO 80247; (720) 443-2522; CopperKettleDenver .com; **Twitter:** @CopperKettleDEN
Founded: 2011 **Founders:** Jeremy Gobien and Kristen Kozik **Brewer:** Jeremy Gobien
Flagship Beer: Mexican Chocolate Stout **Year-round Beers:** Bavarian Helles, Mexican Chocolate Stout **Seasonals/Special Releases:** Better Half IPA, Black IPA, Roggenbier, Copper Mezzina Ale, Summer Ale, Düsseldorf Altbier, Biergarden Dunkel, Smoked Porter, Czech Pilsner, Dortmunder Lager, High Country Breakfast Stout, English Style Black IPA
Tours: No **Taproom:** Mon, Wed, Thurs, and Fri 3 to 9 p.m.; Sat through Sun noon to 9 p.m. Closed Tues. Growlers are available to go.

Copper Kettle founder and brewer Jeremy Gobien and Kristen Kozik moved to Colorado from North Carolina in search of a neighborhood that needed a brewery. After locating one in a western corner of the metro Denver area, the couple set up shop. With an eye to opening a brewery with a welcoming tasting room, they modeled their corner strip mall unit with a aesthetic that could easily be mistaken for a coffee shop. Jeremy, of course, doesn't brew coffee, he brews beer. Award-winning beer.

Copper Kettle opened for business in April 2011. A few short months later the locals had already become accustomed to stopping in to fill their Mug Club trophy cup or to get a couple of growlers filled to go. The word in the neighborhood was out, and Jeremy increased brewing to keep up.

In October 2011 Copper Kettle struck gold, literally, when their much-buzzed-about **Mexican Chocolate Stout** won a gold medal at the GABF. No small feat for a brewery opened just 6 months before.

When the brewery opened, German styles, such as **Bavarian Helles, Dunkelweiss, Dortmunder Lager, Roggenbier, Altbier,** and **Kölsch,** dominated the tap list. Over time, though, the menu gave way to more American, British, and Belgian styles. Jeremy is a busy brewer, and new beers are tapped on a weekly basis. The Mexican Chocolate Stout and Helles are the closest the brewery has to year-round offerings.

Beer Lover's Pick

Mexican Chocolate Stout
Style: American Stout
ABV: 7 percent
Availability: Year-round
    on tap

Mexican Chocolate Stout is a 7 percent ABV robust American stout, brewed with bittersweet chocolate, a blend of three chilies, and cinnamon. The aroma and flavor are exactly what you'd expect from a combination of such distinct flavors. The beer was inspired by traditional Mexican hot chocolate, which is spiked with chile pepper. The beer is rich, not overly boozy, and does a wonderful job of evoking its intended inspiration in beer form.

DEL NORTE BREWING COMPANY

1390 W. Evans Ave., #20, Denver, CO 80223; (303) 935-3223; DelNorteBrewing.com
Founded: 2007 **Founders:** Jack Sosebee and Joseph Fox **Brewers:** Jack Sosebee and
Joseph Fox **Flagship Beer:** Mañana **Year-round Beers:** Mañana, Cinco, Órale **Seasonals/
Special Releases:** Luminaria **Tours:** Fri through Sat 3 to 7 p.m. **Taproom:** None

The story of beer in Colorado is so often a story of innovation and pioneering spirit. Colorado, it seems, is a fertile state for discovering gaps in the market and quickly filling them. Del Norte Brewing Company is another Colorado brewery born of a vacuum in the beer industry. In this case, fresh Mexican-style lagers.

Del Norte opened in 2007 in an industrial area of Denver, southwest of downtown. The founders of the brewery, Jack Sosebee and Joseph Fox, are both fans of Mexican food, but they often found imported Mexican beers to be lackluster and very often stale. So they set about creating the first brewery in America to supply a fresh and interesting selection of Mexican-style lagers to the massive Mexican restaurant and bar industry. During their first year of operation, they only produced 11 barrels of beer exclusively for the Colorado market. Today business is booming, and their beers are sold in Alaska, Colorado, Kansas, New Mexico, Texas, and Wyoming.

Del Norte brews four different lagers, three year-round and one winter seasonal. **Órale** (cerveza clara) is a straw-colored, 4.9 percent ABV Munich Helles, with very low bitterness, a highly effervescent bright yellow-fruit aroma, and a long refreshing lemonade-like body. The beer is designed to complement spicy and complex Mexican dishes. Think of **Cinco** (cerveza clara) as a craft incarnation of Corona. Indeed the beer won medals in aptly named Latin American/Tropical Lager categories at a handful of beer festivals. The light 4.2 percent ABV sunshine-colored lager is all about quaffability and thirst quenching, and it achieves this brilliantly. **Luminaria** is a caramel-forward, German-style, Bock beer. German immigrants to Mexico brought with them more than their love of crisp, bitter Pilsner and golden helles to Central America. Bockbiers in Germany are brewed in the summer and conditioned until the colder months, so they have become a winter tradition in Mexico, as they are in Germany.

Mañana

Style: American Amber Lager

ABV: 5.4 percent

Availability: Year-round on tap and in bottles

In a state that counts as many bold and great beers as Colorado, you might not expect an amber lager to stand out, but that's where you'd be wrong. Mañana (cerveza oscura) is a multi–award winning example of the style that positively shines. It has

a soft nutty and caramel aroma, low bitterness, and a semi-sweet body. The finish is quite crisp. One of the most pint-after-pint drinkable beers in the state.

DENVER BEER CO.

1695 Platte St., Denver, CO 80202; (303) 433-2739; DenverBeerCo.com; **Twitter:** @DenverBeerCo

Founded: 2011 **Founders:** Charlie Berger and Patrick Crawford **Brewers:** Charlie Berger and Patrick Crawford **Flagship Beer:** Graham Cracker Porter **Year-round Beer:** Graham Cracker Porter **Seasonals/Special Releases:** Smoked Lager. New beers weekly. Constantly changes. **Tours:** None **Taproom:** Tues through Thurs 3 p.m. to midnight, Fri through Sat noon to midnight, Sun noon to 9 p.m. Closed Mon. Growlers are available to go.

Located in Denver's much-rejuvenated and now-hip Highland neighborhood, Denver Beer Co. opened for business in late summer 2011. Founders Charlie Berger and Patrick Crawford successfully established a brewery and tasting room with a local, walk-in-and-chat neighborhood feel.

The brewery prides itself on brewing as many new beers as possible, and there is constantly something new on tap. Charlie and Patrick have already brewed a truly

Denver

mind-boggling number of different ales and lagers, some traditional in origin, many with a twist on a classic style, and some wholly experimental. They garnered wide notoriety and buzz when they won a gold medal at the 2011 GABF for their **Graham Cracker Porter.** Yes, it's actually brewed with graham crackers, and yes, it's that good. It's also the only beer to appear consistently on their constantly changing chalkboard beer menu.

To give you an idea of the range of beers you can expect when visiting the brewery, here are a just a few of the beers Denver Beer Co. has brewed since opening: Ichabod's Revenge Pumpkin'd Ale, Kaffir Lime Wheat, 'Tis The Saison, Smoked Lager, and Stormy Summer Stout.

The taproom is spacious and bright and was clearly engineered to be the focus of the space. In a previous life the building was a car mechanic's garage. Charlie and Patrick retained the old-urban charm of the building, including the large vertical doors that once allowed cars to drive in. In warmer months these large glass doors are rolled up to reveal a patio with long German *biergarten*-style communal beer drinking benches. Local food trucks routinely park outside, providing drinkers with a rotating selection of quality cuisines.

Graham Cracker Porter

Style: American Porter

ABV: 5.9 percent

Availability: On tap

This beer really delivers upon its enticing promise. It combines all the best elements of a hearty American stout, with its milk chocolate and espresso coffee notes, buttery vanilla cookie aroma, and the sweetness of an all-American graham cracker. Lovers of such dessert-evoking beers need not ask for much more.

Denver

GREAT DIVIDE BREWING COMPANY

2201 Arapahoe St., Denver, CO 80205; (303) 296-9460 ext. 26; GreatDivide.com;
Twitter: @greatdividebrew

Founded: 1994 **Founder:** Brian Dunn **Brewer:** Brian Dunn **Flagship Beer:** Yeti Imperial Stout **Year-round Beers:** Yeti Imperial Stout, Denver Pale Ale, Titan IPA, Hoss, Claymore Scotch Ale, Hercules Double IPA, Hades, Wild Raspberry Ale, Samurai Rice Ale **Seasonals/Special Releases:** Smoked Baltic Porter, Anniversary Wood Aged Double IPA, Fresh Hop Pale Ale, Rumble Oak Aged IPA, Nomad Pilsner, Grand Cru Belgian-style Dark Ale, Hibernation English-style Old Ale, Old Ruffian Barleywine-style Ale, Colette Farmhouse Ale, Espresso Oak Aged Yeti, Chocolate Oak Aged Yeti, Belgian-style Yeti, Oak Aged Yeti, Barrel Aged Yeti, Barrel Aged Old Ruffian, Barrel Aged Hibernation **Tours:** Mon through Fri 3 and 4 p.m., Sat through Sun every 30 to 45 minutes from 2:30 to 5 p.m. No advance reservations, and space is limited. Please arrive 10 to 15 minutes early. **Taproom:** Sun through Tues 2 to 8 p.m., Wed through Sat 2 to 10 p.m.. Growlers and bottled beers are available to go.

Great Divide is unquestionably Denver's most well-known craft beer export. From Los Angeles to New York and from London to Stockholm, Great Divide and its highly regarded ales and lagers are synonymous with the Mile High City. Located in downtown Denver, Great Divide is a place locals and regular visitors to the city have come to cherish. The brewery taproom is always buzzing with a mix of out-of-towners, lively groups of locals enjoying a postworkday beer or two, or folks like myself, who are lucky to live close enough to stop in and buy a fresh six-pack.

The brewery is probably most well-known for its enduring and ever-popular line of **Yeti** imperial stouts. Over the years the Yeti brand has expanded well beyond its black-as-night, rich-chocolate, and heavily roasted malt-laden roots. **Espresso Oak Aged Yeti** is a January release, brewed with coffee. **Chocolate Oak Aged Yeti** is an April release, brewed with cocoa nibs and cayenne pepper. **Belgian-style Yeti** is a July release, brewed using a Belgian yeast strain for a strong spiced fruit character. **Oak Aged Yeti** is an October release, brewed with an abundance of oak, bringing a soft leather and vanilla character to the otherwise robust bitter beer. The jewel in the crown of the Yeti series, though, is **Barrel Aged Yeti,** an even stronger version of the stout, aged in freshly emptied Stranahan's Colorado Whiskey barrels.

The newest and most surprising standout addition to the brewery's annual release schedule is **Nomad Pilsner.** Nomad, a January seasonal, is a bright, crisp, and thoroughly quaffable pils that falls somewhere between a classic Czech and American interpretation of the style. You could not ask for a more appropriate switch-hitter to one of Great Divide's many heavyweight offerings.

Barrel Aged Yeti

Style: Whiskey Barrel-
Aged Imperial
Stout

ABV: 12.2 percent

Availability: October
in 750-milliliter
bottles

Should you be travel-
ing to Denver for the
annual GABF in Octo-
ber, then chances are you will be able to get your hands on a few bottles of
Barrel Aged Yeti, an outstanding and very limited whiskey barrel–aged imperial stout, before it sells out. Imagine the decadent flavors and the experience of enjoying a bittersweet, alcohol-tinged, tiramisu dessert, and you'll
have some idea of what to expect when drinking this beer. Before it sees the
light of day, this very special version of Yeti, spends upwards of 9 months
conditioning in spent Stranahan's Colorado Whiskey barrels. It is one of rich-
est and most luxurious beers produced in Colorado.

RENEGADE BREWING COMPANY

925 W. 9th Ave., Denver, CO 80204; (720) 401-4089; RenegadeBrewing.com;
Twitter: @RenegadeBrewing
Founded: 2011 **Founders:** Brian O'Connell and Khara O'Connell **Brewer:** Rick Abitbol
Flagship Beer: Ryeteous Rye IPA **Year-round Beers:** Ryeteous Rye IPA, 5' O'Clock Blonde
Ale, Una Mas **Seasonals/Special Releases:** Radiator, Black Gold Imperial Peanut Butter
Cup, Hammer and Sickle, Elevation IPA3 **Tours:** None **Taproom:** Mon through Thurs 3 to
9 p.m., Fri through Sat 2 to 10 p.m., Sun 1 to 6 p.m. Growlers and cans are available to go.

Renegade Brewing is one of a cluster of small neighborhood-focused breweries that
opened in Denver in 2011. Quickly becoming popular, the brewery expanded its
brewing capacity the very next year to meet demand. It also began offering 16-ounce
cans of its **Ryeteous Rye IPA** (7 percent ABV) in the summer of 2012.

Renegade is the brainchild of homebrewers and self-described "craft beer lovers" Brian and Khara O'Connell. Rather than pinning themselves to a certain style set or theme of brewing, they prefer to allow creativity and passion drive what ales and lagers they brew.

A self-descibed Mexican-style, Una Mas amber ale might not be the first beer to snag the attention of an adventurous beer geek, but Renegade adds roasted chili peppers to its Mexican-style amber to up the ante. It is the perfect companion to a breakfast burrito loaded with Colorado green chilis or a hearty plate of pancakes, bacon, and eggs. The semisweet malt backbone of the beer lends it to any number of savory and sweet brunch dishes. The subtle kick from the peppers delivers a seasoned earthiness that brings greater depth to the beer.

5 O'Clock is a 5 percent ABV American-blonde ale with a clean-hop profile and notes of yellow fruit and cereal. The finish has a nice cleanliness about it that invites further drinking. It is an archetypal and well-executed blonde ale.

I've yet to ascertain a significant set of differences between double or imperial IPAs and the newer so-called triple IPAs. Regardless, Renegade's **Elevation Triple**

Beer Lover's Pick

Ryeteous Rye IPA
Style: Rye Beer
ABV: 7 percent
Availability: Year-round on tap and in cans

Ryeteous Rye IPA is Renegade's flagship beer, and it's not hard to taste why. The spicy, deep-amber pour has a vibrant grapefruit and white pepper aroma and a multilayered bitter body. The finish is like the body, bitter to the core, but with a slight fruity kick. The beer clocks in at more than 100 IBUs, so prepare your palate.

IPA (11.2 percent ABV), like its fellow house beer, Ryeteous, registers 100 IBUs and packs a palate-wrecking wallop of hop bite and bitterness. The aroma is dank and reminiscent of a wet forest or bag of mixed fresh herbs. A big beer worthy of attention.

RIVER NORTH BREWERY

2401 Blake St., #1, Denver, CO 80205; (303) 296-2617; RiverNorthBrewery.com
Founded: 2012 **Founder:** Matthew Hess **Brewer:** Matthew Hess **Flagship Beer:** J. Marie Saison **Year-round Beers:** Hello, Darkness Black IPA; River North White Ale; J. Marie Saison; BPR (Belgian-style Pale Red Ale), Hypothesis Belgian-style Double IPA **Seasonals/ Special Releases:** Varies **Tours:** None **Taproom:** Thurs 3 to 9 p.m., Fri 3 to 10 p.m., Sat 3 to 10 p.m., Sun 3 to 9 p.m. Growlers are available to go.

River North Brewery opened for business in downtown Denver in February 2012. It is located in the same building that once housed Flying Dog Brewing Co. before it relocated to Maryland.

River North is a 15-barrel brewery, specializing in brewing beers with a Belgian vibe and an American outlook. Its small, but attractive 40-seat taproom is located within easy walking distance of heavily trafficked Denver beer hot spots, like Falling Rock Tap House, Great Divide Brewing Company, Freshcraft, Wynkoop Brewing Company, and Breckenridge Ball Park Pub. Customers have filled the River North taproom since day one.

The brewery was founded by Matthew Hess, a former Lockheed Martin engineer who worked on future manned space projects. Besides serving patrons at his bustling taproom, Matthew also releases small batches of bottled beer to local liquor stores and sells kegs of beer to bars.

J. Marie is a by-style 7.5 percent ABV saison with a strong woolly aroma, a body that evokes ripe summer fruits, and a suitably dry finish. **Hello, Darkness** is a 6.2 percent ABV pitch black IPA, with a sweeter-than-usual middle and a softer finish for the style, thanks to the use of the estery Belgian yeast strain. **BPR** (or Belgian pale red) is less a traditional Belgian-style amber ale and more an American-style amber, with a juicy fruit Belgian bent. The 6.4 percent ABV ale has nice fresh fruit depth and a clean moderate bitter finish. **River North White** is a clean, ester-forward, 5 percent ABV Belgian-style witbier with a smooth body and a bright Cream of Wheat–like aroma.

Hypothesis
Style: American Double IPA
ABV: 9 percent
Availability: Year-round on tap and in bottles

Hypothesis is a Belgian-inspired take on the enduringly popular American double IPA. The beer clocks in at a projected 130 IBUs and is heavily dry hopped. Despite this, and largely in part to Belgian yeast and malt backbone, the beer has a sweet underbelly and well-rounded overall flavor that temper its bitterness and higher alcohol.

STRANGE BREWING COMPANY

1330 Zuni St., Denver, CO 80204; (720) 985-2337; StrangeBrewingCo.com;
Twitter: @StrangeBrewCo
Founded: 2010 **Founders:** Tim Myers and John Fletcher **Brewers:** Tim Myers and John Fletcher **Flagship Beer:** Strange Pale Ale **Year-round Beers:** IPAphany India Pale Ale, Strange Wit **Seasonals/Special Releases:** Le Bruit du Diable, Bel'Hop'D Belgian Pale Ale, Tainted Black Pale, Paint It Black Honey Coffee Stout, Cherry Bomb Belgian Stout, Cherry Kriek **Tours:** None **Taproom:** Mon through Fri 3 to 8 p.m., Sat noon to 9 p.m. Closed Sun. Growlers are available to go.

The adage goes that as one door closes, another opens, and it definitely sums up how John Fletcher and Tim Myers came to open Strange Brewing Company in May 2010. When the 150-year-old *Rocky Mountain News* newspaper closed for business in February 2009, Fletcher and Myers found themselves unemployed and contemplative. The pair had homebrewed prior to the paper's closing and decided to pool their retirement savings and start a brewery.

Starting small in an industrial unit in a far-flung commercial property zone southwest of downtown Denver, the pair cooked up quite a few interesting recipes in their first three years of operation. They even stumbled across new ideas purely by accident. Their **Cherry Bomb Belgian Stout,** for example, only exists today because Myers used the wrong malt to brew a Belgian witbier.

For the most part, Fletcher and Myers eschew more standard styles, like ambers, light lagers, and golden ales, instead focusing on more esoteric or full-bodied beers, like saisons, *bière de gardes,* stouts with adjuncts, and sours. **Le Bruit du Diable** is an earthy Belgian-style provisional farmhouse ale. Rich with a caramel malt body and warming finish, this 7.5 percent ABV ale delivers sweet summer fruit, exotic spice, and dry-citrus flavors. **Tainted Black Pale** is a bitter, 6 percent ABV pale ale stained black with heavily roasted malt. Bitterness comes from both high hopping and the astringent malt. The potent notes of licorice, charcoal, and pine make this a definite must try for those who enjoy black IPAs. The strange and unusual 6.5 percent ABV **Paint It Black Honey Coffee Stout** uses 6 pounds of Western Slope Ambrosia Honey, 3 pounds of cold-brewed Sumatra coffee, and over 4 pounds of Cascade hops per batch. The resulting inky brew is loaded with semisweet chocolate, espresso coffee, and resinous pine notes.

Beer Lover's Pick

Cherry Kriek
Style: Fruit Lambic
ABV: 4.7 percent
Availability: Occasionally on tap

One of the most popular hard-to-obtain beers for many Americans is Wisconsin Belgian Red, brewed by Wisconsin's New Glarus. It is a semisour cherry ale that has garnered a strong following among beer geeks coast to coast. New Glarus brews a lot of beer, but it does not distribute across state lines. Luckily for those living in or visiting Denver, Strange Brewing Company has a beer called Cherry Kriek that in concept and execution is very similar to Wisconsin Belgian Red. The thoroughly session-able 4.7 percent ABV fruit beer has a bright pink head and a deep dark pink body. The aroma and body are reminiscent of cherry pie filling, with a slightly more acid backbone. The beer has a bright refreshing quality about it, and both fruit beer and sour beer lovers will find the beer of much interest.

WIT'S END BREWING COMPANY

2505 W. 2nd Ave., #13, Denver, CO 80219; (303) 359-9119; WitsEndBrewing.com;
Twitter: @WitsEndBrewing
Founded: 2011 **Founder:** Scott Witsoe **Brewer:** Scott Witsoe **Flagship Beer:** Jean-Claude Van Blond **Year-round Beers:** Jean-Claude Van Blond, Super FL i.p.a., Green Man Ale, Kitchen Sink Porter **Seasonals/Special Releases:** Slam Dunkelweizen, Ugly Sweater, the Mad King **Tours:** None **Taproom:** Thurs 4 to 8 p.m., Fri through Sat 2 to 8 p.m. Growlers are available to go.

Wit's End Brewing Company is one of the newest producers of craft beer in Denver. It is one of the cluster of so-called nanobreweries that opened for business in 2012. Founded by Seattle transplant Scott Witsoe, Wit's End describes its direction and style as new American brewing, a counterpart to the new generation culinary chefs in the restaurant world. What that all means is a brewery that aims to produce beers inspired by traditional beers styles but not bound by brewing them in a necessarily traditional way or with specifically traditional ingredients.

Scott brews all of Wit's End's beers using what is essentially a large homebrew set up. It is one of the smallest commercial brewery operations in Colorado. The small scale of the setup affords Scott enough flexibility to try out new beer recipes in an affordable manner.

Located in a quiet industrial area southwest of downtown, the brewery produces four year-round beers and ongoing experimental creations. Scott can be found manning the taproom himself a few evenings a week. Scott burns with a brewer's passion and lights up at questions about his fledgling brewery. If it's quiet, he'll even offer to show you around and explain his brewing process.

Jean-Claude Van Blond is best described as Wit's End flagship beer. The bright yellow pour bursts with fruity aroma and flavor thanks to the lively Belgian yeast strain used to ferment the beer. It is not your average American blond ale, but a beer brewed to confound and change expectations of what the style can be. **Super FL i.p.a.** is a black IPA brewed with spiky Columbus and Cascade hops. Postfermentation the beer is dry hopped and matured for a time on cedar wood chips. The moderately bitter beer has notes of charcoal, roasted cereal, pine, dry grass, and lemon peel. **Green Man Ale** was inspired by the big IPAs of the Pacific Northwest, beers that balance masses of hop-derived bitterness, aroma, and flavor with a firm biscuit foundation. The drink has a resinous pine forward nose and body, with secondary notes of orange marmalade and candied lemon.

Kitchen Sink Porter

Style: American Porter

ABV: 5.8 percent

Availability: Year-round on tap

Kitchen Sink Porter is aptly named. The beer began life as an American porter, evolving with each subsequent addition. The beer uses some unporter-like malts, including smoked malt and rye. The dry beer has bold notes of dark-roasted coffee, high cocoa dark chocolate, and charcoal. ***Note:*** The Kitchen Sink Porter is pictured on the far right.

Brewpubs

BULL & BUSH PUB & BREWERY

4700 Cherry Creek South Dr., Denver, CO 80246; (303) 759-0333; BullandBush.com;
Twitter: @BandBManBeer
Founded: 1997 **Founders:** Dale Peterson and Dean Peterson **Brewer:** Gabe Moline
Flagship Beer: Big Ben Brown Ale **Year-round Beers:** Big Ben Brown Ale, MAN BEER
IPA, Happy Hop Pilsner, Happy Hop Pilsner, Allgood Ale, Hail Brau Hefeweizen, The Tower
E.S.B., Patio's Vat-Dunkel Weiss **Seasonals/Special Releases:** Legend of the Liquid Brain
Imperial Stout, Justice I.P.A., Tank Town Brown Ale, Release the Hounds Barley Wine,
Royal Oil, Colorado Kolsch, Fyfe's Highland Ale, Don't Mock Maibock, Yule Fuel, Pimp My
Rye, Black Bull Lager, Mind's Eye P.A.

Bull & Bush is a Denver beer institution. The pub, full of dark wood and some screens that pipe in local sports, opened in 1971. It wasn't until 1997, though, that the first Bull & Bush beer was brewed, following the hand over of the business from founders Dale and Dean Peterson to Dale's sons, Erik and David Peterson. The pub now offers six year-round beers and many special one-off pours and seasonals, alongside a healthy rotating list of guest taps. The pub also maintains a good-size bottle list. If whiskey is your thing, they have that covered too, with a well-stocked list of more than 200 choices.

The core beers are mostly skewed toward traditional English styles. **The Tower E.S.B.** (6 percent ABV) is one of the finest examples of the style in the state, if not the country. This beautifully balanced and award-winning beer is definitely a must try when visiting. Another multi-award-winning must-try is their flagship, **Big Ben Brown Ale,** a pretty garnet-colored, 5 percent ABV pour. Like The Tower, this is another nod to classic English-pub styles designed for pint-after-pint enjoyment. The aroma is rich with black treacle, toffee, and caramel. The drink has layers of dried dark fruit and roasted mixed-nut flavor.

The annual tapping of the pub's 11.5 percent ABV bourbon barrel-aged imperial stout, **Legend of the Liquid Brain,** is always a popular event. The beer is something of a local legend among Colorado beer geeks. It is a sticky sweet, chocolate malt bomb, with brilliant notes of toffee and vanilla. The finish is warm and definitely reminds the drinker of its significant ABV.

The food at Bull & Bush is above par and can best be described as Colorado meets British meat and potatoes. Alongside the requisite fish-and-chips, you'll find popular and long-standing house staples like green chili and mashed potato.

DENVER CHOPHOUSE & BREWERY

1735 19th St., Denver, CO 80202; (303) 296-0800; DenverChopHouse.com
Founded: 1995 **Founder:** Frank Day **Brewer:** Kevin Marley **Flagship Beer:** Pilsner
Lager **Year-round Beers:** Pilsner Lager, Dortmunder Lager, Wheat Ale, Dark Munich Lager,
Red Ale, Pale Ale, Dry Stout, Wild Turkey Barrel Conditioned Stout **Seasonals/Special
Releases:** Changes

Kevin Marley has been brewing at Denver ChopHouse & Brewery since 1995, making him a true veteran of Colorado craft brewing. His most-loved and requested creation, and with good reason, is his **Wild Turkey Barrel Conditioned Stout.** The beer breathes and delivers rich, but not overwhelming, notes of coconut, vanilla, leather, cocoa, and butterscotch, while remaining low enough in ABV (6.6 percent)

to be pint-after-pint drinkable. It's an ideal companion to one of the ChopHouse's highly regarded steaks.

Denver ChopHouse is an upscale brewpub and a part of the expansive Rock Bottom chain. Other ChopHouse locations are in Boulder, Washington D.C., Cleveland, and in Terminal A of Denver International Airport.

Today, in addition to the much loved Wild Turkey stout, Kevin brews up a well-executed selection of ales and lagers to accompany the upscale menu of steaks, chops, lamb, seafood, salads, and belt-snapping rich desserts. His full-flavored lagers, like the house **Pilsner,** blonde **Dortmunder,** and hazel-colored **Dark Munich,** are all among the best-kept secrets in Colorado.

While the menu is significantly more expensive at ChopHouse, there is nothing preventing the avid beer lover from stopping in to sample a full flight of the house beers at the bar or buying a growler of Wild Turkey Barrel Conditioned Stout to go.

PINT'S PUB BREWERY & FREEHOUSE
221 W. 13th Ave., Denver, CO 80204; (303) 534-7543; PintsPub.com
Founded: 1993 **Founder:** Scott Diamond **Brewer:** Scott Diamond **Flagship Beer:** Dark Star Ale **Year-round Beers:** Dark Star Ale, Lance India Pale Ale, Czechmate Pilsner, Bitchcraft Blonde Ale, Phonebox Red Ale, Gael Force Scottish Ale, Alchemy ESB, Idyllweiss Wheat, Airedale Pale Ale, John Bull Brown Ale, Black Ajax Stout **Seasonals/Special Releases:** None

Pint's Pub is a British-centric brewpub that is hard to miss thanks to the iconic red English public telephone box and the fluttering Union Jack that mark its entrance. Inside the cozy pub and brewery you'll immediately notice the more than 300 whiskeys that adorn the bar. Not the first thing you expect to see upon entering a brewery, but then Pint's Pub is a known far and wide for what might be the largest whiskey selection in America, as well as its house-brewed beers.

The pub opened in 1993 but did not start brewing until 1996. In the early days all of its beers were modeled on various British ale styles and included what were likely the first cask-conditioned ales in the state. Today Pint's Pub has branched out a little and brews American and German style ales as well. Two of the taps are still dedicated to **Lancer IPA** and **Dark Star Ale,** cask-conditioned beers, or as they are better known in the UK, real ales. These two beers are the main reason most beer geeks initially seek out Pint's Pub, but all of the house offerings are high quality.

Lancer IPA (5.8 percent ABV) can change in complexity and flavor ever so slightly from cask to cask, much like real ales served in the UK. The beer is massively hopped for aroma, flavor, and bitterness, with deep and dank notes of fresh-cut grass, lemon peel, and basil. Dark Star is a 6.4 percent ABV English-style old ale brewed with imported dark treacle and flaked barley. This shadowy dry-hopped beast is unlike any other beer in Colorado. Its soft, cask-conditioned body lends the rich mahogany-colored beer a real smoothness, finesse, and class. Flavor and aroma are predominantly that of a bittersweet fruitcake.

The menu is a curious take on late-night British street food and American pub classics, from wings and lamb kebabs to bangers and mash, burgers, and fish-and-chips.

ROCK BOTTOM RESTAURANT & BREWERY

1001 16th St., #100, Denver, CO 80265; (303) 534-7616; RockBottom.com
Founded: 1991 **Founder:** Frank Day **Brewer:** John McClure **Flagship Beer:** Kolsch
Year-round Beers: Kolsch, Belgian White Ale, Red Ale, IPA **Seasonals/Special Releases:** Changes weekly

The story of the Rock Bottom Restaurant & Brewery empire begins somewhere around 1990 when Frank Day, the owner of a number of Old Chicago Pizza restaurants, noticed that brewpubs were opening in various parts of the country, including Denver. Frank also noticed that patrons of Old Chicago, which served 110 different beers were thirsting for more regional and locally brewed beer versus national domestic and imported brands. Frank gathered a few investors and opened the Walnut Brewery on Walnut Street in downtown Boulder. Walnut was an almost instant success, and it wasn't long before Frank acquired a central location on Denver's 16th Street Mall for his second brewing endeavor. This second endeavor became the Rock Bottom Restaurant & Brewery, located on the ground floor of the Prudential Building, a building commonly known as "The Rock."

The 16th Street Mall location became a busy and vibrant business, and today there are seven Rock Bottom locations in Colorado. Long-time Rock Bottom Denver brewmaster, John McClure retains a little more freedom to brew beyond the four mandated Rock Bottom styles. A constantly rotating selection of interesting beers is always pouring alongside the staples, and depending on when you visit, you might taste everything from an English old ale to a bourbon barrel-aged imperial porter.

WYNKOOP BREWING COMPANY

1634 18th St., Denver, CO 80202; (303) 297-2700; Wynkoop.com; **Twitter:** @Wynkoop
Founded: 1988 **Founder:** John Hickenlooper **Brewer:** Andy Brown **Flagship Beer:** Rail
Yard Ale **Year-round Beers:** Silverback Pale Ale, Light Rail Ale, B3K Schwarzbier, Cowtown
Milk Stout, Wixz Weiss, St. Charles ESB, 2 Guns Pilsener, Patty's Chili Beer, London Calling
IPA, Mile HI.P.A, Cottonwood Organic White **Seasonals/Special Releases:** Changes

Wynkoop Brewing Company opened a brewery and restaurant in 1988 in the
J.S. Brown Mercantile Building, which was constructed in 1899 in Denver's
dilapidated lower downtown Denver neighborhood. At the time, it had been at least
five years since a restaurant had attempted to open for business in the neighborhood. Wynkoop was an immediate success. Not coincidentally, a revival of the neighborhood followed with the opening of other restaurants as well as residential lofts.

Wynkoop was at the cusp of a trend that would play out through the mid-1990s, with brewpubs opening on an almost weekly basis.

The business now includes six Colorado-based craft beer–centric bars and restaurants, and the Phantom Canyon brewpub in Colorado Springs. The house menu is much loved by Denver locals and out-of-town regulars alike. Soups and salads are mainstays, as they are at most brewpubs. Beyond these, diners can choose from the likes of shepherd's pie, fish-and-chips, bangers and mash, buffalo meatloaf, freshly caught Rocky Mountain trout, and grilled lamb sirloin.

In addition to more than 10 house beers, Wynkoop also pours guest beers from mostly local breweries, although far-flung out-of-state beers and European imports also appear from time to time. Whatever style of beer you are in the mood for, Wynkoop more than likely has you covered from mainstays, like its spicy **Patty's Chili Beer** and malty fruitcake-flavored **St. Charles Extra Special Bitter,** to its bright and effervescent cereal forward **Cottonwood Organic White** and bitter, yet balanced **Mile HI.P.A.**

However, the star of Wynkoop's taps is undoubtedly its American black lager, **B3K.** At once roasty, yet refreshing, this beer is light enough to enjoy all evening, and full flavored enough to constantly remind you that you're drinking something with a craft and heritage. It is one of the best examples of a dark lager in Colorado. Much to locals' delight, B3K recently joined Wynkoop's expanding line of canned retail product.

Beer Bars

ALE HOUSE AT AMATO'S
2501 16th St., Denver, CO 80211; (303) 433-9734; AleHouseDenver.com;
Twitter: @AleHouseDenver
Taps: 42

Located a short walk from Denver Beer Co. in Denver's lower highlands, Ale House at Amato's offers up some 42 taps of Colorado craft beer. Fifteen of the taps are dedicated to the beers of owning partners Breckenridge Brewery and Wynkoop, with 25 dedicated to beers from other breweries around the state, with two taps reserved for mead and cider. Amato's also offers some absolutely stunning views of the Denver skyline. If you happen to be visiting on one of Denver's more than 300 blue-sky sunny days, then grab a table outside on the roof.

Amato's menu is a hearty hybrid of modern craft beer–inspired cuisine and American bar classics. Appetizers include wings three ways, calamari fritti, IPA flat bread served with duck confit, blue cheese, arugula and house made berry jam, fresh mussels, elk sausage, crab cakes, edamame and wild boar sliders. Daily soups and inventive salads are supplemented by 10 different sandwiches. Entrees include pork loin, salmon, rib eye, buffalo meatloaf, ale-brined slow-roasted chicken, lobster mac and cheese, and IPA battered fish-and-chips. Diners can also choose from 10 creative half-pound burgers, including the PB&J burger served with creamy peanut butter, chopped bacon, and house-made berry jam.

BRECKENRIDGE COLORADO CRAFT
2220 Blake St., Denver, CO 80205; (303) 297-3644; Breckbrew.com;
Twitter: @BreckBallPark
Taps: 32

Breckenridge Ballpark Pub reopened after a short renovation in May 2012. Part of the renovation was greatly expanding the number of taps. No brewing takes place at Ball Park any longer, with all of Breckenridge's brewing taking place at 700 Kalamath St., south of downtown. In summer 2012 Ballpark Pub was rebranded Breckenridge Colorado Craft. The pub now counts some 32 taps. Breckenridge beers are given a portion of those with the remaining taps used for a wide selection of beers from other Colorado breweries. The pub goes out of its way to secure as many barrel-aged beers as possible. Cider from Denver's Colorado Cider Company and Mead from Redstone Meadery in Boulder are also on tap.

Colorado Craft food consists of an all-American bar and pub grub. Appetizers include dips, nachos, chicken tenders, quesadillas, hummus, chili cheese fries, and more. A broad selection of soups and salads, chicken sandwiches, burgers, and a range of Mexican dishes are also available.

CHEEKY MONK BELGIAN BEER CAFE

534 E. Colfax Ave., Denver, CO 80203; (303) 861-0347; TheCheekyMonk.com;
Twitter: @TheCheekyMonk
Taps: 20 **Bottles/Cans:** 30+

Cheeky Monk's mission is to bring the very best of Belgian beer culture to Denver. The company now counts three locations in the state, but it's the original location on Colfax Avenue that is the business's spiritual and undisputed home. So successful has the Cheeky Monk model been that the business plans to open a brewery and Belgian food market next door. The name of the new brewery will be Three Saints.

A visit to Denver is not complete without a visit to Cheeky Monk. The star of the bar is undoubtedly its 20 taps of prized imported Belgian beer. All styles and major breweries are represented. Supplementing these are more 30 bottled Belgian beers. Being a Belgian-centric restaurant and bar, Cheeky Monk offers a menu heavily inspired by Flemish cuisine. Appetizers include frites aioli with house seasoning, garlic-infused olive oil and Parmesan frites, fried pickles, croquettes de fromage, and carbonnade flamande. Complementing the soups, salads, sandwiches, and burgers are rabbit cassoulet, ratatouille and steamed mussels, and frites served seven different ways. Of course a "trip" to Belgium is not complete without a large Belgian waffle for dessert.

COLT & GRAY

1553 Platte St., #120, Denver, CO 80202; (303) 477-1447; ColtandGray.com;
Twitter: @ColtandGray
Taps: 6 **Bottles/Cans:** 15+

Colt & Gray is located in Denver's professional and affluent lower highlands neighborhood. Emphasizing quality and affordability, it is one of the better places to enjoy good beer in the city. A short and attractive walk from downtown, Colt & Gray is just down the street from Denver Beer Co., so it makes for a great one-two stop and visit. The bar pours rotating taps of carefully chosen craft beer and offers a nice selection of domestic craft and imported bottles and cans, including many one-off small batch brews and special barrel-aged releases by local and out-of-state craft breweries.

The seasonal food menu is as you'd expect of a high-caliber establishment but is in no way intimidating. A few recent highlights include starters such as fried oysters, snails with garlic herb butter, bacon and cashew caramel corn, and crispy pig trotter. A wide selection of house-made charcuterie and cheese is offered a la carte. Small plates include oysters on the half shell, sautéed sweetbreads, mussels, Hudson Valley foie gras, roasted bone marrow, and Colorado grass-fed beef hearts. Example entrees are seared diver scallops, roasted leg of lamb, pan-seared rabbit, roasted squad, and truffle turkey burger.

DENVER BICYCLE CAFE

1308 E. 17th Ave., Denver, CO 80218; (720) 446-8029; DenverBicycleCafe.com;
Twitter: @denverbikecafe
Taps: 6 **Bottles/Cans:** 30+

Denver Bicycle Cafe is one of Denver's most friendly and relaxing places to grab a beer. Although a bicycle repair shop that is also a coffee shop and a beer bar might not seem like an obvious place to enjoy a local craft beer, this place succeeds. It offers six ever-changing taps of craft beer sourced from some of the area's smallest and newest breweries, along with high-quality espresso drinks and homemade tamales and pastries. If that wasn't enough, Denver Bicycle Cafe also sells virtually every canned craft beer produced in Colorado, which, when you consider that the state leads the nation in canning craft beer, is quite a few. Located a few blocks from Vine Street Pub & Brewery, Denver Bicycle Cafe is an absolute must visit, regardless of whether or not you ride a bike.

EUCLID HALL BAR & KITCHEN

1317 14th St., Denver, CO 80202; (303) 534-4255; EuclidHall.com; **Twitter:** @EuclidHall
Taps: 12 **Bottles/Cans:** 40

Founded by Jennifer Jasinski and Beth Gruitch, the owners of two nearby high-end restaurants, Euclid Hall Bar & Kitchen takes the concept of good beer and good food to haute cuisine levels. Located in Denver's picturesque and heavily trafficked Larimer restaurant neighborhood, Euclid serves up more than 10 taps of mostly locally sourced craft beer to pair with its outstanding menu. There is also a cleverly subdivided beer bottle and can list that arranges offerings in increasing levels of boldness and complexity. The first category is "Arithmetic,"which is followed by "Algebra," "Geometry," "Trigonometry," "Calculus," and "Quantum Mathematics." A category called "Library List" offers limited-release beers. Appetizers run the

gourmet gamut from roasted beet ambrosia, through pad Thai pig ears, brûléed center-cut beef marrow bones, fried cheddar curds, and beyond. A mouth-watering selection of Montreal-inspired poutiness—plates of hand-cut french fries covered in melted Wisconsin cheddar cheese curds and gravy—is also offered. Entrees include chicken fried quail and waffles, roasted Alaskan halibut, pork belly and octopus surf n' turf, and grilled Camembert and pear preserve sandwich. The highlight of Euclid's colorful menu, though, is undoubtedly its menu of freshly hand-cranked sausages from around the world. Another speciality of Euclid is craft beer cocktails, of which there are usually eight or so to choose from.

FALLING ROCK TAP HOUSE

1919 Blake St., Denver, CO 80202; (303) 293-8338; FallingRockTapHouse.com;
Twitter: @FallingRockTap
Taps: 75 **Bottles/Cans:** 100+

Falling Rock Tap House is a Denver beer institution. The bar is known far and wide, from Los Angeles to New York City, and beer lovers know its name and respect its reputation. Owner Chris Black is a legend in the beer industry and within craft-beer drinking circles. When the GABF takes over Denver each autumn, Falling Rock becomes the hub of off-site festivities, meet ups, and general rabble-rousing. It's the place you'll find the most-famous brewers in the industry nursing a beer after a gold-medal win. It's the place you'll find newbie beer geeks and seasoned festivalgoers striking up new friendships despite living on opposite sides of the world.

The more than 75 taps of beer that Falling Rock pours year-round are always interesting and often very rare. It's not unusual to walk into the bar on a quiet Wednesday evening and find a five-year-old Belgian Christmas beer on the beer list. Black prides himself on being able to source some of the rarest bottles and kegs of beer in the world. If the more than 75 taps of beer aren't enough to whet the palate, there's always the more than 130 bottled beers in the cooler.

The bar menu is like many craft-beer bars in Colorado, featuring classic American cuisine. Appetizers include beer-battered mushrooms, chicken tenders and fries, quesadillas, and wings. Entrees include salads, sandwiches, burgers, tacos, and hot subs.

FRESHCRAFT

1530 Blake St., Denver, CO 80202; (303) 758-9608; Freshcraft.com;
Twitter: @FreshcraftFood
Taps: 20+ **Bottles/Cans:** 100+

In the short time that Freshcraft has been open, it has firmly cemented itself as one of the most-important, most-loved, and most-respected beer bars in Denver. Freshcraft was founded by three brothers, Lucas, Aaron, and Jason Forgy, in autumn 2010. The bar prides itself on a changing selection of 20 craft beer taps and a bottle list that numbers well over 100 different beers.

Food, too, is an important part of the Freshcraft business. The seasonal menu is of a higher quality than you'll find at other beer spots in the city and is largely designed to pair well with beer. Examples of appetizers include southern fried pickles, tuna watermelon nubbins, garlic chili wings, beer-crusted cheese dippers (see recipe, page 197), and rustic bruschetta. Main plates are offered in small, medium, and large sizes, mostly inspired by American comfort foods. Examples include cocoa chili marinated and roasted crimini mushroom tacos; cheese-crusted, Iowa-style pork tenderloin; mac and cheese made with prosciutto and sun-dried tomatos; chili-glazed Colorado bass; buffalo sausage and kraut; and barbecue meatloaf.

There can be a line out the door waiting to get into Freshcraft during the annual GABF, due in part to an endless list of special beer tappings and its close proximity to the Convention Center, where the main component of the festival takes place.

Denver

HOPS & PIE

3920 Tennyson St., Denver, CO 80212; (303) 477-7000; HopsandPie.com
Taps: 11 **Bottles/Cans:** 50+

Located in Denver's Berkeley neighborhood, Hops & Pie is one of the city's best-kept beer and great food secrets. In addition to Hops & Pie P.A., the house beer brewed by Denver's Strange Brewing Company, the restaurant and bar pours upwards of 10 different craft beers from across the state and country. The beer pours are very carefully curated and are always of an interesting nature and quality. In addition to

the beers on tap, Hops & Pie also has a cellar brimming with choice craft bombers and large format bottles and a cooler full of craft cans.

The food at Hops & Pie is some of the very best in Colorado. The house hand-tossed pizzas are of the highest quality you will find anywhere in the city. A suggested pie of the month is supplemented by a long list of available toppings. Cheeses include feta, fresh mozzarella, blue, goat, ricotta, vegan, swiss, and provolone. Meat toppings extend to prosciutto, smoked ham hock, beer-braised brisket, pulled pork, smoked pork loin, salami, pastrami, and white anchovy. In addition to the usual vegetable toppings you can also opt for dollops of mash potato or corn puree. If some of the best pizza in Colorado isn't enough to whet your appetite, Hops & Pie also makes one of the best mac and cheese dishes in the state (see recipe, page 199). It includes smoked ham, English peas, and herbed bread crumbs. Other menu items of note include the chipotle mango carnitas tacos; house honey-roasted nuts; a pork and apple sandwich; a Reuben; and the B.L.E.A.T., a sandwich with applewood smoked bacon, lettuce, farm egg, avocado, tomato, and aioli.

RACKHOUSE PUB

208 S. Kalamath St., Denver, CO 80223; (720) 570-7824; RackhousePub.com;
Twitter: @RackhousePub
Taps: 20

You'd be forgiven for thinking that you've left Denver entirely when traveling to the outstanding Rackhouse Pub. It's located in a far-flung, industrial corner of southwest Denver next to I-25 in the same building as the famous Stranahan's Colorado Whiskey. The trek is absolutely worth it, though. Rackhouse has quietly built a reputation as one of the best beer and whiskey bars in the state. It's a favorite place for locals to take out-of-town visitors to give them a real taste of Colorado.

Behind the bar, 19 of the 20 beer taps are dedicated to pouring an ever-changing selection of Colorado brewed beer. One tap is reserved for an out-of-state craft beer. If whiskey is your thing, Rackhouse has more than 60 to keep you occupied.

The food menu is big and bold and is focused mainly on big meat and rustic Italian American. Appetizers include street tacos, salmon bruschetta, beef bone marrow, and baked popcorn chicken served with wasabi cream, whiskey barbecue glaze, or cayenne cambozola. Chili is represented by a choice of Colorado beef whiskey, green chicken, and veggie, or a sampler of all three. Rackhouse is famous for its Sea Mac, a rich and creamy mac and cheese made with the addition of maine lobster, gulf shrimp, crayfish, and bacon. For larger appetites there's slow-cooked rack ribs, prime rib, roast chicken, and bison stew. Few places in the city pair such hearty and inspired food with great local beer.

Denver

STAR BAR DENVER

2137 Larimer St., Denver, CO 80205; (720) 328-2420; StarBarDenver.com;
Twitter: @StarBar_Denver
Taps: 14 **Bottles/Cans:** 20+

When is a dive bar not a dive bar? When it's Star Bar Denver, that's when. Star Bar Denver is run by Justin Lloyd, one of Colorado's loudest and proudest good-beer, good-spirit and, not so surprisingly, good-cocktail advocates and specialists. Star Bar has oodles of old-Denver charm, and it's located on a street that seems like it must have been home to well-used watering holes since the days when the city was a busy frontier town. The winner of numerous awards, Star Bar pours 14 taps of mostly Colorado craft beer. But not just any Colorado craft beer—Star Bar is a great place to frequent if you want to taste many of the rarest, one-off, or unusual beers in the state. Justin also initiates one-off creations by occasionally providing spent spirit barrels from small craft distilleries to local area breweries to fill with a beer just for Star Bar.

Star Bar also specializes in local craft spirits, with more than 30 behind the bar. Star Bar has made quite a name for itself nationwide as one of the best places to taste craft beer cocktails. Justin has cooked countless creations and has a real knack for coming up with new cocktails on the fly, as new beers are tapped. A beer field trip to Denver is not complete without a stop at Star Bar.

VINE ST. PUB & BREWERY

1700 Vine St., Denver, CO 80206; (303) 388-2337; MountainSunPub.com;
Twitter: @mountainsunpub
Taps: 21

In addition to being one Denver's best brewpubs to visit Vine St. Pub & Brewery is also one of Denver's best beer bars. (See its sister location, Mountain Sun Pub & Brewery, page 73.) It has a long list of bold and beautiful house-brewed beers to choose from and an extensive and seasonal menu of fresh, carefully prepared food. Vine St. also has six or seven guest craft beers on tap at any one time.

WAZEE SUPPER CLUB

1600 15th St., Denver, CO 80202; (303) 623-9518; WazeeSupperClub.com;
Twitter: @WazeeSupperClub
Taps: 12

Now managed by the same beer-loving business folk who operate Denver's Breckenridge Brewery, Wynkoop Brewing Company in lower downtown, and Phantom Canyon brewpub in downtown Colorado Springs, and more than a dozen other restaurants in the state, the Wazee Supper Club has been a fixture of Denver's historic lower downtown neighborhood, serving beer and pizza, since 1974.

The interior has tons of retro charm, from its vaulted ceilings and black-and-white checkerboard floor to the dumbwaiter that is still used to carry food to the floor. The bar serves up a mix of some 20 taps of beers by Wynkoop, Breckenridge, other Colorado breweries, and some macros, like Guinness, Boddingtons, and Stella Artois. The food menu remains dedicated to the art of pizza making and classic American diner–inspired dishes. Appetizers include Italian breadsticks, white cheddar cheese curds with marinara sauce, wings, and fried pickles. The house burgers, soups, and salads are strongly supported by the main feature of the restaurant, the pizzas and strombolis. All traditional toppings and fillings are thoroughly represented.

Denver

Denver Area

To Boulder
To Fort Collins
To Fort Morgan

Westminster
Thornton

W. 88th Ave.
E. 88th Ave.

Rocky Mountain
Arsenal National
Wildlife Refuge

Denver International Airport

Peña Blvd.

Standley Lake

W. 72nd Ave.

E. 72nd Ave.

E. 56th Ave.

W. 64th Ave.
Arvada

Ward Rd.

1,2

Tower Rd.

Commerce City

Wheat Ridge

W. 38th Ave.

M. L. King Blvd.

Colfax Ave.

3,4
Golden

Colfax Ave.

6th Ave.

6th Ave.

To Idaho Springs

Denver

Alameda Ave.

Alameda Ave.

Aurora

Lakewood

Jewell Ave.
Littleton

Leetsdale Dr.

Cherry Creek

5

Bear Creek Lake

Hampden Ave.

Chambers Rd.
Buckley Rd.
Tower Rd.

Quincy Ave.

Englewood

Quincy Ave.

Marston Lake

Belleview Ave.

Cherry Creek Reservoir

6

W. Belleview Ave.

Greenwood Village

Jordan Rd.

Arapahoe Rd.

Ken Caryl Rd.

Centennial

Littleton

7

Chatfield Reservoir

Lincoln Ave.

Lone Tree
8 ○ **Parker**

E Hess Rd.

CastlePines Pkwy.

Santa Fe Dr.

N Crowfoot Valley Rd.

N

0   3   6 miles

9

To Colorado Springs
Castle Rock

BREWERIES

AC Golden Brewing Company	**3**
Arvada Beer Company	**2**
Coors Brewing Company	**3**
Dry Dock Brewing Company	**5**
Elk Mountain Brewing	**8**
Golden City Brewery	**4**
Lone Tree Brewing Company	**7**

BREWPUBS

Dad & Dudes Breweria	**6**
Rockyard American Grill & Brewing Company	**9**
Yak and Yeti Restaurant & Brewpub	**1**

Denver Area

Arvada, Aurora, Castle Rock, Golden, Lone Tree & Parker

Carefully positioned in the sprawling towns and suburbs surrounding Denver proper is a wonderful selection of newer small-scale breweries all vying for attention in the state's increasingly competitive and busy beer market. Proof that competition can be a great thing, these breweries also brew some of the best beer in country, as they quietly seek to outdo each other while growing and maintaining their respective status as local neighborhood breweries.

Casting a long shadow alongside these new brewing kids on the block is, of course, the globally renowned Coors Brewing Company in Golden. It is the antithesis of the local breweries, but also the flag bearer of the sorts of profits and success that can eventually befall any small brewery that can maintain good standing in the market for long enough.

Breweries

AC GOLDEN BREWING COMPANY (MILLERCOORS)

1221 Ford St. and 13th, Golden, CO 80401; (800) 936-5259; ACGolden.com
Founded: 2007 **Brewer:** Jeff Cornell **Flagship Beer:** Colorado Native **Year-round Beers:** Colorado Native, Herman Joseph's Private Reserve **Seasonals/Special Releases:** Winterfest, Hidden Barrel Kriek, Hidden Barrel Peche, Hidden Barrel Apricot, IPL (India Pale Lager) **Tours:** No **Taproom:** Thurs to Mon 10 a.m. to 4 p.m., Sun noon to 4 p.m.

Launched in 2007 as a stand-alone business and pilot brewery for parent company MillerCoors, AC Golden is definitely one of the more unique members of Colorado's brewing fraternity. Located deep within the belly of the Coors plant in Golden and not open to the public, AC Golden has a small team of skilled full-time brewers who are allowed to experiment with whatever they please. The success stories are then packaged and sold throughout Colorado.

The first AC Golden beer to hit taps and shelves was **Herman Joseph's Private Reserve,** a German Pilsner that pours a brilliant silver-flecked gold color. The beer brewed in 30-barrel batches is an approximation of a recipe brought from Germany by Adolph Coors in the 1860s. Bright with a snappy hop profile, the lager finishes extremely clean and crisp.

The second beer to find a new home at AC Golden was **Winterfest,** a 5.5 percent ABV caramel-colored Vienna lager originally brewed by Coors in the late 1980s for the winter holidays. Winterfest is brewed in September and only sold in Colorado. The beer has a distinct toffee flavor and a semisweet malt forward finish.

The next beer, and the first original recipe, to appear from the secretive AC Golden was **Colorado Native,** an American amber lager brewed almost exclusively with Colorado-sourced ingredients; some of the hops need to be imported into the state from elsewhere. The beer was partly designed to appeal to Coloradoans, increasing interest in locally sourced goods. Colorado Native is brewed with a mix of Chinook, Centennial, and Cascade hops and is decidedly more robust in bitterness and flavor than any other lager brewed at Coors in 2012.

Peche Belgian-Style Ale Aged in Oak Wine Barrels with Peaches Added

Style: American Wild Ale

ABV: Unknown

Availability: Occasionally in bottles

Bottle conditioned with wine yeast and *Brettanomyces (Brett),* this wine-barrel-aged American wild ale was rested on an abundance of Palisade peaches during an extended maturation. The result is a complex, yeast-forward beer with a funky *Brett* edge and soft floral and semisweet summer fruit notes. Peche is one of AC Golden's first Hidden Barrel releases, with more experimental batches to follow. Peche was initially released in the Denver-metro area only, alongside Apricot, a similar beer aged in wine barrels on that fruit.

BREWER NOTES

Our Peche relaxed in a used oak barrel for nearly a year with a hefty dose of fresh peaches from Palisade, Colorado. The use of several strains of brettanomyces and various souring organisms have created a tart, dry Belgian-Style Ale.

We chose a pale base ale to really allow the local peaches to shine through. A pleasant acidity is met with a very dry finish creating a well rounded, peach forward ale. Bottle conditioned with wine yeast and brettanomyces for yet another layer of complexity.

QUESTIONS? (303) 292 3926

AC GOLDEN
BREWING COMPANY™

PECHE

BELGIAN-STYLE ALE AGED IN OAK
WINE BARRELS WITH PEACHES ADDED

1	5/29/2010	8/16/2011	13
BATCH	BREWED	BOTTLED	HBC BARREL

*2012 AC GOLDEN BREWING CO., GOLDEN, CO 80401
750 ml • 1 pint 9.4 Fluid Ounces (25.4 FL. OZ.)

HIDDEN BARREL

COLLECTION™

The Hidden Barrel Collection™ displays our passion for experimenting with a variety of brewing materials and production methods. We experiment with various yeasts in fermentation and in bottle conditioning.

Many beers and ales in the Collection require months to reach maturity. We've been anxiously waiting for this one to be ready to share and now that it is, we hope you enjoy it!

Denver Area

ARVADA BEER COMPANY

5600 Olde Wadsworth Blvd., Arvada, CO 80002; (303) 467-2337; ArvadaBeer.com;
Twitter: @ArvadaBeer
Founded: 2011 **Founders:** Cary Floyd and Kelly Floyd **Brewer:** Adam Draeger **Flagship Beer:** Goldline IPA **Year-round Beers:** Goldline IPA, Poolhall Porter, Ralston's Golden Ale, Olde Town Brown, Water Tower Wheat **Seasonals/Special Releases:** Mexican Lager, Engine 1 Pale Ale, Arvada Pride DIPA, Rotary Red, Renovator Doppelbock, Vanderhoof Barleywine **Tours:** None **Taproom:** Mon through Thurs noon to 10 p.m., Fri through Sat 11 a.m. to 11 p.m., Sun 11 a.m. to 9 p.m. Growlers are available to go.

The appropriately named Arvada Beer Company opened for business in November 2011 and is the second brewery in the small picturesque town of Arvada, located about 15 minutes west of downtown Denver. The other brewery in Arvada is the Indian and Tibetan food-themed brewpub Yak and Yeti, itself only a few blocks from Arvada Beer Company.

Situated in a historic building dating back to 1916, the spacious brewery and taproom can comfortably seat upwards of 130 people. The brewery founders, including co-owner Kelly Floyd, won just about every homebrew award available before they took the commercial brewery plunge. Their roots as hard-core homebrewers come through in their broad and ever expanding selection of ales and lagers. The taproom usually pours six to eight different beers at any one time, with new beers tapped every week.

The 5 percent ABV **59'er Schwarzbier** is a German lager brewed to style, with a strong blackened malt aroma, roasty bitter body, and pleasant milk chocolate finish. Those familiar with style know to expect much less bitterness in this drink than in ales of the same color. The brewery won a gold medal for this beer at the 2011 Colorado State Fair. Arvada's **Goldline IPA** won a bronze medal. This 6.5 percent sunshine-yellow American IPA bursts with orange and yellow citrus fruit character. The beer has an appropriately deep, leafy-green bitterness and a definite earthy finish.

Visitors can order food to eat in from a number of local restaurants, with the menus provided. There is also a beer-centric Belgian-style pomme frites eatery connected to the brewery, providing the perfect accompaniment to the house beers.

Olde Town Brown

Style: American Brown Ale

ABV: 4.8 percent

Availability: Year-round on tap

Olde Town Brown has the character of a beer that was born by seasoned homebrewers clearly familiar with beer foundation beer styles. This walnut-colored American brown ale has a light milk-chocolate and hazelnut-flavor profile, a soft medium malt finish, and an inviting nutty nose. It packs a lot of personality for a 4.8 percent ABV ale and is surely the must try of Arvada's core beers.

COORS BREWING COMPANY (MILLERCOORS)

1221 Ford St. and 13th, Golden, CO 80401; (303) 277-2337; MillerCoors.com; **Twitter:** @MillerCoors

Founded: 1873 **Founders:** Adolph Coors and Jacob Schueler **Brewer:** Various **Flagship Beer:** Coors Light **Year-round Beers:** Too many to list **Seasonals/Special Releases:** Blue Moon Harvest Pumpkin Ale, Blue Moon Spring Blonde Wheat Ale, Blue Moon Summer Honey Wheat Ale, Blue Moon Winter Abbey Ale **Tours:** Yes **Taproom:** Thurs to Mon 10 a.m. to 4 p.m., Sun noon to 4 p.m.

Where to begin with Coors Brewing Company? The best place is with one of the self-guided tours that hundreds of thousands of people enjoy each year when they visit the brewery. Founded in 1893, Coors is one the oldest and most storied breweries in America and is a pillar of the nation's beer history. Located in the old frontier town of Golden at the feet of the Rocky Mountains, it remains the world's single location largest brewery. The size of the facility is humbling by any standard.

During the eye-opening tour, you will witness the vast economies of scale that the historical brewery is able to operate on. It's undeniably breathtaking. Coors malts its own grains for brewing, a feat few breweries around the world can claim. It processes its own water, sourced from nearby mountain springs. It produces its own cans. Coors was the first brewery to use aluminium cans for beer in America. One of the most impressive sights is the farm of traditionally fashioned copper brew kettles that stretch off as far as the eye can see, a stark contrast to the multi-billion-dollar, single-unit stainless system at Anheuser-Busch in Fort Collins.

Denver Area

While Coors can hardly be considered a local Colorado brand anymore given its international stature and reach, Coors Banquet and Coors Light both remain extremely popular with native Coloradoans.

Like the equally monolithic Anheuser-Busch plant in Fort Collins, Coors in Golden is responsible for brewing an almost endless list of lagers, ales, and malt liquors owned by the corporation. The more well regarded of these are poured in the brewery's expansive taproom and are available to enjoy after taking the tour. Seasonals come and go, but the core brands, including **Blue Moon, Killian's Irish Red,** and **Coors Banquet,** are unmoving staples.

Beer Lover's Pick

Coors Banquet
Style: American Adjunct Lager
ABV: 5 percent
Availability: Year-round on tap, in bottles, and in cans
Enjoying a fresh glass of Coors Banquet, which is brewed only in Golden, is an absolute must for any self-respecting beer geek or historian visiting Colorado. Few beers in America are as iconic and or have been brewed in much the same way for so long. The bright, golden-blonde, 5 percent ABV pale lager remains as quaffable and clean as you expect it to be, or indeed, remember it to be.

DRY DOCK BREWING COMPANY

15120 E. Hampden Ave., Aurora, CO 80014; (303) 400-5606; DryDockBrewing.com; **Twitter:** @DryDockBrewing
Founded: 2005 **Founder:** Kevin DeLange **Brewer:** Doug Hyndman **Flagship Beer:** Hefeweizen **Year-round Beers:** Hefeweizen, HMS Victory Amber, Breakwater Pale Ale, Vanilla Porter, USS Enterprise IPA, HMS Bounty Old Ale, Dry Dock Double IPA, Paragon Apricot Blonde **Seasonals/Special Releases:** Savka Poppy Oat Stout, Coffee Milk Stout, Hop Abomination 3, Poor Richard's Colonial Ale, Tripel, Bligh's Barleywine Ale **Tours:** None **Taproom:** Sun through Tues noon to 9 p.m., Wed noon to 9:30 p.m., Thurs noon to 10 p.m., Fri through Sat noon to 11 p.m. Growlers and bottles are available to go.

Dry Dock Brewing Company, located in Aurora, is the brainchild of homebrew store owner Kevin DeLange. In 2005 he rented a unit with just enough square footage in a strip mall, purchased the necessary equipment, and began brewing. As many new brewers quickly discover, success in brewing means you rapidly run out of space, especially if you have a growing taproom. In 2009 Kevin moved to a larger space in the same strip mall, the same year that Dry Dock won the Small Brewery of the Year award at the GABF, another potent catalyst for growth. Dry Dock will open a dedicated production brewery in fall 2012.

Brewed perfectly to style, "best" describes the majority of Dry Dock's beers. That's not to say there aren't also a few that showcase carefully crafted creative flourishes, **Vanilla Porter** (5.4 percent ABV) and **Apricot Blonde** (5.1 percent ABV) being two brilliant examples. For true beer aficionados, it's the likes of Dry Dock's multi-award-winning traditional **Hefeweizen** (4.3 percent ABV), **HMS Victory Amber** (5.8 percent ABV), **HMS Bounty Old Ale** (7 percent ABV), and **Dry Dock Double IPA** (9 percent ABV, see recipe on page 187) that should hold the most appeal.

Dry Dock uses more than 2 pounds of Madagascar and Tahitian vanilla beans in each seven-barrel batch of its Vanilla Porter. The result is a beer that loudly and proudly announces its vanilla addition. The beer greets the expectant imbiber with the sweet aromas of vanilla extract, vanilla wafer cookies, toffee, and confectioner's sugar. The sweet treat vibe continues unabated in the drink. Flavors of milk-chocolate-covered malted milk balls, clove, brown sugar, and molasses all feature prominently.

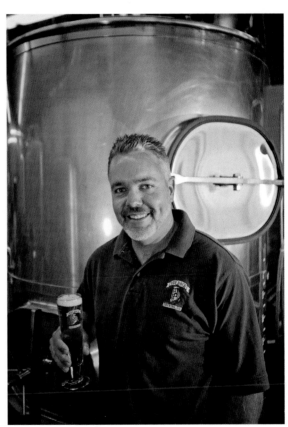

Denver Area

Bligh's Barleywine Ale
Style: English Barleywine
ABV: 9 percent
Availability: Limited fourth-quarter release in 22-ounce bottles

Released in October 2011, Bligh's Barleywine Ale was featured on many "best beers of 2011" lists in Colorado, including my own. The beer was also voted the best Colorado beer of the year by the readers of the popular blog Denver of the Wagon. Bligh's is a hazelnut, brown-colored English-style barleywine, aged for seven months in Stranahan's Colorado Whiskey barrels. The beer breathes welcoming aromas of leather, vanilla, fig, currants, black tea, molasses, and sherry. On the palate, the dominant flavor is unmistakably black licorice, with secondary notes of plum, muscovado sugar, black treacle, baked apples, and peppermint. In keeping with traditional English barleywine style, the beer is very sweet, bitterness low.

ELK MOUNTAIN BREWING

18921 E. Plaza Dr., Parker, CO 80134; (303) 805-2739; ElkMountainBrewing.com
Founded: 2009 **Founders:** Tom Bell and Marcia Bell **Brewer:** Tom Bell **Flagship Beer:** Puma IPA **Year-round Beers:** Puma IPA, Rock Slide Amber Ale, Mine Shaft Kolsch, Wild Wapiti Wheat, Ghost Town Brown, Elk Horn Stout, Ute Bill Pale Ale **Seasonals/Special Releases:** Rotating list **Tours:** None **Taproom:** Mon through Thurs 3 to 9 p.m., Fri through Sat noon to 11 p.m., Sun noon to 8 p.m. Growlers are available to go.

Elk Mountain opened in the summer of 2010. Located in the sleepy commuter town of Parker, Colorado, the brewery was an almost instantaneous hit. It's a story repeated up and down the state: Small brewery opens in otherwise sleepy or quiet locale; locals suddenly appear and rapidly develop a taste for their new home-town brew.

Elk Mountain founder and brewer, Tom Bell, had wanted to open his own brewery for more than a decade. Family and financial obligations hindered that, but the avid hunter and former mechanic did eventually realize his goal and imbued the taproom with a true sense of the local area. All of the beers are named after local wildlife or nearby geographical landmarks. In the center of the spacious room, a large chandelier made from elk horns hangs proudly.

The beers Bell brews are mostly American standards or twists on German or English styles. **Puma IPA** is the brewery's best-selling beer. The American India Pale Ale is bold, with a robust and bitter-tasting green bite, a freshly peeled yellow grapefruit aroma, and a decisive bitter finish. **Ghost Town Brown** is a classic American brown ale, with moderate bitterness, a chocolate belly, and an almost chewy, roasted nut finish. The hazel-colored pour is one of the taprooms most popular pours.

Elk Horn Stout is a hearty oatmeal stout brewed with flaked oats, barley, and five specialty malts. The beer has a thick chocolate-sauce flavor and a smooth mouth feel. Bitterness is low to moderate.

Wild Wapiti Wheat is Elk's take on a traditional Hefeweizen. The beers unfiltered wheat body and sweet clove and freshly peeling banana aroma are perfectly executed. As with all good Hefes, this is engineered for quaffing large glasses of the stuff.

Beer Lover's Pick

Vanilla Caramel Porter
Style: American Porter
ABV: 5.75 percent
Availability: Occasionally on tap
Vanilla Caramel Porter. The very name sounds too good to be true. But the beer more than delivers on its decadent promise. It's big, it's desserty, it's invitingly bittersweet, and demands your prolonged enjoyment. It's a rotating release, so definitely jump on it if you happen to find yourself in the taproom when it's pouring. If you're a fan of lush dark stouts and porters, you will not be disappointed.

GOLDEN CITY BREWERY

920 12th St., Golden, CO 80401; (303) 279-8092; GCBrewery.com; **Twitter:** @goldencitybrew
Founded: 1993 **Founders:** Charlie Sturdavant and Janine Sturdavant **Brewer:** Charlie Sturdavant **Flagship Beer:** Evolution IPA **Year-round Beers:** Evolution IPA, Mad Molly's Brown Ale, Lookout Stout, Clear Creek Gold Pale Ale, Legendary Red Ale **Seasonals/ Special Releases:** Changes **Tours:** None **Taproom:** Mon through Sun 11:30 a.m. to 6:30 p.m. Growlers and bottles are available to go.

At first glance you might be forgiven for thinking that Golden City Brewery was a busy party in someone's backyard garden. The neighborhood brewery resides on a residential side street in the small former frontier town of Golden.

Founded in 1993 by geologists Charlie and Janine Sturdavant, Golden City brewery makes much of its stature as the "second largest brewery in Golden" (the largest being Coors). The brewery is actually an extension of the couple's frontier-era house. The brewing is done in what was once a machine shop, and the taproom is in what was once a conservatory. When the weather complies, drinkers can enjoy their beer outside in the brewery *biergarten,* which is actually the backyard of the property. These are just a few of the many idiosyncrasies, beyond scale, that distinguishes Golden City from the bubbling beer-making behemoth down the road.

Golden City brews five core styles and a host of seasonal and one-off releases; many of these are bottled and are available at area liquor stores or to go, along with growlers at the brewery itself. The IPA and brown ale are both noteworthy. **Mad Molly's Brown Ale** (5 percent ABV) is a brown ale brewed in the northern English tradition. These beers are often refered to in the US as nut brown ales because of their hazelnut color and nutty aroma. Expect an easy drinking smooth body with notes of malted milk balls, mocha, and cocoa powder. **Evolution IPA** is balanced by most American standards for the style, and at 6 percent ABV it is a little lighter than the US norm in 2012. The beer offers up requisite resius pine and muted citrus notes, with bitter, but not overwhelming, hop-derived spiciness.

Anyone planning on visiting the brewery should note its limited hours of operation. Due to its unique license that allows it to brew in a residential area, the brewery is open daily from 11:30 a.m. to 6:30 p.m., so you should plan accordingly.

Beer Lover's Pick

Centurion Barleywine
Style: American Barleywine
ABV: 11.2 percent
Availability: Winter seasonal on tap
 and in bottles

Centurion Barleywine is a hulking winter seasonal strong enough to melt snow. The dark amber pour has an aroma not dissimilar to a European Christmas fruitcake, rich with dried fruit and Sherry notes. Bitterness puts the Centurion somewhere between an abundantly hopped California barleywine and more judiciously hopped English-style barleywine. This is a perfect beer to buy and cellar, so it can be sampled in each passing year as it matures and evolves.

LONE TREE BREWING COMPANY

8200 Park Meadows Dr., #8222, Lone Tree, CO 80124; (303) 792-5822;
LoneTreeBrewingCo.com
Founded: 2011 **Founders:** John Winter and Jason Wiedmaier **Brewers:** John Winter
and Jason Wiedmaier **Flagship Beer:** Hausfrau Hefeweizen **Year-round Beers:** Hausfrau
Hefeweizen, Toots' Oatmeal Stout, Ariadne's Blonde, Puddle Jumper Pale Ale, Hoptree IIPA
Seasonals/Special Releases: Mountain Mama Helles, Black IPA, Hoppy Holiday Brown,
Marienplatz Pilsner **Tours:** None **Taproom:** Mon through Wed noon to 8 p.m., Thurs noon
to 10 p.m., Fri noon to 10 p.m., Sat 11 a.m. to 10 p.m., Sun 11 a.m. to 8 p.m. Growlers
are available to go.

Lone Tree Brewing Company opened for business in December 2011. The brewery
and taproom are located in a bright and spacious retail and business park about 20
minutes south of Denver. Judging by the steady flow of new and seasoned patrons on
a Sunday morning, it has already amassed quite a buzz and following in the local area.

Lone Tree's founding partners, John Winter and Jason Wiedmaier, went into business with the idea of creating a modern, high-quality craft brewery. The space has a welcoming and embracing vibe. Despite its commercial location, the brewery has a neighborhood feel.

The brewery pours seven year-round beers and a raft of seasonal ales and lagers. Most of the beers are brewed very close to style. John especially has a deep respect for German beer styles and the country's approach to beer in general, and that full-flavored, easy-drinking nature definitely comes through in his finely crafted **Hausfrau Hefeweizen** (4.2 percent ABV), **Marienplatz Pilsner** (5 percent ABV), **Mountain Mama Helles** (5.3 percent ABV), **Ariadne's Blonde** (5.7 percent ABV), and **Toots' Oatmeal Stout** (5.2 percent ABV).

It's not just easy-drinking beers under 6 percent ABV that Lone Tree specializes in, though. You are just as likely to find their extremely popular 8 percent ABV double IPA, **Hoptree IIPA** or their dark, citrusy, and bitter 6.5 percent **Black IPA.** The emphasis, though, remains on drinkability and flavor.

Beer Lover's Pick

Puddle Jumper Pale Ale
Style: American Pale Ale
ABV: 5.7 percent
Availability: Year-round on tap
A puddle jumper is a small plane that is used to make short trips. This beer was named to honor John's days as a puddle jumper pilot. The beer is classic American pale ale, with strong yellow citrus, green herbaceous notes, and a quaffable dry swallow. Don't be surprised if you find yourself leaving the brewery with a growler of this stuff.

Brewpubs

DAD & DUDE'S BREWERIA

6730 S. Cornerstar Way, Aurora, CO 80016; (303) 400-5699; Breweria.com
Founded: 2010 **Founders:** Mason Hembree and Tom Hembree **Brewers:** Justin Baccary
and Bard Nielsen **Flagship Beer:** None **Year-round Beers:** None **Seasonals/Special
Releases:** Changes

Breweries in Colorado use brewhouses of every imaginable shape and size. At one
end of the scale, the likes of Coors in Golden and Anheuser-Busch in Fort Collins
brew millions of gallons of beer a day, while the state's burgeoning so-called nanobreweries produce less than 10 barrels a day. Dad & Dude's Breweria in Aurora, south
of Denver, uses the smallest brew system in the state, an in-house, homebrew-size
half barrel set up to brew a revolving selection of creative brews.

The Dad of the operation is longtime restaurateur Tom Hembree, and the Dude is his son, Mason Hembree. The brewpub servers up an enticing selection of rustic Italian pizzas, with crusts made of spent grain from the house-brew batches. Dad & Dude's aims to keep six different beers on tap at all times, but with many proving so popular, it can be a struggle to keep four on tap. In fact, Dad & Dude's is mulling plans to increase the size of their brew house to help meet demand.

The beauty of brewing on such a small scale is that new ideas can be realized in a short space of time. This flexibility means that rather than having to rely upon a core of specific house beers, Dad & Dude's is able to offer up an ever-changing selection of standard styles as well as more outlandish creations. One of the brewery's most requested re-brews is its **Buzzed Weasel Coffee Stout.** But on any given visit you might find anything, such as an IPA brewed with food-friendly ingredients like honey and basil. Much of the Dad & Dude's charm for beer geeks, besides its mouthwatering menu of pizzas, pastas, calzones, and loaded sandwiches, is never knowing what will be on tap.

ROCKYARD AMERICAN GRILL & BREWING COMPANY

880 Castleton Rd., Castle Rock, CO 80109; (303) 814-9273; Rockyard.com;
Twitter: @rockyardbrewing
Founded: 1999 **Founder:** Jeff Drabing **Brewer:** Jim Stinson **Flagship Beer:** Double Eagle Ale **Year-round Beers:** Double Eagle Ale, Redhawk Ale, Lightning Strike Stout, Hopyard IPA, Lynx Light Lager **Seasonals/Special Releases:** Bourbon Barrel Stout, Plymouth Rock Pumpkin Ale, Oktoberfest

As you might expect from a brewpub owned by five siblings, there is a distinct family-oriented vibe to Rockyard American Grill & Brewing Company. Opened in 1999, it's the only brewery in Castle Rock. Rockyard is more than a neighborhood brewpub, though. It bottles and distributes many of its offerings throughout the local area and as far north as Denver.

Jon Stinson has been Rockyard's brewmaster since 2002. He brews up to five year-round offerings and plenty of seasonals and one-off beers, including the most popular Oktoberfest. There is a distinctly lower alcohol content to the core beers at Rockyard, a reflection and understanding by the owners of its place as a brewery that most have no choice but to drive to. **Double Eagle Ale** is a 5 percent ABV American wheat ale with a bold cereal nose, a light body, low bitterness, and mild refreshing fruity finish. **Redhawk Ale** is a 5 percent American amber ale brewed with earthy English East Kent Golding hops and an abundance of caramel malts for an easy-drinking finished product. **Lightning Strike Stout** is a 6 percent ABV

American stout with big roasty charcoal and fresh-brewed coffee notes. The beer has a long dryness that makes it a great stand-in for the more commonly available Irish Dry stout, Guinness.

The food at Rockyard is all-American pub grub. Nachos, lettuce wraps, dips, fried mushrooms, potato skins, onion rings, and ahi tuna round out the appetizers. Mains include soups, salads, pastas, fish-and-chips, teriyaki salmon, burgers, steaks, wings, and a selection of Mexican dishes.

YAK & YETI RESTAURANT & BREWPUB

7803 Ralston Rd., Arvada, CO 80002; (303) 431-9000; TheYakandYeti.com; Twitter: @YakandYetiPub

Founded: 2010 **Founder:** Uday Patel **Brewer:** Adam Draeger **Flagship Beer:** Chai Stout
Year-round Beers: Changes **Seasonals/Special Releases:** Changes

Yak & Yeti is probably the only Indian and Tibetan brewpub in the US. The unlikely combination actually makes a lot of sense. Indian food in its many and varied spicy formats, is a fine and complementary companion to all styles of malty and hoppy ales and lagers. Located in the quiet town of Arvada, the brewpub is situated in a spooky looking old house, with dining rooms on both the first and second floors. Great Indian food isn't always easy to find in the US, but the curries, various complex rice-based dishes, and delicious naan breads served at Yak & Yeti meet with high British and Indian standards.

Of course the beer at Yak & Yeti is the real eye-opener, beginning with the house **Chai Stout.** Aromatically the beer wears its various spice additions on its sleeve. In the drink the spices are all there, but they never overwhelm the palate, or overpower the core roasty and chocolate American stout characteristics. But the one beer you should not leave Yak & Yeti without trying is their **AbominAle Mild.** English milds are a rare find in Colorado, and great ones are an even rarer find. This example has an inviting toffee treacle aroma and a superbly rich caramel and sweet, red-berry body.

There is a second Yak & Yeti location in Westminster, but it does not brew its own beer. It offers the house beers from the original Arvada location.

Boulder

BREWERIES
- ② Asher Brewing Company
- ⑩ Avery Brewing Company
- ③ Boulder Beer Company
- ④ Crystal Springs Brewing Company
- ⑨ Twisted Pine Brewing Company
- ① Upslope Brewing Company

BREWPUBS
- ⑦ Mountain Sun Pub & Brewery
- ⑪ Southern Sun Pub & Brewery
- ⑥ Walnut Brewery

BARS
- ⑧ Backcountry Pizza & Tap House
- ⑤ The West End Tavern

N

1 mile

Boulder

With its vibrant population of college kids, local liberals, outdoors-loving tourists, and affluent international jet-setters, Boulder is easily the most cosmopolitan and colorful city in Colorado. The atmosphere of this magical city at the base of the majestic Rocky Mountains is reflected brilliantly in the beer brewed and served in city. From the upscale beer-centric confines of well-stocked beer bars in the heart of the city to the bustling taprooms of proud new craft breweries in the busy commercial subdivisions that surround the city, great beer in Boulder is never far away but is never taken for granted. Beer appreciation in Boulder is an art form, perhaps not a surprise in a town that the Brewers Association calls home.

Breweries

ASHER BREWING COMPANY

4699 Nautilus Ct., Ste. 104, Boulder, CO 80301; (303) 530-1381; AsherBrewing.com;
Twitter: @AsherBrewing
Founded: 2009 **Founders:** Chris Asher and Steven Turner **Brewers:** Chris Asher and
Steven Turner **Flagship Beer:** Greenade Organic Double I.P.A. **Year-round Beers:** Green
Bullet Organic I.P.A., Green Monstah Organic Strong Ale, Green Lantern Organic Kolsch,
Tree Hugger Organic Amber **Seasonals/Special Releases:** Superfly Organic Oatmeal Stout,
Funbarrel (series) **Tours:** Sat through Sun 4 p.m. **Taproom:** Sun through Wed 3 to 9 p.m.,
Thurs through Sat 3 to 10 p.m. Growlers are available to go.

Asher Brewing Company, located in an area northeast of Boulder known as Gunbarrel, is the first USDA-certified, all-organic brewery in Colorado. Being all organic is a bold choice for a fledgling brewery. Raw material costs of organic hops and malts can be significantly higher than nonorganic materials and sourcing them is more difficult. If being all organic wasn't enough to earn it a green high-five, the brewery is also 100 percent wind powered.

Asher opened for business in 2009. Its ales can be best categorized as balanced. From its best-selling **Green Bullet Organic I.P.A.** to its **Green Monstah Organic Strong Ale,** Asher's year-round offerings share a polite marriage of hop-derived

bitterness and malt-derived sweetness. Asher's beers also share a distinct earthy grit and dark fruitiness, perhaps a byproduct of the more natural way the organic hops are grown.

Tree Hugger Organic Amber is an easy-drinking, 6 percent ABV American amber ale. The copper-hued beer is low in bitterness, with a smooth and toasty malty body. The finish is earthy with soft citrus bite. **Green Lantern Organic Kolsch** is a well-hewn example of the style. The 4.8 percent ABV, straw-colored, traditional German-style beer has a lively cereal nose and a pretty floral sweetness throughout. While not as sessionable as modern English pub ale, Green Lantern is pint-after-pint sessionable by Colorado standards. Green Monstah Organic Strong Ale is a big, chewy, 9.2 percent ABV American strong ale. If the beer reminds you of a sweeter after-dinner spirit, like sherry or cognac, that's intentional. Expect to pick up notes of dark dried fruit and caramelized sugar.

When visiting the Asher tap room, you'll likely see an experimental brew on tap, often under the **Funbarrel** moniker. In the past, Funbarrel beers have included a grape-flavored ale, a kriek-style ale, and a new IPA.

Beer Lover's Pick

Greenade Organic Double I.P.A.
Style: Double IPA
ABV: 9 percent
Availability: Year-round on tap

Greenade Organic Double I.P.A. is a must-savor Asher Brewing Company beer. At 55 IBUs, this big 9 percent ABV imperial IPA is quite a bit less bitter than many of the other examples of the style in Colorado. Its earthy green aroma is complemented by an even bitterness and bready malt character. The balancing act this beer presents between hop and malt belies its high ABV.

AVERY BREWING COMPANY

5763 Arapahoe Ave., Unit E, Boulder, CO 80303; (303) 440-4324; AveryBrewing.com;
Twitter: @AveryBrewingCo
Founded: 1993 **Founder:** Adam Avery **Brewer:** Adam Avery **Flagship Beer:** India Pale
Ale **Year-round Beers:** India Pale Ale, White Rascal, Ellie's Brown Ale, Out of Bounds
Stout, Joe's Premium American Pilsner, Hog Heaven Dry-Hopped Barleywine Style Ale,
the Reverend Belgian Style Quadrupel Ale, Salvation Belgian Style Strong Golden Ale
Seasonals/Special Releases: New World Porter, Karma, Old Jubilation Ale, the Maharaja
Imperial India Pale Ale, the Kaiser Imperial Oktoberfest Lager, Czar Imperial Stout,
Samael's Oak Aged Ale, the Beast Grand Cru Ale, Mephistopheles Stout, Coffeestopheles,
Rumpkin, Anniversary (series) Collaboration, not Litigation Ale **Tours:** Mon through Fri
4 p.m., Sat through Sun 2 p.m.
Taproom: Mon through Sun 11 a.m. to 11 p.m. Growlers and bottled beers are available
to go.

Avery Brewing Company is probably most well-known for a raft of so-called extreme ales. It's a brewery appreciated by many beer aficionados for its heavily hopped, very high alcohol, and barrel-aged sour beers. The truth is, though, that while those beers create a lot of buzz, they are only one part of the Avery story.

Adam Avery founded his namesake brewery in 1993 with a seven-barrel brewhouse tucked away in a small industrial corner of Boulder. The following year the brewery won a gold medal at the GABF for its **Out of Bounds Stout.** By 1995 the brewery was already ramping up production, making the leap to a 30-barrel brewhouse and dramatically increasing its tank capacity. Twelve-ounce and 22-ounce Avery bottles followed.

Avery Brewing Company is best defined by its bold experimentation and vast range of beers. Its year-round releases include staples such as an IPA; **White Rascal,** a Belgian wit; **Ellie's,** an American brown ale; the aforementioned Out of Bounds Stout; and **Joe's,** an abundantly hopped and bitingly bitter American Pilsner.

The first notable Avery beer that every visitor to Colorado should try is the **Maharaja,** a thunderous 10.2 percent ABV imperial IPA. This copper-colored bitter behemoth clocks in at a palate wrecking 102 IBUs, which is about the highest measurable level of bitterness. The beer has a potent herbaceous and resinous nose and a long, almost medicinal bitterness. The Maharaja is available from December through March on tap and in 22-ounce bottles.

Mephistopheles, a 15.1 percent ABV imperial stout that has more in common with a semisweet Italian amaro after-dinner digestif, is another Avery beer that every beer adventurer should endeavor to try. Mephistopheles is one of four beers that comprise Avery's **Demons of Ale** series of extremely high ABV beers. The other ales in the series being **Samael's,** a 14.5 percent ABV oak-aged English stong ale; the **Beast Grand Cru,** a 16.8 percent ABV Belgian strong dark ale; and **Coffeestopheles** (previously known as Mephaddict), a 16 percent ABV coffee-infused imperial stout.

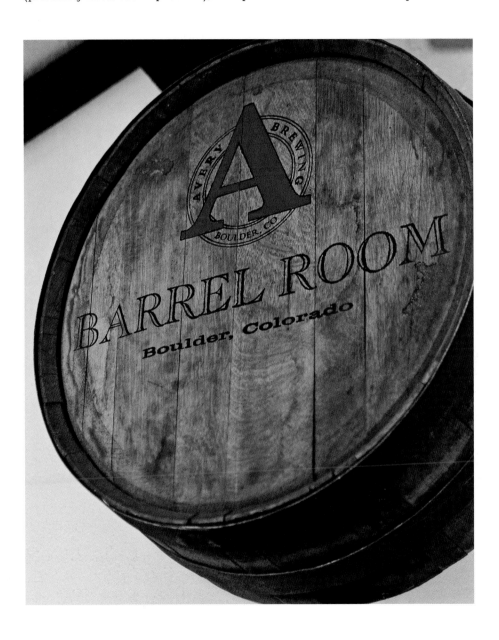

Old Jubilation Ale
Style: Old Ale
ABV: 8.3 percent
Availability: Sept through Dec on tap and in bottles

Cellarable for up to two years, Avery Brewing Company's Old Jubilation Ale is a modern winter classic. This 8.3 percent ABV, ruby-colored, English-style old ale has a beautiful caramel aroma and a body that evokes the flavors of a well-stocked spice rack, despite containing no spices at all. Old Jubilation is brewed with a single British hop called Bullion, and bitterness is low. This is a beer designed to let the malts do most of the talking.

BOULDER BEER COMPANY

2880 Wilderness Place, Boulder, CO 80301; (303) 444-8448; BoulderBeer.com;
Twitter: @BoulderBeerCo
Founded: 1979 **Founders:** David Hummer and Randolph Ware **Brewer:** David Zuckerman
Flagship Beer: Hazed and Infused **Year-round Beers:** Hazed and Infused, Mojo IPA,
Planet Porter, Buffalo Gold, Singletrack Copper Ale, Sweaty Betty Blonde, India Brown Ale
Seasonals/Special Releases: Never Summer Ale, Hoopla Pale Ale, Kinda Blue Blueberry
Wheat, Cold Hop, Obovoid, Killer Penguin, Mojo Risin' Double IPA **Tours:** Mon through Fri
2 p.m., Sat 2 p.m. and 4 p.m. **Taproom:** Mon through Fri 11 a.m. to 10 p.m., Sat noon to
8 p.m. Growlers and bottled beers are available to go.

Boulder Beer Company began way back in 1979, which makes it one of America's longest-running craft breweries. There have certainly been bumps in the road, but today the brewery stands taller, prouder, and stronger than ever. The internationally award-winning brewery is known and respected throughout the US, and its

beers can be found in large swathes of the country. Its most well-known creation, **Hazed and Infused,** is a true modern craft beer icon.

Every once in a while a beer comes along that forever changes the landscape of the beer industry a little bit. In 2011 Boulder brewer Aaron Hickman approached brewmaster David Zuckerman with the idea of professionally brewing one of his best homebrews, a bold dry-hopped amber ale. He called the beer Hazed and Infused. Within 12 months Hazed and Infused had become the brewery's best-selling beer. More bold creations followed, such as **Obovoid,** an oatmeal stout; **Killer Penguin,** an American barleywine; **Mojo IPA;** and **Mojo Risin' Double IPA,** all of which remain mainstays of Boulder's lineup to this day.

Enjoying a glass of Hazed and Infused in the brewery's busy taproom or full-service restaurant, better known to locals as Wilderness Pub, is a must, but before you do that be sure to try the legendary and award-winning **Planet Porter.** The 5.5 percent ABV beer is a classic American porter, which has a bitter chocolate bite and smooth, roasty finish. As porters in Colorado go, it has a drinkability that is unparalleled.

Killer Penguin
Style: American Barleywine
ABV: 10 percent
Availability: Dec in 22-ounce bottles

Killer Penguin is an aggressive take on an aggressive style of beer, the hulking and sometimes intimidating American barleywine. Pouring a rusty color, the beer effervesces a thick, sugar-coated, pine-needle aroma. This big, 10 percent ABV monster has a strata of palate-enveloping scorched caramel and bitter, dark-green herbaceous notes. The finish is fiery and bittersweet. Boulder Beer Company releases the Penguin only when it is ready, after at least six months of conditioning. The bottled version of the beer is handsomely packaged in a wax-sealed bottled with a wooden disc denoting the vintage. This is a beer designed as much for cellaring for enjoyment at a much later date as it is for drinking fresh.

CRYSTAL SPRINGS BREWING COMPANY

876 Sunshine Canyon Dr., Boulder, CO 80302; (303) 884-5602; CrystalSpringsBrewing
.com; **Twitter:** @CrystalSpringsB
Founded: 2010 **Founder:** Tom Horst **Brewer:** Tom Horst **Flagship Beer:** Doc's American
Porter **Year-round Beers:** Doc's American Porter, Stagecoach 1899, Butch Extra (Special)
Pale Ale **Seasonals/Special Releases:** Black Saddle Stout, Uncle Fat, Tic Wit, Crystal
Springs Summertime Ale **Tours:** None **Taproom:** None

This nanobrewery is located in Sunshine Canyon, just west of Boulder. Founder and brewer Tom Horst is one of a small handful of Coloradoans who has taken advantage of laws that permit one to brew commercially on a small scale in their garage, providing they meet certain criteria. His beers can be found under the Crystal Springs Brewing Company label in 22-ounce bottles at liquor stores in Boulder and on tap at some of the more craft beer–centric establishments around town, including the likes of the Kitchen, one of the state's best-reviewed restaurants.

Horst retains a day job as a music teacher. He does have plans to one day relocate to a dedicated brewery space and, who knows, maybe brew full time. **Black Saddle Stout** is a thick 10.3 percent ABV strong, imperial stout winter seasonal designed for cellaring and enjoyment months and even years from now. The bitter beast has coating molasses, licorice, charcoal, and cocoa notes, with a lasting bitter chocolate finish.

Like many American breweries, Crystal Springs releases a German-styled Kölsch as its summer seasonal beer. The aptly named **Crystal Springs Summertime Ale** is a to-style, 5.2 percent ABV, summer fruit-forward golden pour with a lively and slightly barnyard nose. Bitterness is very low, and the finish is moderately dry.

Tic Wit is a Belgian-style witbier brewed with wheat, Indian coriander, and a mix of citrus fruit peel. The hazy white beer is engineered for summer quaffing and pairing with a broad plate of savory foods. The low 5 percent ABV lends the beer to all-day, warm-weather drinking.

Beer Lover's Pick

Doc's American Porter
Style: American Porter
ABV: 7.5 percent
Availability: Year-round on tap and in bottles

Doc's American Porter is a robust, 7.5 percent ABV, bitter American porter, brewed with seven varieties of malts and British and American hops. The beer has a thick, viscous mouthfeel; a deep baker's chocolate creamy bitterness; and a moderate hop-derived bitterness. Occasionally Crystal Springs Brewing Company releases small batches brewed with the addition of hazelnut, raspberry or cherry, and barrel-aged bourbon.

TWISTED PINE BREWING COMPANY

3201 Walnut St., Boulder, CO 80301; (303) 786-9270; TwistedPineBrewing.com;
Twitter: @twistedpine
Founded: 1995 **Founder:** Gordon Knight **Brewer:** Bob Baile **Flagship Beer:** Hoppy Boy
India Pale Ale **Year-round Beers:** Hoppy Boy India Pale Ale, American Amber Ale, Honey
Brown, Cream Style Stout, Rocky Mountain Wheat, Billy's Chilies, Big Shot Espresso Stout,
Ghost Face Killah **Seasonals/Special Releases:** Blond Ale, Raspberry Wheat, Pearl Street
Porter, Reilly's Oak Whiskey Red, Northstar Imperial Porter, Hoppy Man, Le Petit Saison,
Razzy Xpress **Tours:** None **Taproom:** Mon through Fri 11 a.m. to 9 p.m., Sat noon to
9 p.m., Sun noon to 8 p.m. Growlers and bottled beers are available to go.

Boulder's Twisted Pine is the second of three breweries founded by Colorado brewing legend and entrepreneur Gordon Knight. Twisted Pine's taproom offers a wide selection of the brewery's year-round, seasonals, special releases, and one-off experiments. In many ways, experiments define Twisted Pine. From an imperial-strength raspberry stout to a sour IPA aged in bourbon barrels, little if any ideas seem off-limits. That ethos has carried over into the brewery's production beers too.

Billy's Chilies is a light, 5 percent ABV wheat beer infused with a fresh tea made from serrano, habanero, jalapeno, Anaheim, and Fresno chili peppers. The resulting beer has a bright-green, bell-pepper aroma and a multifaceted peppery flavor. Layers of heat and red-vegetal flavor give way to a clean, refreshing finish.

Big Shot Espresso Stout is a hefty American stout conditioned on significant quantities of espresso coffee. Drinking the beer is something akin to enjoying a strong black-iced coffee. Heavily roasted bitterness and chocolate-covered coffee-bean flavors persist to the swallow. If you enjoy trying coffee-infused beers, this is an absolute must.

Le Petit Saison is an unexpected Belgian-styled beer among Twisted Pine's extensive range of American standard and experimental ales. Even the quiet branding belies its connection to the rest of the brewery's bottled offerings. Le Petit is a pretty classical saison, or farmhouse ale, with a woolly nose and sweet fruity body. Bitterness is minimal and the finish gentle.

Beer Lover's Pick

Ghost Face Killah
Style: Chili Beer
ABV: 5 percent
Availability: Occasionally in single 12-ounce bottles

The idea for an even spicier incarnation of Billy's Chilies was seeded in 2009 during Colorado's annual Snowmass Chili Pepper & Brew Fest, when a brazen attendee suggested that Twisted Pine Brewing Company could make an even hotter beer. Not a brewery to shy away from an experiment, Twisted Pine eventually emerged from the brewhouse with a beer that closely resembled Billy's Chilies with one major difference: It was brewed with the addition of, what was at the time, the hottest pepper in the world, the so-called ghost chili, or Bhut Jolokia. The beer is aimed squarely at the more adventurous beer drinker, especially those who enjoy spicy food. In many ways the beer is like a hot Indian curry, packed with atomic heat but full of savory nuance and depth.

UPSLOPE BREWING COMPANY

1501 Lee Hill Rd., #20, Boulder, CO 80304; (303) 449-2911; UpslopeBrewing.com; **Twitter:** @Upslope
Founded: 2008 **Founder:** Matt Cutter **Brewer:** Alex Violette **Flagship Beer:** India Pale Ale **Year-round Beers:** India Pale Ale, Pale Ale, Brown Ale, Craft Lager **Seasonals/ Special Releases:** Belgo, Pumpkin Ale, Foreign Style Stout **Tours:** None **Taproom:** Tues through Thurs 2 to 8 p.m., Fri through Sat 2 to 9 p.m.

Located in an industrial development northwest of Boulder, Upslope is one of a growing number of craft breweries that has wholly embraced the idea of canning its own beers. A once bold concept for small-scale brewers of "good" beer, the idea rapidly became a trend and is now a fully fledged and positively regarded practice.

From the outset, founder Matt Cutter wanted to build a brewery that appealed to active, socially and environmentally conscious people like himself. The cans were chosen because of their smaller carbon footprint and the ease with which they can be recycled. The brewery delivery van was chosen because it is powered by natural gas, and the brewery is designed to use less water.

Upslope found success with its four year-round canned core beers, and a handful of its taproom beers won medals at the likes of the GABF. Pumpkin Ale is the brewery's brilliantly simple take on the now all too often over-spiced pumpkin beer style. Pumpkin Ale won gold at GABF. The beer forwent the usual addition of pumpkin pie spices and was instead just brewed with a mountain of pumpkin flesh.

The four canned core beers are clean and simple yet creative interruptions of their respective styles. **Pale Ale** is 5.8 percent ABV America pale ale. The golden pour is accompanied by a bright-green vegetal aroma. The body is a clean blend of yellow citrus crispness and dank herb notes. **India Pale Ale** is a 7.2 percent ABV American IPA brewed with a very similar eye to crispness and complementary bitterness, albeit, a more potent leafy dankness and gripping bitterness. **Brown Ale** is the highlight of the year-round Upslope beers, with its creamy milk chocolate and mocha aroma and long earthy chicory body. The 6.7 percent ABV beer is far from actually being sessionable, but the beer has easy drinking written all over it. **Craft Lager** is Upslope's newest year-round beer. The 4.8 percent ABV beer is aimed squarely at those still transitioning from mass-produced light lagers to more bitter and full-flavor beers.

Foreign Style Stout
Style: Foreign Extra Stout
ABV: 6.9 percent
Availability: Late winter seasonal on tap and in cans

Released in early 2012, Foreign Style Stout is the first seasonal canned beer from Upslope Brewing Company. The robust, crude oil–colored beer is rich with aromatic notes of prune, black olive, and charcoal. In the drink bitterness rules with dark chocolate, espresso, and burnt-toast notes. The finish is moderately dry.

Brewpubs

MOUNTAIN SUN PUB & BREWERY
1535 Pearl St., Boulder, CO 80302; (303) 546-0886; MountainSunPub.com;
Twitter: @mountainsunpub

SOUTHERN SUN PUB & BREWERY
627 S. Broadway, Boulder, CO 80305; (303) 543-0886

VINE ST. PUB & BREWERY
1700 Vine St., Denver, CO 80206; (303) 388-2337
Founded: 1993 **Founder:** Kevin J. Daly **Brewer:** Brian Hutchinson **Flagship Beer:**
Colorado Kind Ale **Year-round Beers:** Colorado Kind Ale, Isadore Java Porter, FYIPA,
Illusion Dweller IPA , XXX Pale Ale, Annapurna Amber, Blackberry Wheat, Dropkick Stout
Seasonals/Special Releases: Changes weekly

Despite having three locations, Mountain Sun is far removed from typical brewpub chains. The original Mountain Sun location on Boulder's bustling Pearl Street first fired up its brew kettle in 1993. Colorful murals and Grateful Dead posters line the walls, and 20 taps of mostly house-brewed beer flow daily until after midnight. It serves a vibrant mix of college students, professional locals, and tourists, and few restaurants in Boulder feel more Boulder in terms of hippie attitude and welcoming atmosphere.

Mountain Sun's second location, Southern Sun, opened south of Boulder in 2002, and the nature of the location means that the crowd is more family oriented. In 2008 Mountain Sun's third location, Vine Street, opened for business in Denver's restaurant-heavy uptown neighborhood, the perfect location to showcase its high-quality food and first-class service to Denver's more savvy food and beer customers.

Mountain Sun uses fresh and carefully sourced ingredients. The menu offers up wide varieties of both vegetarian- and meat-focused staples that include daily varieties of fresh hummus, exotic grilled-cheese sandwiches, a tempeh Reuben, a BLT, and a vast selection of burgers and veggie burgers. Creative daily dishes and desserts are also offered.

The three locations work together to brew the core and seasonal house beers and a dizzying list of one-off creations, many of which become occasional offerings due to their popularity. February is the ever-popular Stout Month at Mountain Sun. If you're lucky enough to be in Boulder or Denver during February, this yearly

Today's Draught Selection

In addition to our fine house brews, we also feature beers from regional and national craft breweries. In order to provide you with the best selection, we constantly rotate these. From time to time a beer will change mid-day. Please ask your server if any changes have been made in the list below. Enjoy!

MOUNTAIN SUN ALES
Always fresh, always unfiltered

8 oz. glass	16 oz. pint	48 oz. pitcher
$2.80	$4.50	$12.50

Jah Mon Ginger

Annapurna Amber

Kind Ale

Hummingbird *8 oz. pour $4.50 No Happy Hour*

Quinn's Golden Ale

*Nitro Old School Stout

*Nitro Dropkick Stout

Java Porter

Drop Kick Stout

Blackberry Wheat

St. Amos Wit *20oz. pour $5.75 No Happy Hour*

Franklin's Strong Golden *13 oz. pour $4.50*

XXX Pale

F.Y.I.P.A

Illusion Dweller I.P.A

GUEST BEERS

Green Flash Hop Head Red *16 oz. pour $6.25*

Avery's White Rascal *16oz. pour $5.25*

* Belhaven Scottish Ale *16oz. pour $5.75*

Ommegang BPA *13 oz. pour $5.75*

Avery's Kaiser *8 oz. pour $4.95*

SPECIALITY DESSERT

Carrot Cake

Mint Chocolate cake *w/ Old School Stout*

* Indicates beer poured through the nitrogen tap.

Made famous by Guinness Stout, this type of a pour lends an uncommon smoothness and a thick, creamy head to any beer.

celebration of dark beer is an absolute must. Months in advance of Stout Month, the brewers from each Mountain Sun location get together to brainstorm new and different stouts, be they mild, dry, or strong. Interesting adjunct ingredients often include the likes of tangerine, coffee, chai spices, chili, cherry, chocolate, and mint. So popular is this annual toast to America's favorite dark beer family of styles, that beers can change almost daily, as beers kick and are tapped.

If you can't make it to a Mountain Sun brewpub in February, fear not, because every day of the year seasonals and new one-off brews are offered alongside the much-loved, year-round beers. These include **Colorado Kind Ale,** a 6.3 percent ABV American amber ale with a thick, leafy-green, medium-bitter hop profile, and a solid-malt base; the **Illusion Dweller IPA,** a 6.4 percent ABV English-styled IPA brewed with tons of the pungent English hop variety East Kent Goldings; and **FYIPA,** which is possibly Mountain Sun's most requested when not on tap. This big, 7.2 percent ABV hop monster packs bright-yellow citrus and tropical fruit notes, with notes of eucalyptus and mango.

WALNUT BREWERY

1123 Walnut St., Boulder, CO 80302; (303) 447-1345; WalnutBrewery.com
Founded: 1990 **Founder:** Frank Day **Brewer:** Rodney Taylor **Flagship Beers:** Big Horn Bitter, Devil's Thumb Stout, Buffalo Gold, Indian Peaks Pale Ale, Old Elk Brown Ale
Year-round Beer: St. James Irish Red Ale **Seasonals/Special Releases:** Oktoberfest

Frank Day had spent 14 years running Old Chicago restaurants before opening Walnut Brewery, Boulder's first brewpub, in 1990. The 1990s were the heyday of brewpubs in America. The beers most pubs brewed then were simple and unadventurous compared to today's offerings. Pales, reds, ambers, and browns more than sufficed back then and were an earth-shattering move away from light and insipid mass-produced lager.

Following the almost immediate success of Walnut in Boulder, Frank went on to open the first Rock Bottom Restaurant & Brewery on Denver's 16th Street and the rest, as they say, is beer history. Today Walnut is a part of the country-spanning Rock Bottom empire, but it retains its name and continues to pour a similar lineup of ales.

Walnut serves, as it always has, a full menu of American bar and pub classics. Beyond the usual lineup of well-prepared soups and salads, the kitchen offers the likes of hazelnut-crusted chicken, enchiladas, steak, tacos, pasta, burgers, fish-and-chips, mac and cheese with chicken, sandwiches, pizzas, and fajitas.

Boulder

The four unchanging year-round house beers are supplemented by popular seasonals, like the annual Oktoberfest and a rotating "dark" brew. **Buffalo Gold,** a Colorado institution, is brewed with life-giving Willamette and Cascade hops and has big yellow-citrus notes and a suitably dry finish. **St. James Irish Red Ale** is brewed with imported specialty malts and has a toasted-nut body, long biscuit notes, and an earthy, slightly spicy fruit finish. **Indian Peaks Pale Ale** is simply refreshing, sip to swallow. This American pale has pithy citrus fruit flavor, a breezy floral aroma, and a grippy, dry-caramel finish. **Old Elk Brown Ale** has been the recipient of multiple medals at the GABF over the years. This first-class American brown ale has a mocha and milk chocolate forward aroma and flavor and a long smooth finish that lends itself to pint-after-pint enjoyment.

Beer Bars

BACKCOUNTRY PIZZA & TAP HOUSE

2319 Arapahoe Ave., Boulder, CO 80302; (303) 449-4285; BackcountryPizzaandTap
Houses.com
Taps: 50+ **Bottles/Cans:** 100+

In terms of the selection and number of beers offered, Backcountry Pizza & Tap House in Boulder is one of the best beer bars in the US, with more than 50 carefully sourced and curated taps of American and imported craft beer and a detailed and extensive bottle list of good beer from across the globe. This is definitely the place to come to try some of the rarer beers poured anywhere in America, including limited-release domestic and international sour and barrel-aged beers and fresh pale ale IPAs from Europe, New Zealand, and beyond. Being a pizza restaurant, pizzas and calzones are, of course, the main features, but a nice selection of appetizers, soups, salads, sandwiches, and burgers is also available.

THE WEST END TAVERN

926 Pearl St., Boulder, CO 80302; (303) 444-3535; TheWestEndTavern.com;
Twitter: @westendtavern
Taps: 24 **Bottles/Cans:** 20+

The West End Tavern is one of the finest beer establishments in all of Colorado. Located in Boulder's posh West End, a retail and restaurant neighborhood, it does everything right, from the carefully curated tap selections to its bottle list and perfectly prepared food. The West End Tavern is a part of the Big Red F Restaurant Group, which also owns the Jax Fish House restaurants in Boulder, Denver, and Fort Collins; Zolo Grill; Centro Latin Kitchen; Lola; and the Bitter Bar, all highly rated and regarded Boulder eateries.

In addition to the 25 brilliantly curated beer taps, which often includes pilot batches from local breweries and very hard-to-find imports, the West End Tavern also prides itself on its menu of more than 75 bourbons. The bar can also whip you up a delicious beer cocktail if you ask politely (see the Rusty Bus recipe on page 203). The West End Tavern even boasts its own excellent stout brewed by Victory in Pennsylvania.

Diners and drinkers can chose to sit downstairs at the bar and get some beer or bourbon schooling from the knowledgeable bar staff as they drink, or get comfy at one of the adjacent booth-style tables, or better yet, go upstairs to the heated roof terrace that has its own bar and service.

Dinner, lunch, and brunch are all served at the West End Tavern. Dinner highlights include yam chips, wings, house-smoked pork ribs, picnic eggs, and wet fries for appetizers and soups, salads, burgers, market-style barbecue of pulled pork, hot links, bourbon-smoked brisket, and barbecue chicken for entrees.

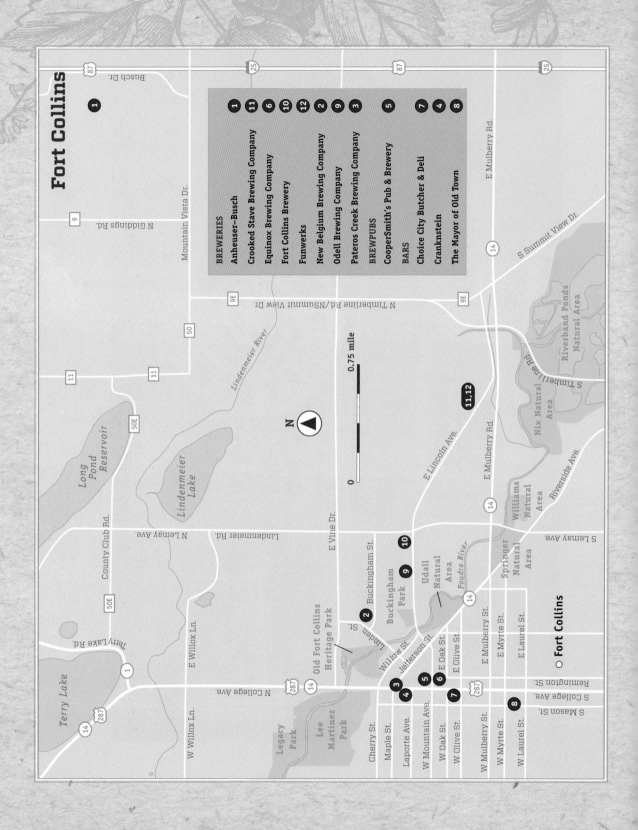

Fort Collins

BREWERIES

1. Anheuser–Busch
11. Crooked Stave Brewing Company
6. Equinox Brewing Company
10. Fort Collins Brewery
12. Funwerks
2. New Belgium Brewing Company
9. Odell Brewing Company
3. Pateros Creek Brewing Company

BREWPUBS

5. CooperSmith's Pub & Brewery

BARS

7. Choice City Butcher & Deli
4. Cranknstein
8. The Mayor of Old Town

0.75 mile

N

Fort Collins

On the flat prairie that stretches east to west from I-25 toward downtown Fort Collins, you'll pass brewery after brewery, of all sizes, shapes, and styles. There is a peaceful and idyllic quality about Fort Collins and the landscape that surrounds despite the close proximity and density of so many beer makers in such a small city. Quite simply, Fort Collins feels like a model beer mecca. It is easy to navigate, inexpensive, aesthetically appealing, and filled with taprooms and establishments pouring fresh local and regional beer every few yards.

Breweries

ANHEUSER-BUSCH, FORT COLLINS

2351 Busch Dr., Fort Collins, CO 80524; (970) 490-4691; Anheuser-Busch.com
Founded: 1988 (1852) **Founder:** Adolphus Busch **Brewer:** Various **Flagship Beer:** Bud
Light **Year-round Beers:** Too many to list **Seasonals/Special Releases:** Shock Top
Pumpkin Wheat, Michelob Pumpkin Spice Ale, Michelob Winter's Bourbon Cask Ale **Tours:**
June through Sept daily 10 a.m. to 4 p.m., Oct through May Thurs through Mon 10 a.m.
to 4 p.m. **Taproom:** June through Sept daily 10 a.m. to 4 p.m., Oct through May Thurs
through Mon 10 a.m. to 4 p.m.

Colorado has such a widespread reputation as a craft-beer capital that many
might be very surprised to learn that the third-oldest operating brewery in the
state is actually the monolithic, 130-acre, Anheuser-Busch facility in Fort Collins.

The brewery came online in 1988. The scale of brewing undertaken at Anheuser-Busch is truly breathtaking. Constructed on a rail line with direct access the arterial I-25, the brewery was purposely positioned to deliver fresh beer to the Rocky Mountain region, the West Coast, and the Midwest as quickly as possible. The brewery operates around the clock, 7 days a week, brewing upwards of 30 different beers, including the various Michelob and Shock Top brands.

Somewhat in keeping with Colorado's position as a pioneering beer state, beers like **Budweiser American Ale, Shock Top Belgian White,** and **Michelob DunkelWeisse** were all developed at the Fort Collins brewery before being rolled out nationally.

Upwards of 100,000 people visit the brewery every year. The tours are informative and deliver a surprisingly up close and personal experience, especially if you choose to pay for the Brewmaster Tour. One of the highlights of the tour is a visit to the stables, where one of Anheuser-Busch's famous Clydesdale horse display teams is in residence. Every person of drinking age who takes the tour is afforded three full pours of any of the beers pouring in the taproom after the tour.

Michelob AmberBock
Style: Bock
ABV: 5.2 percent
Availability: Year-round on tap and in bottles
Michelob AmberBock is definitely the highlight of a visit to Anheuser-Busch in Fort Collins. The 5.2 percent ABV hazelnut-colored lager is brewed to broadly replicate the key characteristics of the wider German bock beer family. The aroma and flavor is caramel forward, with a lingering earthy hop spiciness.

CROOKED STAVE BREWING COMPANY

1900 E. Lincoln Ave., Unit B, Fort Collins, CO 80524; CrookedStave.com;
Twitter: @CrookedStave
Founded: 2011 **Founder:** Chad Yakobson **Brewer:** Chad Yakobson **Flagship Beer:** Surette
Year-round Beers: Surette, Petite Sour **Seasonals/Special Releases:** Wild Wild Brett
(series), Fertile Soil Fresh Hopped Golden Ale, Blackberry Petite Sour, Surette Reserva,
L'Brett d'Or, Persica, Nightmare on Brett Street (series), Batch #1, Oculus **Tours:** None
Taproom: None

Colorado native Chad Yakobson knows a thing a two about the naturally occurring yeasts known as *Brettanomyces,* probably as much as anybody in the US does. *Brettanomyces,* commonly called *Brett,* is the bane of many winemakers the world over, but for an increasingly number of fringe brewers, *Brett* has become something of a muse. Indeed, it has even become the foundation of a clutch of fascinating breweries like Colorado's Crooked Stave, Chad's bold brewing venture that seeks to explore and showcase beers brewed with *Brett* and various souring bacteria.

Brewers like Chad have taken this wild yeast indoors, taming its various strains as they see fit to bring forth all manner of "funky" aromatics and flavor characteristics. Descriptors such as woolly, horse-blanket, floral, earthy, and dusty are often associated with beers that possess inherent *Brett* characteristics. Indeed Chad looks after what might be one of the largest libraries of propagated *Brett* in the US. It's a palette he uses to a most vibrant effect in his ongoing **Wild Wild Brett** series of releases, which are all 100 percent fermented with *Brett.* The series is inspired by the seven colors of the rainbow, each beer drawing ingredients of a specific color.

One of the common misconceptions that *Brett*-centric brewers like Chad are keen to dispel is that *Brett* makes beers sour. It does not. *Brett* is often confused with the various souring bacteria that give lambics and such their tart and acidic personality.

Wild Wild Brett Rouge, the first of Crooked Stave's "rainbow of *Brett*" beers, is a hazy, ruby-hued ale, brewed with whole hibiscus flowers, hawthorn berries, and rose hips. The 5.2 percent ABV has an aroma of dusty rose petals, earthy radish, tart cranberry, and roasted green tea. In the drink, the spritzy body effervesces flavors of bitter lemon pith, beetroot, red currant, and passion fruit. The finish is dry but not without a nice hit of tartness.

Surette
Style: Saison
ABV: 6.2 percent
Availability: Year-round
on tap and in
bottles

Surette is a take on a
forgotten and esoteric
Belgian style of farm-
house provision ale that
underwent extended oak
maturation that resulted
in some mildly tart and
richly funky character-
istics. Aged in large
oak foeders at Crooked
Stave Brewing Company,
Surette is brewed with
malted barley, wheat,
oats, rye, and spelt.
The beer has a unique
personality that sets
it apart from the many
farmhouse-style saisons

and bière de gardes brewed in Colorado and well beyond the state's borders.
The aroma bristles with noble *Brett* personality of wet wool, dust, barnyard,
and brilliant sunny floral notes. The same follows for the drink, with the
addition of light autumnal acidic fruit flavors. It's a superb beer and will
evolve further in the cellar should the idea of buying a case to take home
strike you.

Fort Collins

EQUINOX BREWING COMPANY

133 Remington St., Fort Collins, CO 80524; (970) 484-1368; EquinoxBrewing.com;
Twitter: @equinoxbrewing
Founded: 2010 **Founder:** Colin Westcott **Brewer:** Colin Westcott **Flagship Beer:** Eclipse
Brown **Year-round Beers:** Eclipse Brown, Sunrise Golden Ale, Remi's Saison IPA, O'Rion
Irish Red, Red Dwarf Amber Ale **Seasonals/Special Releases:** Atom Smasher Wee Heavy
Tours: None **Taproom:** Mon through Wed noon to 8 p.m., Thurs through Sat noon to
9 p.m., Sun noon to 7 p.m. Growlers are available to go.

The only problem regular visitors to Equinox Brewing might ever encounter is being able to order their favorite beer with any sense of regularity. Owner and brewer Colin Westcott, also the owner of Hops & Berries, the homebrew shop next door, likes to keep new offerings coming thick and fast. There are very few American, British, German, or Belgian styles he hasn't confidently tried.

Before opening his storefront operation in the picturesque, brewery rich, college town of Fort Collins in April 2010, Westcott had been a brewer at breweries in Alaska and Montana. His depth of experience and championing of homebrews is apparent. The level of description that each of the 10 beers pouring is afforded on the beer menu is uncommon, even in today's beer-savvy marketplace. It's clear Westcott is keen to educate. Homebrew books can also be found on a bookshelf in the brewery, as if to further inspire.

Golden Sunrise Ale (5.2 percent ABV) is Equinox's lightest regular pour. The straw-color beer has an inviting golden breakfast-cereal aroma and light-to-moderate bitterness. Pops of lemon zest, lime, and white pepper are present throughout. **Red Dwarf Amber Ale** (5.3 percent ABV) is a prototypical American amber ale, with a soft head, pungent pine nose, and moderate bitterness. The body brings balance to the resinous aroma, with some caramel-apple malt sweetness. **Haver Scottish Ale** (6.3 percent ABV) is a rich, export-strength beer with strong caramel and bitter-sweet molasses notes. All of the beer's malty bombast is balanced by a surprisingly lengthy dry finish.

Eclipse Brown
Style: American Brown Ale
ABV: 5.3 percent
Availability: Year-round on tap

Eclipse Brown is the closet Equinox Brewing Company has to a flagship beer. The homebrew recipe for this beer can be found in the BYOB: Brew Your Own Beer chapter of this book. Eclipse Brown is dry with medium-roast coffee, toasted mixed nut, and chewy toffee notes. Equinox suggests allowing the beer to slightly warm for best enjoyment.

FORT COLLINS BREWERY

1020 E. Lincoln Ave., Fort Collins, CO 80524; (970) 472-1499; FortCollinsBrewery.com; **Twitter:** @FortCollinsBrew

Founded: 2003 **Founders:** Tom Peters and Jan Peters **Brewer:** Tom Peters **Flagship Beer:** Rocky Mountain IPA **Year-round Beers:** Rocky Mountain IPA, 1900 Amber, Major Tom's Pomegranate Wheat, Kidd Black Lager, Z Smoked Amber Lager, Red Banshee, Chocolate Stout **Seasonals/Special Releases:** Big Shot Seasonal Ale, Maibock, Hellesbock, Wheat Wine, Common Ground, Dopplebock, Double Chocolate, Incredible Hop (series) **Tours:** Sat 1, 2, 3, 4, and 5 p.m. **Taproom:** Mon through Thurs 11 a.m. to 6 p.m., Fri through Sat 11 a.m. to 7 p.m. Closed Sun. Growlers and bottles are available to go.

Fort Collins Brewery opened for business in 2003 after its owners purchased the defunct H. C. Berger brewery. Seven years later, in 2010, the brewery moved a mile down the road into an expansive and new purpose home. Fort Collins Brewing still owns its original property and now rents the space to Funkwerks, a fledgling saison-centric brewery.

Brewing core German-style lagers has been a mainstay of Fort Collins Brewery for many years. It brews two in particular: **Kidd Lager,** an earthy *schwarzbier,* and **Z Lager,** a traditional *rauchbier,* remain popular.

In the years since brewing those first successful lagers, the brewery massively expanded its portfolio. **Rocky Mountain IPA** is a 6.2 percent ABV American-style IPA with an aroma of fresh-cut grass and menthol and a tangy and quenching body. **Major Tom's Pomegranate Wheat** is a popular 4.2 percent ABV year-round release. The tart addition of pomegranate in the beer brings forward the tart quality inherent in a lot of wheat beers.

In addition to year-round releases, the brewery releases many seasonal, speciality, and experimental ales and lagers throughout the year. You might come across anything from a sticky sweet wheat wine to an ashy imperial black IPA, both on tap or for sale in 22-ounce bottles.

Fort Collins is one of only a handful of breweries in the US to have purchased an Austrian-built, Alfred Gruber counter-pressure growler filler machine. The impressive device uses the same principles as an industrial bottling line, using CO_2 to purge the growler before filling it with beer. The resulting growler will stay fresh and carbonated for significantly longer than a normal taproom or bar-tap filled growler. You can see the impressive growler filler in action and purchase a growler to go at the bar in-house restaurant, Gravity Ten Twenty.

Double Chocolate Stout

Style: American Double Stout

ABV: 8.1 percent

Availability: Winter seasonal on tap and in bottles

Bitter baker's chocolate and black coffee are the calling cards of American Double Stout, a hefty imperial-strength stout. The tar-colored pour has thick treacle toffee aroma, and the body has additional hints of black licorice, molasses, and brown sugar. Taking a few bottles of this home for later enjoyment is highly recommended.

FUNKWERKS

1900 E. Lincoln Ave., Unit B, Fort Collins, CO 80524; (970) 482-3865; Funkwerks.com; Twitter: @Funkwerks

Founded: 2010 **Founders:** Gordon Schuck and Brad Lincoln **Brewers:** Gordon Schuck and Brad Lincoln **Flagship Beer:** Saison **Year-round Beers:** Saison, Southern Tropic, Tropic King **Seasonals/Special Releases:** Belgian White, Cherry Saison, Hibiscus Resistance, Key Lime Rye, Helter Spelter, Casper, Aurora, Chai White **Tours:** None **Taproom:** Mon through Thurs noon to 8 p.m., Fri through Sat noon to 10 p.m., Sun noon to 6 p.m. Growlers and bottles are available to go.

Funkwerks was founded by Gordon Schuck and Brad Lincoln, graduates of the Siebel Institute of Technology brewing academy program in Chicago. The brewery opened for business in late 2010 with a focus on brewing saisons and farmhouse provision ales. Funkwerks set up shop in the building previously occupied by Fort Collins Brewery, which upscaled and relocated to a new purpose-built brewery down the road. Fort Collins Brewery still owns the building and leases the space to Funkwerks.

Saison ales are said to have originated from the French-speaking region of Belgium called Wallonia. *Saison* is French for "season." It is said that saison ales were the drink of seasonal farm laborers known as saisoniers. The lack of refrigeration or easy temperature control meant that the optimal time to brew in the region was between autumn and the start of spring, when warm weather would not impede fermentation. These provisional beers were brewed in these cooler months and laid down in the cellar for consumption throughout the year.

Alongside a handful of year-round core saisons, the brewery releases many small batches of bottled product each year. New experimental beers are also tapped regularly at the brewery taproom.

Saison (6.8 percent ABV, see recipe on page 189) is Funkwerks flagship year-round release, and it forgoes exotic or unusual adjunct ingredients and is instead an excellent interpretation of a modern Belgian saison. Its dusty lemon-meringue-pie nose gives way to an instant dryness on the palate. The beer has endless lemon juice, white pepper, and lime peel flavors. There is a refreshing brilliance to the drink, sip through swallow.

Tropic King
Style: Saison
ABV: 8 percent
Availability: Year-round on tap and in bottles

Brewed with a New Zealand hop called Rakau, Tropic King is an 8 percent ABV saison with lots of tropical fruit aroma and flavor. The nose is ablaze with notes of peach melba, mango, sweet peppers, and fresh ginger. The same follows for the flavor, with strong yeast-derived fruity notes and a less-dry-than-expected finish. In many respects this is the saison equivalent of a Belgian tripel.

NEW BELGIUM BREWING COMPANY

500 Linden St., Fort Collins, CO 80524; (970) 221-0524; NewBelgium.com;
Twitter: @newbelgium
Founded: 1991 **Founders:** Jeff Lebesch and Kim Jordan **Brewer:** Peter Bouckaert
Flagship Beer: Fat Tire **Year-round Beers:** Fat Tire, 1554, Sunshine Wheat, Blue Paddle, Trippel, Ranger IPA, Belgo IPA, Abbey, Mothership Wit, Shift **Seasonals/Special Releases:** Snow Day, Dig, Le Terroir, Abbey Grand Cru, Super Cru, Kick, La Folie, Le Fleur Misseur, Biere de Mars, Cluth, Cocoa Mole Ale, Pickly Passion, Fresh Hop, old Cherry Ale, Ken's Beer **Tours:** Tues through Sat 11 a.m. to 4 p.m. by reservation only. Reservations can only be made through the brewery's website. Book well in advance, as tours are popular. **Taproom:** Tues through Sat 10 a.m. to 6 p.m. Growlers and bottled beers are available to go.

In 1986 homebrewer, electrical engineer, and future New Belgium Brewing Company cofounder, Jeff Lebesch was riding his mountain bike through Belgium when he had a beer epiphany at a bar called Brugge Biertje. On that day the breadth and dynamic nature of Belgian beers changed his perception of beer for good. Upon his return to the US, Jeff brewed an Abbey-style ale and an amber ale called Fat Tire in

honor of his life-changing journey and his fat tire. *Fat tire* is eighties Colorado slang for a mountain bike.

People didn't like the name Fat Tire but loved the beer. Jeff stuck to his guns, though, kept the name, and brewed the beer for another six years. The rest, to put it mildly, is history.

Fat Tire is New Belgium's flagship beer and remains one of the most requested beers in markets where it is still unavailable. Some beer geeks claim that the 5.2 percent ABV Belgian-styled amber ale has changed over the years and doesn't match the profile of batches of old. The more likely reason, though, is that beer drinkers' palates have changed and become more sophisticated, specifically because of crafted beers like Fat Tire. Fat Tire endures as a perfect gateway beer for those immigrating from lighter offerings. Drinking a fresh Fat Tire at New Belgium's taproom is a right of passage for any serious beer adventurer.

Easily the most fascinating of New Belgium's year-round beers is **1554,** an enlightened black ale. In 1997 the recipe for the beer was destroyed in a flood. New Belgium brewer Peter Bouckaert and researcher Phil Bernstien journeyed to Belgium to dig up whatever they could on the forgotten style of beer in an attempt to revive it. The result is a 5.4 percent ABV, medium-bodied, chocolate-colored ale, fermented with a lager yeast strain. Bitterness is low, and a toasted-biscuit flavor is significant. The beer has a pleasant lightness about it, while being full in flavor.

La Folie

Style: Flanders Red Ale

ABV: 6 percent

Availability: Jan in 22-ounce bottles

By far the most celebrated and hotly anticipated Lips of Faith series release from New Belgium Brewing Company was La Folie. The 2012 vintage has a nose that bleeds cider vinegar, toffee apple, sweet strawberry ice cream, and dark chocolate. The body is pin sharp, with notes of tart cranberry, sour white grape, balsamic vinegar, tart cherry juice, and lime.

ODELL BREWING COMPANY

800 E. Lincoln Ave., Fort Collins, CO 80524; (970) 498-9070; OdellBrewing.com; **Twitter:** @OdellBrewing

Founded: 1989 **Founder:** Doug Odell **Brewer:** Doug Odell **Flagship Beer:** 90 Shilling **Year-round Beers:** 90 Shilling, 5 Barrel Pale Ale, Easy Street Wheat, IPA, Levity Amber Ale, Cutthroat Porter **Seasonals/Special Releases:** Red Ale, St. Lupulin, Isolation Ale, Woodcut (series), Bourbon Barrel Stout, Saboteur, Avant Peche, Friek, Hiveranno, Myrcenary, Double Pilsner, Mountain Standard **Tours:** Mon through Sat 1, 2, and 3 p.m. **Taproom:** Mon through Thurs 11 a.m. to 6 p.m., Fri through Sat 11 a.m. to 7 p.m. Growlers and bottled beers are available to go.

Founded in 1989 by Doug Odell, Odell Brewing Company is the sixth-largest production brewery in America. Together with breweries like New Belgium, Oskar Blues, Boulder, Fort Collins, Left Hand, Great Divide, and Avery, Odell has grown to international recognition and helped make Colorado a globally renowned beer-making epicenter.

Balance is the order of the day at Odell. From imperial strength beers to many small pilot creations, many of the brewery's creations exhibit a well-crafted nuance

of character. Hop bombs arrive with solid malty foundations, and stouts and porters have a smoothness and sweetness.

Odell's state-of-the-art facility, opened in 2010, was built with environmental issues in mind. The building uses solar power and natural light wherever possible, and the new, large-scale, cold-storage warehouse constantly adapts to the external temperature of the building, drawing cold air in when available instead of using electricity to power refrigeration.

Two beers, **90 Shilling** and **Easy Street Wheat,** have been Odell staples since 1989, but you quickly get the sense that Odell gets the most joy and satisfaction from offering up a vast array of styles. In addition to a consistent flow of new seasonals and experimental beers, the brewery has a dedicated barrel program focused on producing wood-aged beers. The annual **Woodcut** series and exotic Belgian-inspired beers brewed with *Brettanomyces* and souring bacteria have become highly regarded and valuable assets of the business.

In the brewery's colorful and busy taproom, 20 taps pour a mix of year-round, seasonal, barrel-aged, and experimental pilot beers. Odell prides itself on brewing beers with nonbrewing employees and friends of the brewery, as evidenced by the ever-changing list of interesting small-batch pilot brews.

Friek

Style: Fruit Lambic

ABV: 6.5 percent

Availability: Occasionally in 750-milliliter bottles

Friek is a tasteful and sour ode to the traditional cherry (kriek) and raspberry (framboise) lambics of the Pajottenland region of Belgium. Elements of these beers take a long time to reach agreeable maturation. Various batches of Friek are brewed and aged for up to three years, before being blended for a perfect balance of tart and sweet characteristics. Friek is one of the most impressive American interpretations of a fruit lambic.

PATEROS CREEK BREWING COMPANY

242 N. College Ave., Unit B, Fort Collins, CO 80524; (970) 484-722; PaterosCreekBrewing
.com; **Twitter:** @paterosbrew
Founded: 2011 **Founder:** Steve Jones **Brewer:** Steve Jones **Flagship Beer:** Cache la
Porter **Year-round Beers:** Cache la Porter, Stimulator Pale Ale, Old Town Ale, and Car 21
Seasonals/Special Releases: Rustic Red Irish Red, Snowy River Vanilla Porter, Sharktooth
Black Chili Ale, Greyrock GF Cream Ale, Outlaw Tap (series) **Tours:** None **Taproom:** Mon 4
to 8 p.m., Tues through Thurs noon to 8 p.m., Fri through Sat noon to 9 p.m. Closed Sun.
Growlers are available to go.

Fort Collins is one of busiest brewing cities in America, and it's not just the well-known brewing likes of New Belgium and Odell that helped put Fort Collins on the brewing map. Smaller upstarts, like Pateros Creek and Equinox, are doing just as much to capture Colorado's craft-beer drinkers' attention.

Steve Jones founded Pateros Creek with a desire to produce sessionable beers of the sort that beer folks could drink a few of and then safely drive home afterward. Steve's four year-round beers, **Cache la Porter** (see recipe, page 192), **Stimulator Pale Ale, Old Town Ale,** and **Car 21,** range in ABV from 4.5 to 5.3.

Steve grew up in Fort Collins, and a respect of the local permeates the small taproom and the beers it pours, from the abundance of local wood used in the space to the story behind each name of the beers. A celebration of the local is the order of the day.

Car 21 is that unusual of styles in Colorado, an English Bitter. This 4.5 percent, malt-forward beer has a toasty nose and a body bursting with caramel, dried red fruit, and soft-hop bitterness. **Stimulator Pale Ale** adds a healthy amount of rye malt to the usual pale ale mix to spice things up. The base of the beer is malty enough to complement and balance out the peppery-rye character and abundant use of leafy Cascade hops. **Cache la Porter** is a well-rounded, English-style porter with inviting milk chocolate and earthy hazelnut flavors. Bitterness is low, and the finish is smooth and toasty. The beer is pint-after-pint sessionable.

Beer Lover's Pick

Snowy River Vanilla Porter
Style: American Porter
ABV: 5 percent
Availability: Winter seasonal on tap
Vanilla is not an uncommon beer ingredient these days, but it is an uncommon ingredient in lower ABV beers, more often turning up in imperial strength stouts, browns, and porters. Snowy River Vanilla Porter uses local vanilla to brighten and sweeten the dark base cocoa and roasted-malt flavor of the beer. The result is a beer that is brilliant, sweet, and dessert-evoking.

Brewpub

COOPERSMITH'S PUB AND BREWERY

5 Old Town Sq., Fort Collins, CO 80524; (970) 498-0483; CooperSmithsPub.com;
Twitter: @CooperSmithsPub
Founded: 1989 **Founder:** Scott Smith and Brad Page **Brewer:** Dwight Hall **Flagship
Beer:** Punjabi Pale Ale **Year-round Beers:** Punjabi Pale Ale, Sigda's Green Chile, Poudre
Pale Ale, Dark Knight HBA, Columbine Kolsch, Mountain Avenue Wheat, Not Brown Ale,
Albert Damm Bitter, Horsetooth Stout, Cerveza Del Verano, Beire Blanche Du Fort, Tippet
American Lager, Steamship Ale, #13 Apricot Ale **Seasonals/Special Releases:** Changes

CooperSmith's Pub and Brewery opened in Old Town Fort Collins in 1989, the year
after Wynkoop opened for business in a dilapidated downtown Denver neighborhood. CooperSmith's founders, Scott Smith and Brad Page, had looked to Wynkoop's
owners for help with their business plan before pulling the trigger on their own
brewpub. Scott and Brad eventually found themselves at the heart of the revival of
Old Town Fort Collins.

The brewery and restaurant were constructed in an old grocery store in the
heart of the town. Today the brewery feels so at home that you might assume that
CooperSmith's had occupied the location for 100 years. Today, thanks in part to pioneering businesses like CooperSmith's, downtown Fort Collins is a bustling middle-
class college town.

CooperSmiths, of course, has its staple beers. One of the boldest is **Sigda's
Green Chile** ale, thought to be the first year-round chili beer served anywhere in
the country. The 5.4 percent ABV golden pour is brewed with Anaheim and serrano
chilies, and rather than burning the palate with pepper derived heat, it delivers a
pleasant and breezy vegetal freshness.

Over the course of a year CooperSmith's brews and serves upwards of 70 different beers, with styles running the gamut from Belgian sours to seldom-brewed,
cask-conditioned English styles served from a traditional hand pump. CooperSmith's
leaves few styles unbrewed and that includes ciders and meads. On any given day
you might find a cherry cider or blueberry mead pouring on one or two of the pub's
16 taps.

CooperSmith's is divided into two sides: the Pubside and the Poolside. The
Pubside menu offers up an extremely wide and encompassing selection of British-,
American-, and Mexican-inspired pub fare from burgers and fish-and-chips to pastas
and brick-oven pizzas. The Poolside offers up more American bar classics, with a
greater emphasis on burgers, pizzas, wings, nachos, and the like.

Fort Collins

Beer Bars

CHOICE CITY BUTCHER & DELI

104 W. Olive St., Fort Collins, CO 80524; (970) 490-2489; ChoiceCityButcher.com
Taps: 40 **Bottles/Cans:** 20+

Choice City Butcher & Deli, in the beautiful college town and brewery nirvana of Fort Collins, is probably one of the only craft beer–centric New York–style deli-catessens in America. No surprise then that this excellent and well-executed concept has been rated as not only one of the best beer restaurants in America but also one of the very best in the world, on two separate occasions by readers of RateBeer.

Behind the register, the wall is lined with 40 taps, pouring the likes of hard-to-find imports; rare, barrel-aged American offerings; and a small one-off batch beer by a local Colorado brewery. In addition to the jaw-dropping tap list, Choice City also has a bottle list of intriguing and often limited-release beers.

In terms of food, Choice City is a butcher as well as a restaurant and as such is a true meat lovers' Valhalla. The breakfast menu includes the likes of corned beef or buffalo hash with eggs, savory stuffed crepes, eggs Benedict, and chicken-fried steak. For lunch, how about a Colorado buffalo Reuben, Italian multi-meat sub, sausage sandwich, grilled cheese, or philly cheesesteak? Dinner could include a buffalo chicken salad, buffalo meat and bacon sliders, rib-eye crepes, or chile rellenos raviolis.

CRANKNSTEIN

215 N. College Ave., Unit A, Fort Collins, CO 80524; (970) 818-7008;
Twitter: @cranknstein; **Taps:** 12

Cranknstein in Fort Collins is similar in concept to Denver Bicycle Cafe: a perfect combination of a love of bike riding, great coffee, and good local beer. The 12 taps behind the bar pour a selection of the region's best IPAs, stouts, reds, wheats, porters, and even small, one-off pilot batches from area breweries. The daily food menu is small but always perfectly formed. Hungry customers can usually select from the likes of fresh quiche, sweet and savory scones, fruit crumbles, and pies. Cranknstein is an essential part of any Fort Collins bar crawl. After you've visited, you'll be green with envy and demanding that your hometown have an establishment of similar stylings.

THE MAYOR OF OLD TOWN

632 S. Mason St., Fort Collins, CO 80524; (970) 682-2410; TheMayorofOldTown.com;
Twitter: @mayorofoldtown
Taps: 100 **Bottles/Cans:** 20+

The Mayor of Old Town is one Fort Collins's best places to go if you want to sample a lot of local, national, and international beers. The bar has an impressive array of 100 taps. While there are plenty of chain beer restaurants that boast 100 taps, their offerings usually leave a lot to be desired. The Mayor is different. Here you will find one-off pilot batches from local Fort Collins breweries and rare barrel-aged beers from the East Coast and West Coast. The owners clearly care about getting their hands on the best and most-interesting beers out there. Quality imported beers from Belgium, Germany, the UK, and beyond are also well represented. If 100 taps of carefully selected beer from around the world isn't enough for you, then fear not. The Mayor also has a cooler or two stocked with even more selections in bottles and cans. Yes, the Mayor is a legitimate beer paradise.

The menu at the Mayor of Old Town is all-day American diner meets Italian American pizzeria and sub shop. A wide selection of breakfast burritos, Italian deli sandwiches, breakfast sandwiches, and bagels supplement the list of traditional pizzas, soups, and salads.

Fort Collins

Front Range

BREWERIES

Big Beaver Brewing Company	2
Crabtree Brewing Company	4
Estes Park Brewery	1
Grimm Brothers Brewhouse	3
Left Hand Brewing Company	7
Oskar Blues Brewery	9
Tommyknocker Brewery	10

BREWPUBS

Pitcher's Brewery & Sports Shack	5
Pumphouse Brewery & Restaurant	6

BARS

Oskar Blues Home Made Liquids & Solids	8

0   10   20 miles

Front Range

Estes Park, Greeley, Idaho Springs, Longmont & Loveland

In the small cities that dot the vast and impressive Front Range landscape between the larger metro areas of Denver, Boulder, and Fort Collins, you'll find that community after community has a quality local brewery and often more than one. Few states in the US are even close to having as many breweries as Colorado, and this fertile wealth of brewing is not confined to the larger cities. In fact many a Front Range town is home to one of Colorado's better-known breweries, such as Left Hand, Oskar Blues, and Tommyknocker.

Breweries

BIG BEAVER BREWING COMPANY

2707 W. Eisenhower Blvd., Unit 9, Loveland, CO 80537; (970) 818-6064; BigBeaverbrew .com; **Twitter:** @big_beaver_brew

Founded: 2010 **Founder:** Peter E. Villeneuve **Brewer:** Peter E. Villeneuve **Flagship Beer:** Beaver Stubble Stout **Year-round Beers:** Beaver Stubble Stout, Potent Peter IPA, Shaved Tail Ale, Bust-A-Nut Brown Ale, Red Arse Ale, Whiskey Dick Stout, Breezy Bean Bag Scottish Ale **Seasonals/Special Releases:** Bock, Doppelbock, Fruity Booty Brew, Screw the Pooch Pale Ale, Burning Beaver Ale **Tours:** None **Taproom:** Mon through Sun 2 to 8 p.m. Growlers and Tap-A-Draft containers are available to go.

*Q*uirky and *cheeky* are the two words that best describe Big Beaver Brewing Company. This small, four-barrel brewery and taproom in Loveland offers a smorgasbord of beers whose names are designed to make the customer simultaneously blush and chuckle. Big Beaver clearly relishes the reactions its risqué beers provoke.

The brewery is the brainchild of Peter E. Villeneuve, who started homebrewing while penning a PhD dissertation on the practicalities of using yeast as a source of nutrition for astronauts undertaking prolonged space travel. Big Beaver is located in an unassuming storefront office of the sort you would expect to find a small local law firm or a dental practice in. After walking through an empty front room, you emerge into a wider rear space, where a sizeable bar and taproom is situated. Large chalkboards list the 13 beers pouring that day. House-boiled beer brats can also be ordered at the bar.

Big Beaver does not bottle its beers, but 64-ounce growlers and 6-litre Tap-A-Draft containers are available to go. The beers themselves range from traditionally styled pales, stouts, IPAs, Belgian ales, and German lagers to more experimental offerings brewed with adjuncts like fruit and spice.

Potent Peter IPA is a moderately bitter American IPA, dry hopped to boost its grassy green aroma. At 6.2 percent ABV, it is moderately balanced in terms alcohol and lighter than the 7 to 7.5

Beaver Stubble Stout

Style: Foreign Extra Stout

ABV: 6.9 percent

Availability: Year-round on tap at the brewery taproom

Beaver Stubble Stout is the clear standout of Big Beaver Brewing Company's many brews. A foreign export stout, Stubble has a weighty espresso nose; light bitterness; a soft, cocoa-butter body; and a short, dry finish. Given its strength, the beer has a surprisingly sessionable quality about it. It's definitely worth considering taking home a growler of Beaver Stubble Stout.

percent of many other Colorado IPAs. **Burning Beaver Ale** is an interesting speciality beer. It's essentially a Belgian witbier with a strong clove and sweet herb aroma but brewed with the addition of cayenne chilies. The chilies add a piquant white-pepper quality to the aroma and deliver a swelling heat on the finish but never become overwhelming.

CRABTREE BREWING COMPANY

625 3rd St., Greeley, CO 80631; (970) 356-0516; CrabTreeBrewing.com; Twitter: @Crabtreebrewing

Founded: 2006 **Founder:** Jeff Crabtree **Brewer:** Jeff Crabtree **Flagship Beer:** Ginger Bee **Year-round Beers:** Ginger Bee, Serenity Amber Ale, Boxcar Brown, Jeff's Pale Ale, Twisted Creek Wheat **Seasonals/Special Releases:** Oatmeal Stout, Chunkin Pumpkin, Eclipse Black IPA, Braggot, Dearfield Ale, Golden 8, Berliner Weisse Ale, Cézanne Saison, Barrel Aged (series; various one offs) **Tours:** None **Taproom:** Mon to Thurs 1 to 10 p.m., Fri and Sat noon to midnight, Sun noon to 6 p.m.

The Crabtree Brewing Company story begins in 2003, the year that owner and founder Jeff Crabtree brewed his first batch of homebrew. Soon after, the Union Colony Brewery, which at the time was the only brewery in the small industrial farm community of Greeley, Colorado, went out of business. In a bold move, Jeff, freshly bitten by the brewing bug, took out a loan and purchased much of Union's equipment. At the time, Jeff was studying business at a local college, and he shrewdly leveraged his assignments to explore the viability of opening a small craft brewery in the local area.

Front Range

Upon graduation, Jeff did not jump headfirst into full-time brewery management but instead decided to hedge his bets by taking a job in the corporate world and operating the brewery part-time in a small and gritty well-worn corner of Greeley. Unfortunately, success didn't come overnight. The turning point occurred when Jeff decided that he needed to quit his corporate day job and dedicate himself full time to the brewery. Soon after, he began focusing more on brewing styles of beers that interested him.

Crabtree's GABF silver medal–winning **Oatmeal Stout** and its **Eclipse Black IPA** can now be found in local stores along Colorado's Front Range. The aforementioned 7.5 percent ABV Oatmeal Stout is a definite must try for any self-respecting stout or porter lover. It's not difficult to understand why this smooth milk-chocolate and toffee-treacle rich dark delight grabbed the palates of beer judges at the GABF.

Come September, the shelves of liquor stores are full of pumpkin and other autumn seasonals. If you're lucky enough to be visiting Colorado at this beautiful time of year, sampling Crabtree's **Chunkin Pumpkin** should be toward the top of your "to taste" list. This evocative, rich, pumpkin pie–like beer is brewed with an abundance of season-appropriate spices and roasted and chunked pumpkin flesh.

Berliner Weisse Ale
Style: Berliner Weisse
ABV: 4.3 percent
Availability: Occasionally on tap and in bottles

The Crabtree Brewing Company beer you simply cannot leave Colorado without trying, especially if you enjoy sour beers, is the GABF gold medal–winning tart and effervescent Berliner Weisse. The highly refreshing, quaffable, sour, wheat-based beer is a style

that until recently was only brewed by a handful of breweries in its homeland, Germany, or more specially, in and around Berlin. The style is traditionally served with a shot of raspberry, or woodruff syrup. Sour lovers will likely prefer the beer sans syrup, but Crabtree does offer house-made organic raspberry and woodruff syrups for those interested in trying the beer that way.

ESTES PARK BREWERY

470 Prospect Village Dr., Estes Park, CO 80517; (970) 586-5421; EPBrewery.com
Founded: 1993 **Founder:** Gordon Knight **Brewer:** Eric Bratrud **Flagship Beer:** Redrum Ale **Year-round Beers:** Trail Ridge Red (Redrum) Ale, Longs Peak Raspberry Wheat, Park Gold, Stinger Wild Honey Wheat, Gold, Staggering Elk Lager, Porter, Renegade IPA, Samson Stout, Barley Wine, Shining Pale Ale, Blackberry Wheat **Seasonals/Special Releases:** Rotating list **Tours:** None **Taproom:** Sun through Thurs 11 a.m. to 10 p.m., Fri through Sat 11 a.m. to 11 p.m. Growlers and bottles are available to go.

The modern Estes Park Brewery was born in 1994 out of a merger of two other businesses, Gordon Knight's High Country Brewery, which relocated from Boulder to Estes a year after it opened, and Ed Grueff's Events Center, already in the city of Estes Park. The bold craft recipes that Colorado beer guru Knight brought with him were an eye-opener to many existing patrons, so new "lighter" options were added to the brewery's repertoire, including **Longs Peak Raspberry Wheat** (4.2 percent ABV), a beer that became a year round offering.

Park Gold is a 4.2 percent ABV German-style Kölsch, with an fruity apricot and dry grass aroma, and clean low to medium bitter body. Kölsch make for great first beers of the day if you're planning on tasting everything the brewery has to offer. **Staggering Elk Lager** (4.8 percent ABV) is brewed in the California-common style made famous by Anchor Steam Beer. The brew uses Pilsner malt and Saaz hops, and like any good Pilsner is a quaffable, clean, and refreshing drink that is also a food-friendly choice.

In addition to its house offerings, Estes Park also brews two beers for the nearby Stanley Hotel, the locale that inspired the *The Shining*, a movie based on a novel by Stephen King. **Trail Ridge Red (Redrum) Ale** is a 4.5 percernt ABV English-style session bitter, with an appropriately low bitterness and soft-biscuit malt and bramble fruit notes. The **Shining Pale Ale,** a 6 percent ABV, moderately bittered, English-American hybrid pub ale, is reminiscent of an ESB.

Barley Wine
Style: American Barleywine
ABV: 10 percent
Availability: Winter seasonal on tap and year-round in bottles
Estes Park Brewery's Barley Wine is only brewed once a year and is allowed to condition for 12 months before being sold the following year. The 10 percent ABV is designed to be cellared for up to five years. The amber pour is initially suffused with heat, resinous hop burn, and finally sticky sweetness. If you're lucky enough to be in area in the winter, this is a definite must-try offering.

GRIMM BROTHERS BREWHOUSE

623 Denver Ave., Loveland, CO 80538; (970) 624-6045; GrimmBrosBrewhouse.com;
Twitter: @grimmbrosbrew
Founded: 2010 Founders: Don Chapman and Aaron Heaton Brewer: Don Chapman
Flagship Beer: Little Red Cap Year-round Beers: Little Red Cap, Snow Drop, The Fearless
Youth, Master Thief, The Griffin Seasonals/Special Releases: The Farmers Daughter
Oktoberfest Lager, Hare's Bride Hefewein, Biere De Grimm, German Barleywine, Magic
Mirror, 7 Ravens, The Owl, The Count Tours: None Taproom: Mon through Thurs 1 to
7 p.m., Fri 1 to 9 p.m., Sat noon to 9 p.m., Sun 1 to 5 p.m. Growlers and bottles are
available to go.

In an effort to avoid opening a brewery that simply served yet another IPA and
pale ale, Don Chapman and Aaron Heaton wanted to go in an entirely different direction. The aspiring brewery owners decided to specialize in brewing only
German beer styles, or German-inspired beers. Any thought of them adhering to
Germany's strict *Reinheitsgebot* (beer purity laws) was immediately dismissed. One

Beer Lover's Pick

The Griffin
Style: Hefeweizen
ABV: 4.7 percent
Availability: Year-round on tap
and in bottles
The Griffin, a brewed-to-style
unfiltered Hefeweizen, is one of
the best examples of the beer type
in Colorado. The hazy off-white
lively pour is an explosive drink
of lemon peel, clove, white pepper, and soft dry-grass notes. The
finish is a touch dry and invites
further quaffing.

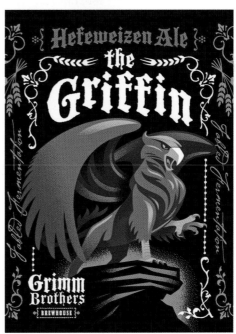

Front Range

of their most successful beers is **Snow Drop** (see recipe, page 190), a *kottbusser,* which is a long-forgotten German style brewed with the addition of honey, oats, and molasses.

The branding aesthetic of Grimm Brothers is an eye-catching one; the brewery paid a skilled agency to create new fairy-tale character for every beer. The uniform look and feel of the beers is supported by a new taproom full of gothic dark wood.

In addition to Snow Drop, Grimm Brothers's other year-round beers include **Little Red Cap,** a 5.2 percent ABV Düsseldorf altbier; the **Fearless Youth,** a spritzy 5.2 percent ABV dunkel; **Master Thief** (6.7 percent ABV), an English-style porter brewed with German ingredients; and **The Griffin** (4.7 percent ABV), a bright and flavorful traditional Hefeweizen.

LEFT HAND BREWING COMPANY

1265 Boston Ave., Longmont CO 80501; (303) 772-0258; LeftHandBrewing.com; Twitter: @LeftHandBrewing
Founded: 1993 **Founders:** Dick Doore and Eric Wallace **Brewer:** Ro Gunzel **Flagship Beer:** Nitro **Year-round Beers:** Nitro, Milk Stout, Sawtooth Ale, 400 Pound Monkey, Polestar Pilsner, Black Jack Porter, Stranger Pale Ale, Wake Up Dead Stout **Seasonals/Special Releases:** Good JuJu, Oktoberfest, Warrior IPA, Fade to Black (series), Wake Up Dead Stout, Chainsaw, Twin Sisters, Smokejumper, TNT Weisen Doppelbock **Tours:** Sat through Sun 1 and 2 p.m., Mon through Fri by appointment only, call (303) 772-0258 ext. 110 **Taproom:** Mon through Thurs 3 to 8 p.m., Fri noon to 9 p.m., Sat noon to 8 p.m., Sun 1 to 8 p.m. Growlers and bottled beers are available to go.

The Left Hand Brewing Company story began in 1990 after its future cofounder, Dick Doore, brewed his first homebrew from a kit he received for Christmas from his brother. Three busy homebrewing years later, his obsession had blossomed, and he found himself in Colorado, where he and a former college friend, Eric Wallace, brainstormed the brewery that would one day become Left Hand Brewing Company.

In 1993 Dick and Eric set up shop in a former sausage factory in Longmont. The name of their fledgling brewery was Indian Peaks. The name was short-lived, however, as it came to light that another brewery was using the name Indian Peaks for one of its beers. After going back to the drawing board, the pair settled on Left Hand Brewing Company, which honors Chief Niwot and his tribe that spent the winter in the local area. "Left Hand" is taken from the Arapahoe word for left hand, *Niwot.*

Left Hand opened under its new name on January 22, 1994. The first beer under the new name was **Sawtooth Ale,** which remains a popular year-round release for

the brewery to this day. Later that year, Left Hand won two medals at the GABF, a bronze medal in the robust porter category for their **Black Jack Porter** and a gold medal for Sawtooth in the bitter category. A big accomplishment for such a new beer maker.

By the close of 2010, the brewery had brewed more than 24,000 barrels of beer, and by 2011 that number had shot up to more than 36,000 barrels. In late 2011 Left Hand unleashed the world's first nitrogen pressure-filled glass bottle. Nitrogen-presented beers previously required a widget like the gas-dispensing examples used by Guinness and Boddingtons in their cans and bottles to provide a thick white head and creamy body. Simply called the **Nitro,** the beer is a creamy and smooth nitro-carbonated incarnation of the brewery's best-selling milk stout.

Beer Lover's Pick

Wake Up Dead Stout
Style: Russian Imperial Stout
ABV: 10.2 percent
Availability: Year-round on tap and in bottles

A trip to Colorado, or to Left Hand Brewing Company itself, isn't complete without enjoying a glass of Wake Up Dead Stout. This potent 10.2 percent ABV Russian imperial stout is brewed to cellar for up to and beyond four years. The thick, crude-oil pour has tight, earthy licorice root; espresso bean and baker's chocolate notes; and a warm alcohol finish. This tightly bundled big beer will, if cellared correctly, mellow and really open up over time.

OSKAR BLUES BREWERY

1800 Pike Rd., #B, Longmont, CO 80501; (303) 776-1914; OskarBlues.com;
Twitter: @oskarblues
Founded: 1997 **Founder:** Dale Katechis **Brewer:** Dale Katechis **Flagship Beer:** Dale's
Pale Ale **Year-round Beers:** Dale's Pale Ale, Old Chub, Mama's Little Yella Pils **Seasonals/
Special Releases:** Ten FIDY, Gubna, G'Knight Imperial Red, Deviant Dale's **Tours:** Mon
through Thurs 4 p.m., Fri through Sun 2, 3, 4, and 5 p.m. **Taproom:** Mon through Fri 2 to
8 p.m., Sat through Sun noon to 8 p.m. Growlers and cans are available to go.

Oskar Blues is synonymous with being the first craft brewery to put its beer in cans. The brewery blazed the trail at a time when most in the craft-beer community thought cans were only appropriate for cheap, light lagers. With a single bold move, Oskar Blues owner and founder Dale Katechis elevated his small brewery in Lyons, Colorado, to be a business of national interest. That was 2002. Ten years

later Oskar Blues was not only one of the fastest growing breweries in America, but also one of the fastest growing businesses in the nation, period.

There are a few qualities that might ultimately make modern lined cans more appealing to a craft brewery owner than glass bottles. One of the most appealing aspects of cans, though, is that they do not allow light in to strike the beer. They also have a much tighter space between the fill and cap than bottles do. This means there is less oxygen in the container that could eventually spoil the beer and also means that cans have a longer shelf life.

In 1997 Dale didn't have any Oskar Blues beers to worry about canning. He had recently leveraged himself to open a Cajun restaurant in Lyons. Despite Dale being a homebrewer, Left Hand Brewing Company made the Oskar Blues house beer. Following the suggestion of a homebrewing customer, Dale partnered with the man to craft a beer that would eventually become **Dale's Pale Ale.** The beer rapidly gained a following and word of Dale's Pale Ale began to spread well beyond the small mountain town.

Beer Lover's Pick

Deviant Dale's
Style: American IPA
ABV: 8 percent
Availability: Year-round on tap
  and in cans

Oskar Blues Brewery's Deviant Dale's won a silver medal in its category at the 2011 GABF, and once you've tasted it, you'll understand exactly why. The beer is an impressive and memorable example of the American IPA style. It has a brutish aroma of fresh citrus peel and extracted pine oil, and the body is no less savage, with appetizing flavors that are in line with the aroma; pine, orange marmalade, and menthol notes all play a central role. Deviant Dale's is also the first beer to be packaged in 16-ounce cans.

The colorfully named HYA (Here's Your Ass) followed. Today this full-bodied, malty, Scottish-style ale can be found in cans and on tap year-round by the name **Old Chub.**

More than any other brewery of its success and size, Oskar Blues has a tightly focused product line. **Mama's Little Yella Pils** is a brilliant, sunshine yellow–colored American Pilsner with a bitter pithy bite from sip to swallow. For most beer geeks, though, it is Oskar Blues' stronger ales that command the most interest. **G'Knight Imperial Red** is a 8.7 percent ABV American amber ale, with a potent nose of seaweed and tarragon and a body thick with the flavor of anise and eucalyptus. It's one of those ales that blurs the line between the ambers and IPAs.

TOMMYKNOCKER BREWERY
1401 Miner St., Idaho Springs, CO 80452; (303) 567-2688; TommyKnocker.com; **Twitter:** @TKBrew
Founded: 1994 **Founder:** Steve Indrehus **Brewer:** Steve Indrehus **Flagship Beer:** Maple Nut Brown **Year-round Beers:** Maple Nut Brown Ale, Jack Whacker Wheat Ale, Alpine Glacier Pilsner Lager, Pick Axe India Pale Ale, Butt Head Bock Lager, Vienna Amber Lager **Seasonals/Special Releases:** Imperial Nut Brown Ale, Hop Strike Black IPA, Cocoa Porter Winter Ale, Tundrabeary Summer Ale **Tours:** None **Taproom:** Mon through Sat 11 to 2 a.m., Sun 11 a.m. to midnight. Growlers and bottles are available to go.

Tommyknocker's reputation and beers reach far beyond its small ski-town home of Idaho Springs. The brewery distributes to many states in the US, but its attitude, ambience, and beers remain proudly Coloradoan. When visiting the brewery on the pretty main street of Idaho Springs, you would be forgiven for thinking Tommyknocker was anything more than another of Colorado's small-town brewpubs. There are few clues to its stature as a brewery that sends large pallets of beer far afield.

Tommyknocker is named after the mythical little creatures that were said to pester the Cornish miners who settled in Idaho Springs to work the mines. The gremlins of the Cornish mining world, as it were.

Interestingly, Tommyknocker uses oak chips in the brewing of many of its beers, using the wood as an active ingredient alongside malt and hops to impart subtle and sweet vanilla and coconut flavors.

Tommyknocker has gained the most momentum and buzz thank to its tawny-colored, 4.5 percent ABV **Maple Nut Brown Ale.** The maple is present as a background note and serves to soften the bitter dark chocolate–covered Brazil-nut flavors that permeate the beer.

The 6.5 percent ABV **Hop Strike Black IPA** is a black IPA with a spicy, rye-malt twist. The addition of rye malt brings notes of white and black pepper to the moderate-to-high bittered, charcoal-black pour. The nose has potent notes of tar and earthy pine.

A popular Colorado winter release, **Cocoa Porter Winter Ale** is a low bitterness American porter, brewed with a healthy amount of cocoa. The resulting dark-brown pour is a smooth drink, laden with milk chocolate and mocha aroma and flavor. This 5.7 percent ABV beer is a must try for chocolate beer lovers.

Butt Head Bock Lager
Style: Bock
ABV: 8.2 percent
Availability: Year-round on tap and in bottles
Butt Head Bock Lager is a strong bock beer, brewed in the style of a traditional German doppelbock. The strong, malt-heavy, Brazil-nut brown pour has thick bittersweet notes of muscovado sugar, toffee, and treacle. The finish has a smooth, warming, caramel finish.

Brewpubs

PITCHER'S BREWERY & SPORTS SHACK

2501 S. 11th Ave., Greeley, CO 80631; (970) 353-3393
Founder: Gus Christopoulous **Brewer:** Gus Christopoulous **Flagship Beer:** 808 Wheat
Year-round Beers: Baja Mexican–style Lager, 808 Wheat, Sunset Amber, Apricot Ale,
Sensuous IPA **Seasonals/Special Releases:** Changes

Pitcher's Brewery & Sports Shack in Greeley is one of the more off-the-beaten-path breweries in Colorado. It's an unusual brewery, and one worth putting on your radar if you're planning a visit to the more well-known Greeley brewery, Crabtree, located about 10 minutes away.

I'm not entirely sure what a shack is, but it conjures up images of a casual bar on a sun-drenched beach, somewhere exotic. Thanks to some surf memorabilia

mounted on the walls and a vague Hawaiian-themed interior aesthetic, Pitcher's does at least have an element of the beach about it. The "sports" in the name is well represented by the many televisions blaring the games of day.

The food is limited to standard American bar fare, such as burgers, sliders, wings, and such, but to be honest the food really isn't the reason to visit Pitchers. The reason to visit Pitchers is, of course, the house beer.

The best offerings at Pitchers are the brewery's lighter brews. **Baja Mexican–style Lager,** served with a generous wedge of lime bursts with citrus effervescent, has a clean cereal body and a refreshing light bitter finish. The brewery's flagship beer, **808 Wheat,** is an American pale wheat ale served with a slice of orange and like Baja, acts as a pleasingly drinkable refresher. The beer has clearly been designed to be pint-after-pint drinkable. A comfortable companion to an afternoon or evening of sports watching. **Sunset Amber** is a brewed-to-style American amber ale. The brilliant copper pours with soft notes of biscuit, bitter lemon, and caramel. This is a polite beer that is more than at home paired with American bar classics offered on Pitcher's menu.

PUMPHOUSE BREWERY & RESTAURANT

540 Main St., Longmont, CO 80501; (303) 702-0881; PumphouseBrewery.com; **Twitter:** @PumphouseBrew
Founded: 1996 **Founders:** Dennis Coombs, Craig Taylor, Dave D'Epagnier, and Thomas Charles **Brewer:** Dave Mentus **Flagship Beer:** Wildfire Wheat **Year-round Beers:** Wildfire Wheat, Flashpoint IPA, 4-Alarm Copper Ale, Red Alert Amber, Shockwave Scottish Ale, Spotted Dog Milk Stout **Seasonals/Special Releases:** Hooligan Double IPA, Backdraft Imperial Stout, Survivor Cream Ale, Blueberry Wheat, Tripel, Brushfire Belgian Pale Ale, Wildland Sour #7, Pyro Chocolate Porter

Pumphouse Brewery & Restaurant in Colorado's picturesque Longmont is one of the state's well-established and highly rated brewpubs, proudly independently owned and operated since 1996. The brewery and restaurant sit at one of the central crossroads of the town and was constructed in a spacious and historic building that dates back to 1918. In 2004 the owners decided to expand into the ever-popular sports-bar business, but instead of changing the vibe of the original space, they simply added a sports bar, called the Red Zone, onto the existing space.

Red Zone and the restaurant, Pumphouse, share the same menu. Appetizers include artichoke dip, hot wings, southwestern eggs rolls, crab cakes, and smoked mozzarella. Entrees include a selection of hearty burgers, sandwiches, soups, salads, and pub staples, like fish-and-chips, burritos, fajitas, tacos, enchiladas, fried chicken, ribs, steak, and pasta.

The food is all high quality, but it's the beers that are the real highlights. There are six well-executed, year-round beers that are supplemented by a nice selection of revolving creations. **Wildfire Wheat** is a 5 percent ABV American pale wheat ale, with refreshing unfiltered citrus forward aroma and flavor and a tart cereal finish. **Flashpoint IPA** is a 6.6 percent ABV American IPA with a strong yellow citrus nose and a long herbaceous and menthol body. This makes for a great pairing with the house hot wings or any of the Mexican dishes. **Spotted Dog Milk Stout** is a sessionable 4.6 percent ABV milk stout, with a milk chocolate nose and sweet mocha body. Notes of toffee, caramel, and coffee all contribute to the desserty finish.

Beer Bar

OSKAR BLUES HOME MADE LIQUIDS & SOLIDS

1555 S. Hover Rd., Longmont, Colorado 80501; (303) 485-9400; OskarBlues.com
Taps: 43

You'd think Oskar Blues, one of the fastest growing craft breweries, would have enough on its hands running a massive production brewery, a hop and cattle farm, a cajun restaurant, and a small brewery in its spiritual home of Lyons, Colorado, but owner Dale Katechis decided to open a large-scale craft-beer restaurant in Longmont. The brilliantly named Oskar Blues Home Made Liquids & Solids counts 43 of the best curated taps of craft beer in Colorado. Most of the beers are sourced from Colorado breweries, but some of the finer out-of-state breweries get a look in as well. There are no imported or bottled beers stocked at the restaurant.

The southern barbecue–inspired menu is perfectly Oskar Blues and comes courtesy of Jason Rogers, a James Beard Foundation recognized chef. Appetizers include beer steamed mussels, bayou meatballs with crawfish, crab cakes with green tomatoes, fried pickles, shrimp and grits, and two pounds of smoked wings. Mains include 12-ounce flatiron steak, grilled trout, blackened mix grill of salmon, jumbo shrimp and andouille sausage, chicken and andouille jambalaya, beer can chicken, spare ribs, and fried chicken. If all that isn't enough to whet your appetite, Liquids & Solids also offers up an extensive menu of hearty salads, pizzas, burgers, sandwiches, and decadent Southern-style desserts.

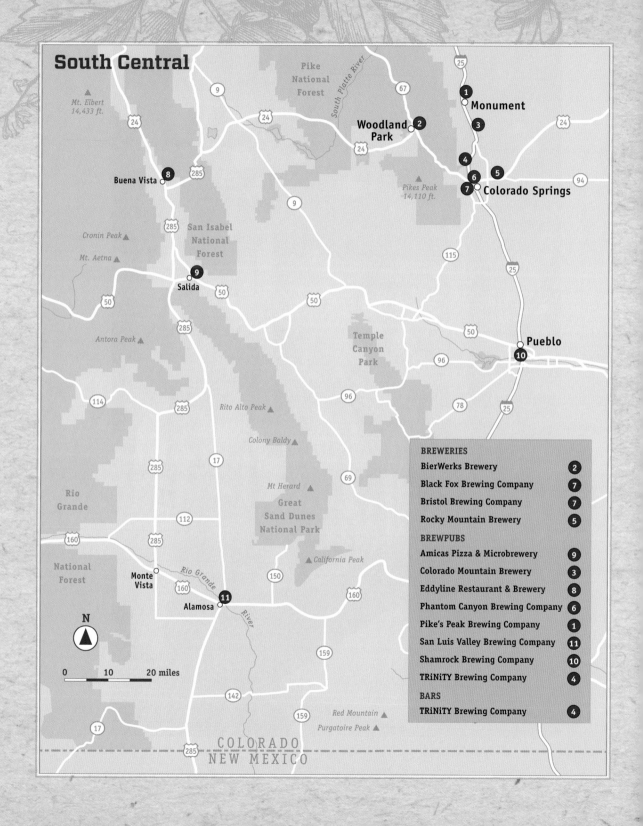

South Central

Mt. Elbert
14,433 ft.

Pike
National
Forest

South Platte River

1 ○ Monument

Woodland
Park **2**

3

4

Buena Vista **8**

6
5
7 ○ Colorado Springs

Pikes Peak
14,110 ft.

San Isabel
National
Forest

Cronin Peak

Mt. Aetna

9
Salida

Antora Peak

Rio
Grande

Temple
Canyon
Park

Pueblo **10**

Rito Alto Peak

Colony Baldy

Mt Herard

Great
Sand Dunes
National Park

California Peak

National
Forest

Monte
Vista

Rio Grande River

Alamosa **11**

N

0   10   20 miles

Red Mountain

Purgatoire Peak

COLORADO
NEW MEXICO

BREWERIES

BierWerks Brewery	**2**
Black Fox Brewing Company	**7**
Bristol Brewing Company	**7**
Rocky Mountain Brewery	**5**

BREWPUBS

Amicas Pizza & Microbrewery	**9**
Colorado Mountain Brewery	**3**
Eddyline Restaurant & Brewery	**8**
Phantom Canyon Brewing Company	**6**
Pike's Peak Brewing Company	**1**
San Luis Valley Brewing Company	**11**
Shamrock Brewing Company	**10**
TRiNiTY Brewing Company	**4**

BARS

| TRiNiTY Brewing Company | **4** |

South Central

Alamosa, Buena Vista, Colorado Springs, Monument, Pueblo, Salida & Woodland Park

If there is a theme that ties together the brewing and beer sensibility of the larger area south of Denver, it is creativity and an unspoken rule that one should never be bound by rules. Many of Colorado's most ingenious and experimental breweries can be found in this region, from the likes of TRiNiTY, Black Fox, and Rocky Mountain Brewery in the Colorado Springs area to the vast number of close-knit and family-run brewpubs that tap new creations every week in the towns that pepper the region.

Breweries

BIERWERKS BREWERY

121 E. Midland Ave., Woodland Park, CO 80863; (719) 686-8100; BierWerks.com;
Twitter: @Bierwerks
Founded: 2010 **Founders:** Jeff Aragon and Brian Horton **Brewers:** James McGraw
Flagship Beer: Helles **Year-round Beers:** Helles, Altbier, Dunkel, Latzenbier **Seasonals/
Special Releases:** Weissbier, Oktoberfest, Dunkelweiss, Weihnachtsbier, Doppelbock,
Weizenbock, Maibock, Dortmunder, Double IPA, Baltic Porter, Double Red, Wee Heavy,
Imperial Stout **Tours:** None **Taproom:** Mon through Thurs 2:30 to 10 p.m., Fri through
Sat 1 to 10 p.m., Sun 1 to 8 p.m. Growlers are available to go.

BierWerks Brewery owners Brian Horton and Jeff Aragon are not your average brewery upstarts. For more than a decade, they owned and operated Trinidad Brewing Company in southern Colorado, which went out of business when the economy crashed. Brian and Jeff moved farther north and in August 2010 opened BierWerks in Woodland Park, near Colorado Springs. Instead of replicating their previous business model and brewing American and English beer styles, they decided to go German.

To man the mash tun, Brian and Jeff hired James McGraw as their brewmaster. McGraw trained at the prestigious Doemens Academy in Munich, Germany, and worked for BJ's Brewhouse and a brewery called Tustin in California before answering the call to brew German styles, his passion, year-round at BierWerks.

The range of German-style beers that BierWerks brews is all encompassing, and many of them are put on tap during the seasons they are traditionally released in. A helles, an altbier, a dunkel, and a darker, stronger, incarnation of an altbier called a latzenbier make up BierWerks's selection of year-round offerings. The **Helles** (5.5 percent ABV) is brewed in much the same fashion it has been in Munich for generations. The blonde lager has a sweet underbelly, a light cereal aroma, and minimal bitterness. It is a beer engineered for ongoing drinkability. The **Altbier** (5.8 percent ABV) is a style that Düsseldorf, a city in the Rhineland region of Germany, proudly proclaims as its own. The amber-hued style is unusual in that it is an ale that is cold fermented and conditioned in much the same way as a lager. Bitterness is light to moderate, the finish dry. Sweetness is as important in this beer as the bitter bite.

BierWerks does occasionally brew beers that aren't German in origin. It explores high-gravity versions of American and British styles with its series called **Brewers Reserve.** Past releases include a double IPA, a Baltic porter, a double red ale, a Scottish-styled wee heavy, and an imperial stout.

Beer Lover's Pick

Latzenbier
Style: Latzenbier
ABV: 6.9 percent
Availability: Year-round
 on tap

The most unique of Bier-Werks Brewery's year-round taps is undoubtedly its Latzenbier (6.9 percent ABV). The potent and esoteric style is seldom brewed in the US. It is a beer with tight monastic brewing heritage in Germany. The beer is stout and extremely rich, with chewy toffee-caramel and molasses-like characteristics. Highly unusual and definitely worth trying.

BLACK FOX BREWING COMPANY

1647 S. Tejon St., Colorado Springs, CO 80905; (719) 964-4676; BlackFoxBrewing.com
Founded: 2009 **Founder:** John Schneider **Brewer:** John Schneider **Flagship Beer:** None
Year-round Beers: None **Seasonals/Special Releases:** La Noche Del Diablo, Cracked, Somnombulance, Don't Call Me Wit, Faust Part 2, Black Fox Saison, Samhain **Tours:** None **Taproom:** None. Black Fox beers are poured in at Bristol Brewing Company (same location). Mon through Fri 10 a.m. to 9 p.m., Sat 9 a.m. to 9 p.m., Sun noon to 6 p.m. Growlers are available to go.

Funkwerks is Colorado's most widely known saison brewery, but Black Fox Brewing Company, which operates out of Bristol Brewing Company in Colorado Springs, was Colorado's first all saison-style beer maker in the state. The venture was founded by John Schneider, a man who fully embraces the idea that saison is less a style and more a practical and seasonal approach to brewing. Virtually no adjunct ingredients are off-limits. If it's around, is easily accessible, or just seems like a great idea, then it can find its way into one of Black Fox's provisional farmhouse ales.

John launched Black Fox at the Bristol taproom in early 2009, and from the beginning there was no concern that his beers would be confused with Bristol's beers. They included **Somnombulance,** an 8 percent ABV dark saison, matured on coffee, vanilla, and Ghirardelli caramel; and **Siempre Loco,** a 7 percent ABV saison brewed with cumin, lime zest, and pepper, for release on Cinco de Mayo.

One of Black Fox's most popular beers is **La Noche Del Diablo,** a dark saison, aged on cherries and dark chocolate. The beer is a mysterious farmhouse ale with an unusual chocolate sundae dessert-like personality.

An avid skateboarder and punk-music aficionado, John has imbued his small brewing operation with much of the spirit and vibe of his pastimes, from the names of his beers to the general forthright attitude and outlandish nature of the beers themselves.

Black Fox does not bottle at present, so if you're interested in trying any of John's colorful creations, look first to the Bristol taproom. You may also find them in any of the more serious craft beer–centric bars recommended in this book.

Black Fox is currently in the process of relocating to a new, as yet undisclosed location in Denver. Production is on temporary hiatus.

Beer Lover's Pick

Don't Call Me Wit
Style: Witbier
ABV: 6.6 percent
Availability: Occasionally on tap

Don't Call Me Wit is a spritzy, peppery, saison-like take on the traditional witbier, and it is positively Champagne-like on the palate. Bursting with pithy fruit aroma, bite, and crispness, it would seem a perfect and lively companion to any number of breakfast foods you care to name. As this book attests, Colorado has no shortage of fascinating breweries making interesting beers of every beer style imaginable. Finding a witbier like this in the middle of the state at a small brewery within another brewery is an example of how far beer making in America has come.

BRISTOL BREWING COMPANY

1647 S. Tejon, Colorado Springs, CO 80906; (719) 633-2555; BristolBrewing.com;
Twitter: @Bristol_Brewery
Founded: 1994 **Founder:** Mike Bristol **Brewer:** Mike Bristol **Flagship Beer:** Laughing
Lab Scottish Ale **Year-round Beers:** Laughing Lab Scottish Ale, Red Rocket Pale Ale,
Beehive Honey Wheat, Mass Transit Ale, Compass IPA **Seasonals/Special Releases:** Old
No. 23 Barley Wine, Winter Warlock Oatmeal Stout, Yellow Kite Summer Pils, Christmas
Ale, Cheyenne Canon Pinon Nut Ale, Local 5 Ale, Octoberfest Lager, Smokebrush Porter,
Venetucci Pumpkin Ale, Edge City Kolsch, Edge City Dunkelweiss Bier, Edge City Small
Beer, Edge City 1.5 IPA, Edge City Wit Bier, Edge City Mild Ale, XXX Warlock **Tours:** None
Taproom: Mon through Fri 10 a.m. to 9 p.m., Sat 9 a.m. to 9 p.m., Sun noon to 6 p.m.

Bristol was founded in 1994 by Mike Bristol, another refugee of the corporate world who decided that opening and operating a brewery was more his speed. Located in Colorado Springs, Bristol and his namesake brewery are known for many things locally. To some people Bristol is known for brewing **XXX Warlock,** an 18.4 percent ABV stout and the strongest beer ever released in Colorado. To other people, Bristol is known for all of the money it raises and donates to local charities through its special beer releases. If you're a beer judge or the kind of person who pays attention to such things, Bristol might be synonymous with **Laughing Lab Scottish Ale,** the most-awarded beer in GABF history. In every sense Bristol exemplifies what a small business with the right attitude can achieve.

If you're visiting Colorado from out of state, one of the most appealing things about Bristol is the exclusivity of its beers. The brewery only distributes within the state, so sampling its beers

Winter Warlock Oatmeal Stout
Style: Oatmeal Stout
ABV: 6 percent
Availability: Dec on tap and in 12-ounce bottles
Bristol Brewing Company's Winter Warlock Oatmeal Stout is one of the more impressive winter seasonals released in Colorado each year. The coal-colored pour is suffused with dark chocolate and espresso notes. The significant flaked oatmeal addition lends the beer a lengthy silk-textured body.

while visiting is an absolute must, beginning with the aforementioned Laughing Lab.

Laughing Lab is a rust-colored, 5 percent ABV, Scottish-style malt showcase that eschews bitterness in favor of sweet fudge, hazelnut, biscuit and caramel notes, and a smooth velvety finish. Laughing Lab is available year-round on tap and in bottles.

Old No. 23 Barley Wine is another of Bristol's GABF award winners. The 10.1 percent ABV strong ale is patterned on the sticky sweet, brandy-like English barley-wine style once brewed abundantly in the UK. The toffee-colored beer is designed as a sipper to be enjoyed during the colder months. Old No. 23's annual appearance seems timed almost perfectly with the first snowfalls of the Front Range.

ROCKY MOUNTAIN BREWERY
625 Paonia St., Colorado Springs, CO 80915; (719) 528-1651; RockyMountainBrews.com
Founded: 2009 **Founder:** Duane Lujan **Brewer:** Duane Lujan **Flagship Beer:** Da' Yoopers **Year-round Beers:** Blonde Lager, Spirit Hill Amber, Brunette Nut Brown, Redhead **Seasonals/Special Releases:** Da' Yoopers, Eat a Peach, Tatonka Blueberry Cobbler, Key Lime Cheesecake, PB&J Sammich, S'mores **Tours:** None **Taproom:** Mon to Sat 5 to 10 p.m.

I first heard about Rocky Mountain Brewery while at the GABF in 2010, when a local proclaimed that I simply could not leave Colorado without trying the local "cherry pie beer." The beer, it turns out, is called **Da' Yoopers,** brewed by Rocky Mountain Brewery located in Colorado Springs.

Rocky Mountain Brewery was founded by Duane Lujan, who segued into the brewing business after running a homebrew supply store. He owned and operated My Home Brew for 12 years before brewing commercially. As luck would have it for Duane, another local brewery called Blicks Brewing had recently gone out of business in the area. Duane moved into its space, took over its equipment, and began brewing all manner of outlandish creations, brewed with the likes of curry, jelly beans, and chai.

As for the cherry pie beer, Da' Yoopers, it does indeed smell and taste exactly like a cherry pie reincarnated as beer. It's uncanny. And if all that wasn't impressive enough, it turns out that Da' Yoopers is part of a series of tap-only dessert-inspired beers released under the **Bakeshop series** name. The beers defy most explanation in terms of how accurately they replicate their intended sweet goods. This series has included **Eat a Peach,** a beer designed to replicate the aroma and flavor of peach cobbler; **Tatonka Blueberry Cobbler; Key Lime Cheesecake; PB&J Sammich;** and **S'mores.** The Backshop series releases always come as a surprise, and the possibility of tasting one is worth the trip to the brewery.

Key Lime Cheesecake
Style: Fruit Beer
ABV: Unknown
Availability: Occasionally on tap
The level to which **Key Lime Cheesecake,** brewed by Rocky Mountain using a secret recipe, tastes exactly like a cool, refreshing, and creamy bite of key lime pie is hard to believe. Few beers in the US, except for the others produced by this very brewery, taste so uncannily like an actual dessert. Outstanding.

Brewpubs

AMICAS PIZZA & MICROBREWERY

136 E. 2nd St., Salida, CO 81201; (719) 539-5219; Amicassalida.com
Founded: 2002 **Founder:** Kathie Younghans **Brewer:** Mike LaCroix **Flagship Beer:**
Headwaters IPA **Year-round Beers:** Bomber Blonde Ale, Headwaters IPA, Rex's Amber Ale,
Single Speed Red, Big S Brown **Seasonals/Special Releases:** Double Wide Oatmeal Stout,
Mocha Joe Porter, Momma's Milk Stout

Originally a franchise location of the Il Vicino brewpub chain, Amicas Pizza & Microbrewery came into being when the parent company decided that the small, but tourist-rich town of Salida could no longer financially justify their business there. Kathie Younghans begged to differ, and the independent business was reborn as Amicas.

Amicas brews a wide variety of beer styles, many being bold interpretations of archetypal brewpub classics, like blondes, pales, Indian pales, ambers, browns, and stouts, with a rotating selection of adjunct-laden beers and strong ales.

Bomber Blonde Ale is a reliable, 5.2 percent ABV American blonde, brewed with German Halletau hops. The beer has low bitterness, a consistent cereal body, and a mild clean finish. Perfect for pizza, panini, and calzone pairing. **Headwaters IPA** is a robust, 7 percent ABV American IPA with a heavy bitter bite and a bright, yellow-citrus nose. **Rex's Amber Ale** is actually brewed in the English ESB style. The malts provide the main aromatic and flavor profile of this 6 percent ABV beer. Hints of caramel, toffee, biscuit, and red fruit all make their presence felt in the drink. The finish is more biscuit, with a low bitterness and mild dryness. **Big S Brown** is a bold American brown ale, with a thick, nutty aroma and body. This 6 percent ABV beer is well engineered to pair with food, including sweeter dishes and desserts.

Amicas brews quite a few seasonal and speciality offerings throughout the year, such as **Double Wide Oatmeal Stout,** a hearty 6 percent ABV winter stout with big dark-chocolate, roasted-nut, and espresso-coffee notes. The pub menu is a made up of Italian-American staples: pizzas, calzones, paninis, pastas, salads, and desserts.

COLORADO MOUNTAIN BREWERY

11202 Rampart Hills View, Colorado Springs, CO 80921; (719) 434-5750; CMBrew.com;
Twitter: @cmbrew
Founded: 2010 **Founders:** Scott Koons and John Bauer **Brewer:** Andy Bradley **Flagship Beer:** Panther India Pale Ale **Year-round Beers:** Panther India Pale Ale, 7258 Blonde Ale, UniBrau Hefeweissen, Ole 59er Amber Ale, Monumental Stout **Seasonals/Special Releases:** None

Colorado Mountain Brewery is a brewpub shaped from the get-go by its proximity to the neighboring US Air Force Academy. The brewery and restaurant owners, John Bauer and Scott Koons, are themselves academy graduates. The clientele is drawn heavily from the academy, and the air force influence can be spotted in the names of some of the house beers. **Panther India Pale Ale** is named after the special forces unit of the same name; **Ole 59er Amber Ale** is a nod to the academy's first graduating glass of 1959; and **7258 Blonde Ale** refers to the elevation of the academy.

Brewmaster Andy Bradley designed the six house offerings to be appealing to a wider beer-drinking crowd, without sacrificing flavor and body. All six beers share an ease and quaffability.

The standout beers at Colorado Mountain are the biscuity Ole 59er, a 5.2 percent ABV, malty, American amber ale, with a soft caramel and orange peel finish; and the bitter-chocolate and coffee flavored **Monumental,** a fairly traditional take on the American stout style. Both in keeping with their design and intent, these beers are pint-after-pint quaffable.

The menu offers up solid American pub favorites and classic bar food. The house beers, designed to be evenhanded and drinkable, pair easily with many items on the menu.

EDDYLINE RESTAURANT & BREWERY

926 S. Main St., Buena Vista, CO 81211; (719) 966-6000; EddylinePub.com;
Twitter: @eddylinepub
Founded: 2009 **Founders:** Mic Heynekamp and Molley Heynekamp **Brewer:** Scott Kimball
Flagship Beer: Crank Yanker IPA **Year-round Beers:** Crank Yanker IPA, Drag Bag Lager, Kickin' Back Amber Lager, Midland Trail Colorado Pale Ale **Seasonals/Special Releases:** Inner Glow Red Chili Porter, Cherry Wheat, Pumpkin Patch Pale Ale

Eddyline Restaurant & Brewery is located in the outdoor activities hub of Buena Vista. The pub offers up pecan wood–fired pizzas and a broad selection of house-brewed ales and lagers. In 2011 the brewery began canning its showcase IPA, **Crank Yanker.**

The brewpub takes great pride in being a local business in Buena Vista and does much to support and encourage local events and clubs. The beer, though, is what people come back for time and time again.

The aforementioned Crank Yanker is a bold, 7.8 percent ABV, high-IBU American IPA. That's not to say that the beer forgoes a malt backbone in favor of a purely hop-driven profile, though, as it strikes a pleasing balance with a residual malt sweetness and layered pine-evoking, hop-derived bite and aroma.

If you're lucky enough to visit during the autumn, a glass of **Pumpkin Patch Pale Ale** is exactly what the beer doctor prescribes. This 6 percent ABV, low bitterness, spice and pumpkin-flesh enhanced American pale is a delight. The brewery uses one pound of pumpkin for every three gallons of the beer brewed. Holiday spices are used in abundance here to provide a more pumpkin pie–like, pumpkin-beer experience.

Another must order, and possibly the best beer to accompany one of the pecan wood–fired pizzas, is **Kickin' Back Amber Lager.** This 5.5 percent ABV, American

red lager is brewed in the Vienna style. It has a soft toffee profile and moderate, but subtle, bitterness.

PHANTOM CANYON BREWING COMPANY

2 E. Pikes Peak Ave., Colorado Springs, CO 80903; (719) 635-2800; PhantomCanyon.com;
Twitter: @PhantomCanyon
Founded: 1993 **Founders:** Mark Schiffler and John Hickenlooper **Brewer:** Alan Stiles
Flagship Beer: Phantom IPA **Year-round Beers:** Phantom IPA, Zebulon's Peated Porter,
Hefeweizen, Cascade Amber Ale, Queen's Blonde Ale, Railyard Ale **Seasonals/Special
Releases:** Changes

When you wander through the corner street doors of Phantom Canyon Brewing Company, positioned proudly in the heart of scenic Colorado Springs, you might be forgiven for questioning the fact that the majestic historic building was once hours away from demolition. Its future as one of the first brewpubs in Colorado was thankfully secured in large part by John Hickenlooper, the founder of Wynkoop Brewing Company who went on to become the mayor of Denver and the governor of Colorado. John bought the building with his own cash, and in 1993 Phantom Canyon opened for business. Hickenlooper and founding partner Mark Schiffler folded Phantom Canyon into their Wynkoop Holding company.

In much the same way that Hickenlooper's Wynkoop project helped inspire a revitalization of Denver's downtown, the opening of Phantom Canyon in downtown Colorado Springs inspired a new generation of restaurant owners to begin utilizing the long-ignored buildings in the area. It wasn't just restaurants that began to appear in and around Colorado Springs either. With a few years a cluster of breweries had also set up shop.

Phantom Canyon offers six year-round beers: **Phantom IPA, Zebulon's Peated Porter, Hefeweizen, Cascade Amber Ale, Queen's Blonde Ale,** and **Railyard Ale.** All have clearly been honed over many years and are solid renditions of their respective styles. For the true geek adventurer, though, it's the ever-changing and exciting selection of special beers that pour at Phantom Canyon that will hold the most appeal. Depending on the timing of your visit, you might be lucky enough to enjoy an ESB, a historical recreation of an old English strong ale, a barleywine, a braggot, or perhaps a Belgian-style tripel, alongside samples of the six well-crafted house beers.

The brewpub serves brunch, lunch, and dinner. Menu choices include the lighter likes of freshly baked muffins, granola, and bacon and eggs to more hearty offerings, such as full cheese plates, beef tips, brisket, and jerk chicken. A full line of desserts is also offered.

PIKES PEAK BREWING CO.

1756 Lake Woodmoor Dr., Monument, CO 80132; (719) 208-4098; PikesPeakBrewing.com; **Twitter:** @pikespeakbeer

Founded: 2011 **Founder:** Chris Wright **Brewer:** Chris Wright **Flagship Beer:** Summit House Barrel Stout **Year-round Beers:** Pikes Peak Gold Rush Ale, Rocky Wheat Ale, Devil's Head Red Ale, Summit House Barrel Stout; Brits Are Back **Seasonals/Special Releases:** Summit House Barrel Stout, East India Porter, Pike Hot Shots Green Chili

Pikes Peak Brewing Co. opened for business in May 2011. Located just off I-25, it is perfectly located for those traveling between brewing hubs of Denver to the north and Colorado Springs to the south. Of course, as with most breweries that open in Colorado, the local community has fully embraced the idea of a hometown brewery and make up the majority of the regular customers.

Founder and brewer Chris Wright wanted the brewery taproom to evoke the comfortable and welcoming vibe of a cozy and bright coffee shop, and upon entering the space, you'd be hard pressed not to agree that he has done just that. Two large

tap banks dominate the bar, pouring a diverse selection of beer styles. All of the standard American styles are present and accounted for.

Pikes Peak year-round ales and lagers include **Devil's Head Red Ale,** a potent and spicy 7.9 percent ABV American red ale; **Summit House Stout,** a 6.5 percent ABV, roasty oatmeal stout with a thick and palate-coating body; **Rocky Wheat Ale,** a 5.1 percent ABV, hazy, clove-forward Hefeweizen; **Pikes Peak Gold Rush Ale,** a 7.4 percent ABV, sweet-and-fruity, Belgian-style golden ale; and the **Brits Are Back,** a 5.2 percent ABV, English-style pub ale that, flavorwise, falls somewhere between an English mild and an ESB.

As well as brewing a broad selection of interesting and well-executed beers, Pikes Peak serves up some great bar food. Enjoy the likes of a full meat and cheese platter, fresh German-style pretzels, pulled-pork sandwiches, soups and chili, paninis, and a German chocolate cake made with the house stout.

SAN LUIS VALLEY BREWING COMPANY

631 Main St., Alamosa, CO 81101; (719) 587-2337; SLVBrewCo.com
Founded: 2006 **Founders:** Scott Graber and Angie Graber **Brewers:** Scott Graber and Angie Graber **Flagship Beer:** Grande River IPA **Year-round Beers:** Alamosa Amber, Grande River IPA, Valle Caliente, Hefe Suave, Valle Especial, Ol' 169 Oatmeal Stout
Seasonals/Special Releases: Changes

San Luis Valley Brewing in the rural town of Alamosa opened for business in 2006 under the watchful eye of owners Scott and Angie Graber. It's unique in that it's as much a missionary for the religiously curious as it is a place that happens to serve good house-brewed beer and good food. The Grabers have a past in community service and ministerial services: Scott as a youth pastor and Angie as a substance abuse counselor. Indeed customers are encouraged to discuss theology and God with the owners over a pint whenever they feel the need. Although that is certainly not a requisite to enjoying the beer and food on offer.

There are six year-round brews and plenty of revolving seasonals and one-offs. The brewery does offer many of their beers to go in 12- and 22-ounce bottles. **Alamosa Amber** is a 5 percent ABV, American amber ale designed to be as balanced and food friendly as possible. The beer pops with notes of biscuit, caramel, and fresh-cut grass. **Valle Caliente** (5.5 percent ABV) is that wonderful Southwestern-style of beer, the chili lager. This refreshing sunshine-colored beer is infused with chili to lend the beer a vegetal edge, as well as a kick of peppery heat. **Valle Especial** (4.2 percent ABV) is a light and bright Mexican-style Pilsner. An award winner for the brewery, it offers up an earthy nose of fresh-cut grass and a quick and clean body.

The menu is broadly classic American with the likes of warm spinach artichoke dip, nachos, crab cakes, hot wings, chili, french onion soup, and quesadillas, all well represented as appetizers. Entrees are catered for with a healthy mix of steaks, burgers, big salads, jambalaya, fresh trout, ribs, pastas, and sandwiches.

SHAMROCK BREWING COMPANY

108 W. 3rd St., Pueblo, CO 81003; (719) 542-9974; ShamrockBrewing.com; **Twitter:** @ShamrockBrewery
Founded: 2005 **Founder:** Shawn Sanborn **Brewer:** Jason Buehler **Flagship Beer:** Steel City Blonde **Year-round Beers:** Steel City Blonde, Irish Red Ale, Extra Plain Porter, Arch City Pale Ale **Seasonals/Special Releases:** Scotch Strong Ale, English Pale Ale, Johnson Brothers Pilsner, Black Eye PA

Shamrock Brewing is a vaguely Irish-themed brewpub in downtown Pueblo. The brewery serves up four year-round beers alongside a colorful and award-winning mix of German-, English-, Irish-, Belgian-, and American-inspired seasonal and special beers.

The four house beers are all sessionable by American standards and make for great pairings almost across the board with the meat-and-potatoes-centric Irish-inspired foods. **Steel City Blonde** is a 4.8 percent ABV, straw-colored, Munich-style helles lager with a soft cereal profile, low bitterness, and thoroughly quaffable character. It's light but certainly not lacking in flavor or polish. **Irish Red Ale** represents the Gaelic style confidently with plenty of biscuit and caramel malt sweetness and low to nonexistent bitter hop profile. **Extra Plain Porter** was designed to replicate the inky, pre-Irish dry stouts of the late 1700s. The everyman's daily pub beer, it offers a bold hearty body of roasted chocolate malt flavor. **Arch City Pale Ale** is a 5 percent ABV American pale ale that bursts with leafy green, herbaceous, Northwest hop–derived bitterness and flavor.

Shamrock serves a brunch, lunch, dinner, and late-night menu of food. For brunch diners can select from the likes of a traditional Irish breakfast, pancakes, corned beef hash, huevos rancheros, eggs Benedict, loaded biscuits, french toast, and omelets. Lunch and dinner include such items as wings, mussels, Irish ale cheese soup, burgers, fish-and-chips, shepherd's pie, steaks, and chops.

TRINITY BREWING COMPANY

1466 Garden of the Gods, # 184, Colorado Springs, CO 80907; (719) 634-0029;
TrinityBrew.com; **Twitter:** @TRiNiTYBrewing
Founded: 2008 **Founder:** Jason Yester **Brewer:** Jason Yester **Flagship Beer:** Farmhouse
Saison **Year-round Beers:** Sunna Wit, Awaken Stout, Flo IPA, Farmhouse Saison, Soul
Seasonals/Special Releases: Pappy Legba, Wee Banshee Irish Heather Ale, Emperor
Wears No Clothes, Southern Hospitality, Libidinous, Slap Your Mammy, Didgeribrew, Kinky
Reggae, Cherry Awaken Stout, Chilly Water Baltic Porter, Passed Stout, Emma's Pumpkin
Saison (new name), Stop Making Sense, Old Growth, Farmhouse Provisional, TPS Report,
the Flavor, Brain of the Turtle

Jason Yester is truly the guru and master of his domain. He's the founder and brewmaster of the colorful TRiNiTY Brewing Company, a brewery that specializes in brewing a dizzying number of envelope-bending saisons and adventurous and confounding Belgian sours. The brewery is located in the corner lot of a business strip mall in a suburb of the supposedly conservative Colorado Springs. Not the sort of place you'd expect to find a liberal, slow-food eatery, pouring some of the most creative and unusual beers in America. But the location and concept were embraced from the outset. Upon opening in 2008, TRiNiTY sold out of beer within two days.

While best known for his raft of outlandish saisons and sours, Yester is just as passionate about the creative selection of year-round beers on offer at TRiNiTY. **Sunna Wit** is a unique take on the traditional Belgian wheat-ale style. Brewed with tangerine, lemon, and lime zests and coriander, the beer is then aged on rose petals. Sunna is also fermented with 50 percent saison yeast, which lends the quaffable and refreshing beer a soft woolly nose and a decidedly deeper and drier fruity body. **Soul** is quite possibly the only regularly available horkey in the US. Horkey, in terms of aroma, color, and flavor, falls somewhere between an English brown ale and an English mild. The mostly forgotten British beer type was brewed to mark the end of the harvest season. TRiNiTY's horkey is steeped in long malty caramel and biscuit notes.

Many of Yester's saisons and sours are released in beeswax-sealed 750-milliliter bottles. All of them have been designed to be cellared for at least five years. Each release is highly anticipated and usually sells out in a short amount of time. No small feat for beers that cost upwards of $25 a bottle.

Beer Bar

TRINITY BREWING COMPANY

1466 Garden of the Gods, #184, Colorado Springs, CO 80907; (719) 634-0029;
TrinityBrew.com; **Twitter:** @TrinityBrewing
Taps: 34 **Bottles/Cans:** 4+ (special TRiNiTY 750-milliliter release)

In addition to pouring 10 taps of its own brilliant creations, TRiNiTY Brewing also happens to pour a changing tap list of 24 guest beers, making it one of the best all-round beer bars and beer-centric restaurants in all of Colorado Springs. Adding to its cache, it is also one of the best places in the state to get rare tappings of out-of-state beers, like Russian River Pliny the Younger.

The food at TRiNiTY is of a high quality and inventiveness. As you sip your way through the 34 taps of beer at the bar, you can dine on the likes of authentic Belgian frites or American sweet potato fries with curry ketchup and cracked-pepper buttermilk ranch dipping sauces, poutine frites topped with hearty boar gravy, Irish cheddar and mozzarella cheese curds, bison jerky, falafel salad, and Colorado lamb or Kobe beef sliders with a choice of creative toppings.

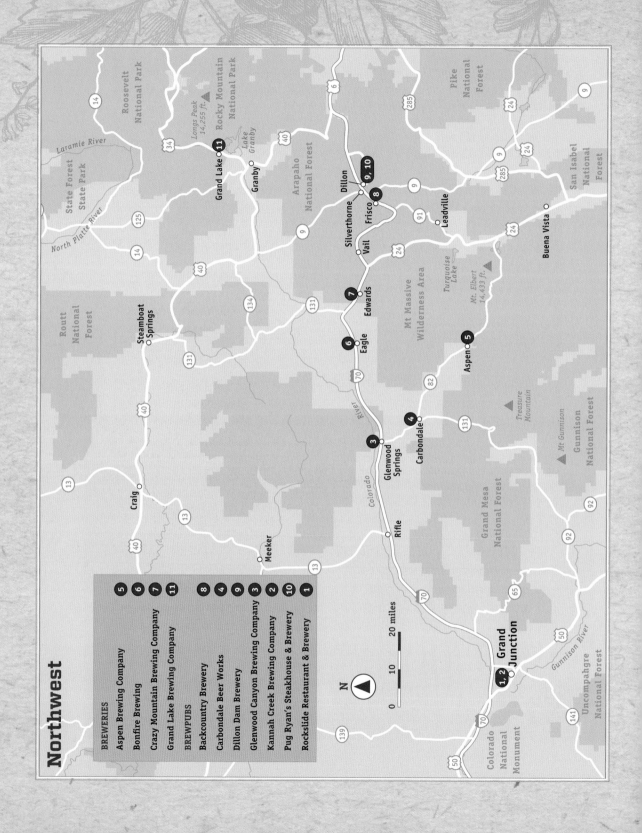

Northwest

BREWERIES

- **5** Aspen Brewing Company
- **6** Bonfire Brewing
- **7** Crazy Mountain Brewing Company
- **11** Grand Lake Brewing Company

BREWPUBS

- **8** Backcountry Brewery
- **4** Carbondale Beer Works
- **9** Dillon Dam Brewery
- **3** Glenwood Canyon Brewing Company
- **2** Kannah Creek Brewing Company
- **10** Pug Ryan's Steakhouse & Brewery
- **1** Rockslide Restaurant & Brewery

Northwest

Aspen, Carbondale, Dillon, Eagle, Edwards, Frisco, Glenwood Springs, Grand Junction & Grand Lake

It seems that every good ski town and mountain-bike hot spot in the Rocky Mountain region has a buzzed-about local brewpub. Some are new and bold and want to be heard far and wide, while others have been quiet local institutions for many years and prefer to stay that way. With much of beer tourism and interest in Colorado focused on the Denver, Boulder, Fort Collins, and Colorado Springs areas, the brewpubs of the mountains and western slope are an exciting and highly recommended untapped goldmine of new beer-drinking experiences for visitors as well as native Coloradoans.

Breweries

ASPEN BREWING COMPANY

304 E. Hopkins Ave., Aspen, CO 81611; (970) 920-2739; AspenBrewingCompany.com;
Twitter: @AspenBrewingCo
Founded: 2008 **Founders:** Duncan Clauss and Brad Veltman **Brewer:** Chase Engel
Flagship Beer: Independence Pass IPA **Year-round Beers:** Independence Pass IPA, Ajax
Pilsner, Brown Bearale, Conundrum Red Ale, This Season's Blonde, Smuggler Wheat Ale
Seasonals/Special Releases: Pyramid Peak Porter, Midnight Mine Imperial Stout **Tours:**
Coming soon **Taproom:** Mon through Sat noon to midnight, Sun noon to 11 p.m. Growlers
are available to go.

Founded in 2008 by Brad Veltman and Duncan Clauss, two young, twenty-something University of Colorado graduates, Apsen Brewing Company sells beer in the rich and glamorous ski resort from which it takes its name. Partnered with their brewer, Chase Engel, Brad and Duncan offer five year-round offerings, some of which are from recipes they honed after much practice as homebrewers during college. The five beers are stand-style offerings but are designed to be anything but bland or forgettable.

More and more craft breweries are looking to lagers as a way to diversify their annual lineup of beers. For decades ales have ruled at craft breweries. As a rule of thumb, ales are quicker and cheaper to produce because they do not require extended cold fermentation. Despite this, the popularity of lagers, especially Pilsner styles, cannot be ignored by many smaller breweries looking to stake a claim in an increasingly competitive industry. Aspen's year-round, 4.5 percent ABV **Ajax Pilsner** is brewed to model the traditional German incarnation of the style. It does not skimp on hop aromatics or bitterness. Why the name Ajax? It's the town's local name for the nearby Aspen Mountain.

Pronounced "Brown Barrel," **Brown Bearale** was named to honor the many black bears that inhabit the Aspen region. Many of these black bears are actually more of a hazel-brown color than black. The beer was also so named, because a pack of brown-black bears busted through the garage of the house where Brad, Duncan, and Rory were living and began eating their homebrew grain supply. The 6 percent ABV American brown ale is thick with a smokey wood note and was fashioned to be pint-after-pint drinkable.

Independence Pass IPA

Style: American IPA

ABV: 7.5 percent

Availability: Year-round on tap

Independence Pass IPA is Aspen Brewing Company's best-selling year-round beer. Named after the narrow road that traverses the Continental Divide at a peak of 12,095 feet, this American IPA was meant to wow in much the same respect. Designed with the hophead firmly in mind, the beer is heavily hopped in every regard, for bitterness, flavor, and aroma. At 7.5 percent ABV, it is on

par alcoholwise with the majority of the IPAs in Colorado. Aromatically, the beer breathes expected notes of citrus and bitter resinous pine.

BONFIRE BREWING

127 Second St., Eagle, CO 81631; (970) 306-7113; BonfireBrewing.com; **Twitter:** @bonfirebrewing

Founded: 2010 **Founders:** Andy Jessen and Matt Wirtz **Brewers:** Andy Jessen and Matt Wirtz **Flagship Beer:** None **Year-round Beers:** None **Seasonals/Special Releases:** Two Hands Wheat, Blonfire!, Demshitz Brown Ale, Firestarter IPA, Mystery IPA, Dark Dog India Black Ale, Second St. Stout, High-Altitude Pale Ale (H.A.P.A.), Save Christmas, Yellow Chair Peach, Miramonte Mild, Tent Pole Porter, Tent Pole Porter S.E, PINK-I, Stranger Blonde, Gyptoberfest, The Cleve, Awry, Mistress Winter Wheat, TEBREW Sunday Sipper (American Barleywine) **Tours:** None **Taproom:** Mon through Wed 5:30 to 10 p.m., Thurs 4 to 10 p.m., Fri through Sat 4 p.m. to midnight, Sun 3 to 8 p.m. Growlers are available to go.

Located in the small town of Eagle, Bonfire Brewing is built around the concept of a campfire, a place where people can gather and feel welcome.

Virtually every craft brewery in America, the truly successful and well-regarded ones at least, had some sort of humble beginning. Bonfire is no different. Matt Wirtz and Andy Jessen started the brewery when they needed to raise a little extra cash to cover the cost of an exiting roommate. Already avid garage homebrewers, the two set about raising enough capital to go small-scale commercial. Their one investor was Andy's father. Matt and Andy then moved into a small storefront and started building their campfire.

The Bonfire taproom pours up to 10 beers, with a leaning toward hoppier styles, browns, and some lighter fare for those who have no idea why anyone would proudly label themselves a hophead.

Firestarter IPA is a 6.6 percent ABV American IPA brewed with leafy Columbus hops and brilliantly aromatic Cascade hops. This beer has a touch of heat and layers of green herbaceous bitterness. **Two Hands Wheat** is Bonfire's take on an American pale wheat ale. Definitely a beer skewed to those drinkers who find the likes of Firestarter too intense. The beer is lighter in alcohol too.

A winter favorite, **Save Christmas,** was originally released on Christmas Eve 2010. The beer began life as accident, when a batch of the house brown ale, **Demshitz Brown Ale,** finished too watery. Ever the experimenters, Matt and Andy brewed a honey and cinnamon beer and blended it with low gravity brown. The result, or a least a tweaked derivative of it, is now brewed each holiday season and sold as Save Christmas.

Beer Lover's Pick

Stranger Blonde
Style: American Blonde Ale
ABV: 4.8 percent
Availability: Occasionally on tap
Brewed with orange citrus–evoking nugget hops and earthy Willamette hops, Stranger Blonde is a bright, sunshine-colored pour with layers of cereal base malt smoothness and grit and a soft complex bitter depth that is lacking from so many other American blonde ales.

CRAZY MOUNTAIN BREWING COMPANY

439 Edwards Access Rd., #B-102, Edwards, CO 81632; (970) 926-3009; CrazyMountainBrewery.com; **Twitter:** @crazymtnbrewery **Founded:** 2010 **Founders:** Kevin Selvy and Marisa Aguilar **Brewer:** Kevin Selvy **Flagship Beer:** Amber Ale **Year-round Beers:** Amber Ale, Lava Lake Wit, Old Soul, Cara de Luna Black Ale, Mountain Livin' Pale Ale, Hookiebobb IPA **Seasonals/Special Releases:** Horseshoes & Hand Grenades; Stout; Lawyers, Guns and Money Barley Wine; Saison **Tours:** None **Taproom:** Mon through Sat 11 a.m. to 8 p.m., Sun 11 a.m. to 5 p.m. Growlers and cans are available to go.

Crazy Mountain made a big splash before it even brewed its first batch of beer in Vail. **Old Soul,** brewed at a brewery in California and driven to Vail, won rave reviews in 2010 at the highly regarded Big Beers, Belgians and Barleywines Festival, which is held annually in Vail. The success of the beer at the festival solidified the remaining investors that founders Kevin Selvy and Marisa Aguilar needed to set about building the first production brewery in the much-traveled ski resort. They fashioned the brewery in an empty warehouse and began to expand their lineup. They opened a taproom in October 2010 and completed a second major expansion in early 2012.

In the years since, Crazy Mountain's **Amber Ale** (5.2 percent ABV) in cans has become a firm fixture and bestseller in liquor stores across the state. Canned versions of **Lava Lake Wit** (5.2 percent ABV) and **Mountain Livin' Pale Ale** (5.7 percent ABV) followed in 2012.

The brewery has six year-round offerings. Pouring alongside Amber Ale, Lava Lake, and Livin' Pale are the aforementioned Old Soul (7.5 percent ABV), brewed with juniper berries; **Cara de Luna Black Ale** (5 percent ABV), an eye-opening black pale ale that the brewery affectionately calls a mutt of beer being as it is brewed with German hops, Belgian malt, and American yeast; and lastly **Hookiebobb IPA** (6.7 percent ABV), a robust bitter American IPA with a firm biscuit backbone. Bitterness is significant, clocking in at 87 IBUs.

Further expanding the brewery repertoire is a clutch of seasonal beers. **Horseshoes & Hand Grenades** is a 6 percent ABV designed for the snowy Vail winters. The beer plays five different malts off of each other, with light-to-medium bitterness derived from Chinook and Amarillo hops. **Stout** is Crazy's interpretation of an Irish dry stout. Bitter and roasty, the 5.25 percent ABV beer is squarely aimed at those who want their Guinness and some added flavor too.

Northwest

Amber Ale

Style: American Amber Ale

ABV: 5.2 percent

Availability: Year-round on tap and in cans

Crazy Mountain's Amber Ale is a ubiquitous canned offering in Colorado. The 5.2 percent ABV American red ale has soft herbaceous bitterness throughout, a pretty spring flower floral aroma, and a balanced biscuit finish.

GRAND LAKE BREWING COMPANY

9921 U.S. Hwy. 34, Grand Lake, CO 80447; (970) 627-9404; GrandLakeBrewing.com;
Twitter: @grandlakebrew
Founded: 2003 **Founders:** Richard Wood and Karen Wood **Brewer:** Eric Kohl **Flagship Beer:** Plaid Bastard Scotch Ale **Year-round Beers:** Plaid Bastard, Stumpjumper India Pale Ale, Wooly Booger Nut Brown Ale, Rocky Mountain Red Ale, White Cap Wheat, Shadow Mountain Oatmeal Stout, Hoppy's One Ton Pale Ale, Pumphouse Lager, Rebel Pale Ale **Seasonals/Special Releases:** Super Chicken, Holy Grail Final Cask **Tours:** None **Taproom:** Thurs through Fri 4 to 9 p.m., Sat noon to 9 p.m., Sun noon to 8 p.m. Closed Mon through Wed. Growlers and bottles are available to go.

Grand Lake has the quiet honor of being the highest-altitude packaging brewery in the US, located a staggering 8,339 feet above sea level in a small town of the same name.

Richard and Karen Wood opened the small brewery in 2003. Since the beginning, the business has been a hands-on labor of love. Richard and Karen brew, bottle, and distribute the beer all themselves. No small feat when big markets like Denver and Boulder are up to 100 miles away. To say the couple is dedicated is a massive understatement.

Grand Lake brews nine different beers on a regular basis every year. A few come and go with the seasons, but all can usually be found throughout the year in larger liqor stores in the state.

Of immediate interest to most beer geeks is the **Stumpjumper India Pale Ale.** The 7 percent ABV, American-style IPA uses more than three pounds of hops per barrel brewed. The beer is not without a malt backbone to balance the bags of hops added to the brew kettle. Common style notes of pine, lemon peel, and earthy grass are all present.

Shadow Mountain Oatmeal Stout is the first Grand Lake beer that dark beer lovers should seek out. This 5 percent ABV, creamy ale has an inviting, soft, milk-chocolate nose and a long, silky-smooth, mocha-flavored body. More chocolate is present on the finish but more of the high cocoa bitter baker's variety, though.

For those who enjoy stronger beers, Grand Lake has you covered. **Plaid Bastard** is one of the brewery's most popular beers, a potent 8 percent ABV, Scottish-styled wee heavy. The beer is a massive malt bomb with nary a hint of bitter hop bite. This beer is a warming semisweet delight.

Northwest

Super Chicken

Style: American Barleywine

ABV: 11 percent

Availability: Winter seasonal on tap and year-round in bottles

One of the more off-the-radar barleywines in Colorado, Super Chicken is definitely worth hunting down if you enjoy the style. This 11 percent ABV beast is loaded with dried fruit, toffee, and caramel character. It is not without a good thwack of hop-derived bitterness, either. The brewery occasionally releases a special version aged in whiskey barrels. Both varieties are noteworthy.

Brewpubs

BACKCOUNTRY BREWERY

720 Main St., Frisco, CO 80443; (970) 668-2337; BackcountryBrewery.com;
Twitter: @backcountrybrew
Founded: 1996 **Founders:** Woody Van Gundy and Anthony Carestia **Brewer:** Alan Simons
Flagship Beer: Telemark India Pale Ale **Year-round Beers:** Wheeler Wheat, Ptarmigan
Pilsner, Telemark India Pale Ale, Switchback Amber, Peak One Porter **Seasonals/Special
Releases:** Maybock German Lager, Whiteout Barelywine, Breakfast Stout

Backcountry Brewery is located in Summit County, the same county that the original Breckenridge Brewery, Dillon Dam, and Pug Ryan's, call home. All this makes for one of the less well-known but no less brilliant beer scenes in Colorado. Backcountry opened some six years after the original Breckenridge brewpub and as such is one of the state's earlier craft beer businesses.

The core of Backcountry's beers are a familiar selection of common styles. The brewery has won no less than eight GABF medals between 1998 and 2011. High praise indeed. Award winners include the 4.7 percent ABV **Ptarmigan Pilsner,** a vibrant pils with an appropriately delicate hop profile and a long, refreshing, bright malt body and finish. **Telemark India Pale Ale** is 5.6 percent ABV British IPA with a fresh leafy aroma and lengthy bitter body. The finish is dry, with a robust and noticeable malt backbone. **Switchback Amber** is brewed in the traditional German Oktoberfest lager style. The deep amber pour has a pretty floral hop aroma and a carefully balanced bittersweet caramel body. Bitterness is low at a somewhat sessionable 5.3 percent ABV. **Maybock German Lager** is a multi–award winning, classical 6.5 percent ABV strong spring lager brewed in the traditional Bavarian style. The beer has a firm, golden-malt foundation and a floral finish.

Backcountry also brews smaller batches of occasional special and strong beers. The most popular of these is **Breakfast Stout,** a rich black coffee stout with deep-roasted espresso and baker's chocolate notes. Mouthfeel is smooth and hearty, with a medium dry finish. Coffee-beer lovers will definitely want to seek this out when in Colorado.

If you cannot make it to the brewery itself, Backcountry beers often appear on tap at better beer bars in and around Denver and Boulder.

CARBONDALE BEER WORKS

647 Main St., Carbondale, CO 81623; (970) 262-7777; CarbondaleBeerWorks.com;
Twitter: @CdaleBeerWorks
Founded: 2010 **Founder:** Jeff Dahl **Brewer:** Jeff Dahl **Flagship Beer:** None **Year-round Beers:** Langer Irish Stout, Dirty Blonde Ale, Tomahawk IPA, Monkey's Uncle Dunkle Wheat **Seasonals/Special Releases:** Old Man Winter Barley Wine, English Bitter, Little Tinker ESB, Off-Beat Lemon Wheat

Carbondale Beer Works was founded by Jeff Dahl in 2010. Despite being located near the ski epicenters of Glenwood Springs and Aspen, Carbondale Beer Works is more local centric. Jeff had wanted to start a brewery for many years. The idea that held the most appeal was that of brewery and taproom with the atmosphere of an English pub. Indeed Jeff traveled to the UK to better his brewing skills before he opened his brewery. While in the UK, he discovered an affinity for traditional cask-conditioned ales—beers with much softer effervescence thanks to natural conditioning rather than the modern forced carbonation of their American and German brethren.

Carbondale's beers range in style from a very British-focused **Little Tinker ESB** to a **Langer Irish Stout.** The brewery also prides itself on being a self-described "wienery," serving up mostly locally sourced sausages to accompany its selection of house brews.

DILLON DAM BREWERY

100 Little Dam St., Dillon, CO 80435; (970) 262-7777; DamBrewery.com;
Twitter: @damgoodbeer
Founded: 1997 **Founder:** Cory Forster **Brewer:** Cory Forster **Flagship Beer:** Extra Pale Ale **Year-round Beers:** Extra Pale Ale, Dam Lyte, Wildernest Wheat, Paradise Pilsner, Dam Straight Lager, Sweet George's Brown, McLuhr's Irish Stout **Seasonals/Special Releases:** Lenawee IPA

Like many brewpubs in Colorado, Dillon Dam Brewery remains successful thanks to a mix of dedicated year-round locals and seasonal skiers. The brewery opened for business in 1997 and routinely offers a selection of eight or so beers that include standard ales and a light lager, as well as interesting experimental takes on traditional beer style using creative adjunct ingredients, like fruits, herbs, and spices.

While Dillon Dam is located in a small, but busy town, its annual beer production in the region of 2,000 barrels ranks it as not only one of the largest brewpubs in the state, but also within the top 40 producing brewpubs in the nation. The brewery's location near the popular resort towns of Vail, Steamboat Springs, and Aspen also contributes to the brewpub's success.

The food is a mix of modern American appetizers, like wings, nachos, quesa-dillas, soups, and salads; pub classic entrees, like fried chicken, mac and cheese, chili, ribs, burgers, pastas, steaks, and chicken; and stalwart American desserts, like brownie sundaes, root beer floats, apple pie, and bread pudding.

The tried-and-true menu of beers runs the gamut from the award-winning lagers to full-bodied and bitter ales. On the lighter side there is the straw-colored and highly effervescent **Dam Lyte** lager; noble-hopped **Wildernest Wheat,** brewed with a lager yeast strain; a well-balanced house Pilsner, **Paradise Pilsner;** and GABF silver medal–winning **Dam Straight Lager,** a bright amber beer with a soft medium body, caramel backbone, and light bitterness.

GLENWOOD CANYON BREWING COMPANY

402 Seventh St., Glenwood Springs, CO 81601; (970) 945-1276; GlenwoodCanyon.com;
Twitter: @GlenwoodBrewPub
Founded: 1996 **Founders:** Steve Carver and April Carver **Brewer:** Ken Jones **Flagship
Beer:** Vapor Cave IPA **Year-round Beers:** Vapor Cave IPA, Hanging Lake Honey Ale, Grizzly
Creek Raspberry Wheat, St. James Irish Red, Old Depot Porter, No Name Nut Brown Ale
Seasonals/Special Releases: Strawberry Daze

During the 1990s brewpub boom, you would have been forgiven for losing track of every new opening. For a time it seemed like every town of more than a few thousand was toasting or ribbon cutting the opening of new restaurant that also happened to offer up a healthy lineup of its own beers. Glenwood Springs is one such town. Glenwood Canyon brewpub might not have been one of the first brewpubs in Colorado, but it has definitely outlasted many of them. It offers up a solid selection of core beers, rotating seasonals, and one-off brews to complement its classic American pub menu of appetizers, salads, soups, stews, chilies, burgers, sandwiches, pastas, fish-and-chips, pizzas, and steaks.

Be it the easy-eating likes of the house mozzarella sticks or egg rolls or the more hearty likes of the beef stroganoff or chicken enchiladas, Glenwood Canyon has a beer to match. **Grizzly Creek Raspberry Wheat** is a beer of vibrant body, with a bright semitart red fruit finish. **St. James Irish Red** delivers confidently and coherently the style's requisite biscuit foundation, light bitterness, and clean, dry finish. Irish reds are broadly food-friendly beers. **Hanging Lake Honey Ale** has delicate pops of complementary residual floral sweetness thanks to an addition of local honey in the brew. The beer was designed to be food-friendly and pint-after-pint quaffable and assuredly delivers. For the hop lover there is **Vapor Cave IPA.** This abundantly bittered India pale has layers of green herbal bite and lively pine needle aroma. Pair this with any of the spicier or cheese-heavy items on the menu.

The specialty beer seeker will want to visit the brewpub in June when **Strawberry Daze** is tapped. This American amber ale is brewed with 300 pounds per batch of strawberries and is brewed in honor of the local festival of the same name.

KANNAH CREEK BREWING COMPANY

1960 N. 12th St., Grand Junction, CO 81501; (970) 263-0111; KannahCreekBrewingCo
.com; **Twitter:** @KannahCreekBrew
Founded: 2005 **Founder:** Jim Jeffryes **Brewer:** Jim Jeffryes **Flagship Beer:** Broken Oar
IPA **Year-round Beers:** Black's Bridge Stout, Broken Oar IPA, Highside Hefeweizen, Island
Mesa Blonde, Lands End Amber, Pigasus Porter, Standing Wave Pale Ale **Seasonals/Special
Releases:** Angus Og, Cascadian Dark Ale, Chill Pils, Crossed Irons Irish Ale, Fresh Hopped
ESB, Hopplebock, Huckleberry Wheat, Indian Creek Brown Ale, Not Yers Maibock, Nutty
Brewnette, Octoberfest, Peachy Wheat, Soulstiz Winter Ale, Stolen Saison, Stumplifter
Barley Wine, The Defrostor, The Scottish, The Strong Ale, Three Fjords, Vanilla Stout

When looking to try the best beers in the world, it is often wise to begin by looking outside the box. Dig a little deeper and you will frequently discover that little-known local brewpubs, like Kannah Creek, pop up multiple times on the annual list of World Beer Cup medal winners. While often not as flamboyant or driven by ever-increasing growth and expansion as their larger craft-brewing brethren, these small local enterprises perfect their craft year in and year out, brewing some of the most consistent and high-quality beers in the world.

Former tech industry employee and homebrewer Jim Jeffryes decided to open a brewery after being diagnosed with multiple sclerosis. The city of Grand Junction, on Colorado's expansive Western Slope, is better known for its wine and fruit than its more brew-savvy eastern counterpart, the Front Range. Despite this, Jim brews and pours upwards of 20 experimental beers at Kannah Creek throughout the year alongside more-familiar and less-intimidating styles of beer.

Kannah Creek offers seven year-round staples to complement its Italian American menu of pizzas, pastas, and calzones. **Black's Bridge Stout** is a bold, chocolate brown–colored pour, served like Guinness on a nitrogen tap to give it a smooth creamy body and thick fluffy head. The roasty beer has deep notes of freshly brewed filter coffee, charcoal, and bitter baker's chocolate. **Broken Oar IPA** is brewed more in the bright hop-forward American style than the maltier English model. This hoppy bitter offering has layers of pine needle and yellow citrus fruit depth, with notes of sweet tropical fruit. **Island Mesa Blonde** is like so many blonde ales at American brewpubs and breweries, designed to appeal more to the American light lager drinker than seasoned hophead. Nevertheless, this vibrant yellow pour has an appealing and refreshing cereal brightness and works well as a pairing for Kannah's menu.

PUG RYAN'S STEAKHOUSE & BREWERY

104 Village Place, Dillon, CO 80435; (970) 468-2145; PugRyans.com;
Twitter: @pugsposse
Founded: 1997 **Founders:** Travis and Annie Holton **Brewer:** Dave Simmons **Flagship Beer:** Pallavicini Pilsner **Year-round Beers:** Pallavicini Pilsner, Great Scott Scottish Ale, Morningwood Wheat **Seasonals/Special Releases:** Oatmeal Vanilla Stout

Opened as a steak house in 1975, Pug Ryan's was already a known and highly respected entity in the mountain town of Dillon when it became Pug Ryan's Steakhouse & Brewery in 1997. Fifteen years and a healthy clutch of GABF medals later, Pug Ryan's is known throughout Colorado by beer fans. A good part of Pug

Ryan's notoriety can be attributed to the canning and distribution of its excellent and award-winning **Pallavicini Pilsner** and **Morningwood Wheat.**

There are a few brewpubs in Colorado that are as memorable for their high-quality food as well as for their excellent house beer, and Denver ChopHouse and TRiNiTY in Colorado Springs are two that immediately come to mind. Pug Ryan's definitely falls into that same category. Appetizers include sushi grade ahi tuna pan seared, fresh calamari fried golden brown, and crab cakes made with fresh snow crab meat.

Entrees are well covered with the usual selection of soups, salads, and various American pub classics, but it's the high-end grill where Pug Ryan's really impresses. Seafood highlights include salmon Oscar, pesto-encrusted cod, Rocky Mountain rainbow trout, and wheat beer–battered shrimp. While red meat lovers can indulge with Scottish ale and whiskey slow-roasted baby back ribs, bacon-wrapped filet mignon, rib eye steak, top sirloin, or perhaps the house specialty, the King Cut prime rib.

ROCKSLIDE RESTAURANT & BREWERY
401 Main St., Grand Junction, CO 81501; (970) 245-2111; RockslideBrewpub.com
Founded: 1994 **Founder:** Justin Bauer **Brewer:** Justin Bauer **Flagship Beer:** Widow Maker Wheat **Year-round Beers:** Widow Maker Wheat, Rabbit Ears Amber Ale, Big Bear Stout, Cold Shivers Pale Ale, Raspberry Wheat, Kokopelli Cream Ale **Seasonals/Special Releases:** Holiday Porter, Irish Red Ale, Honey Blonde Ale

Open since 1994, Rockslide Restaurant & Brewery is a true feature of downtown Grand Junction, an important old frontier town in western Colorado. The brewery pours nine of its own brewed beers to complement its archetypal menu of American pub food. Classic appetizers include nachos, onion rings, buffalo wings, and calamari. Entrees are well served with big salads, burgers, pork and chicken sandwiches, tacos, fish-and-chips, pizzas, calzones, chicken fried steak, steaks, meatloaf, and various fish dishes.

While the styles of beers that Rockslide brews are nothing earth-shattering, they are all brewed with an obvious care and quality. There are six year-round house beers and a shifting list of seasonals, occasionals, and one-offs. **Widow Maker Wheat** is an American pale wheat ale, with a brilliant fruit nose and a clean, slightly tart, yellow-and-green citrus finish. **Rabbit Ears Amber Ale** is an American amber ale, offering a smooth and quaffable balance of soft nut and caramel notes and medium-to-low earthy bitterness. **Big Bear Stout** is robust American stout, perfect for pairing with any of the heavier meat dishes on the restaurant menu. It has notes of espresso, dark chocolate, and black pepper. **Cold Shivers Pale Ale** is an American pale ale with a floral nose and deep notes of mango, passion fruit, and kiwi. Bitterness is moderate, and the finish has a nice dryness. **Raspberry Wheat** is like many of its ilk with a tart fruity twist on the popular house wheat beer. This is best paired with a salad. **Kokopelli Cream Ale** is the everyman's house beer. It was engineered to be pint-after-pint sessionable, refreshing, and polite in both aroma and flavor.

A local favorite come holiday time is the **Holiday Porter,** a dark brew made with Christmastime spices, brown sugar, molasses, and apple cider juice.

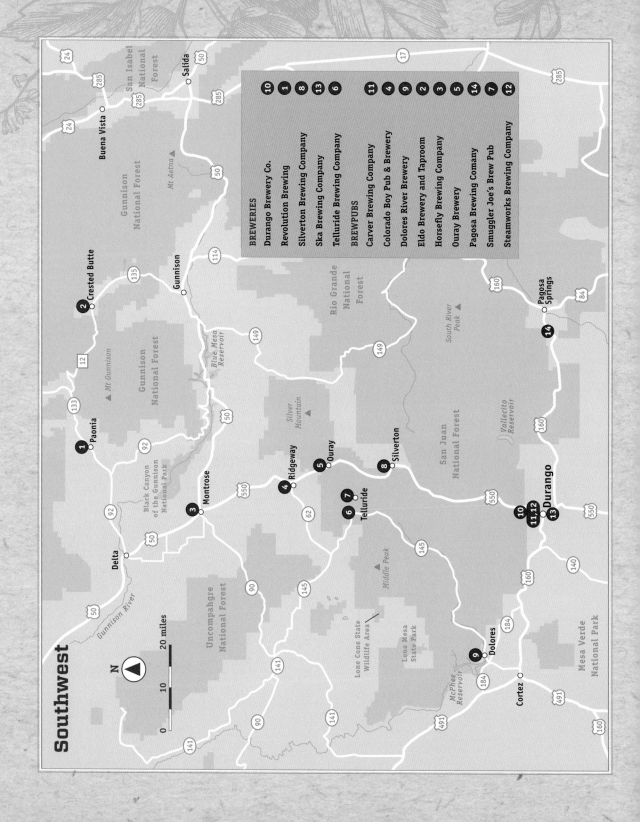

Southwest

N

20 miles

10

0

BREWERIES

- ⑩ Durango Brewery Co.
- ① Revolution Brewing
- ⑧ Silverton Brewing Company
- ⑬ Ska Brewing Company
- ⑥ Telluride Brewing Company

BREWPUBS

- ⑪ Carver Brewing Company
- ④ Colorado Boy Pub & Brewery
- ⑨ Dolores River Brewery
- ② Eldo Brewery and Taproom
- ③ Horsefly Brewing Company
- ⑤ Ouray Brewery
- ⑭ Pagosa Brewing Comany
- ⑦ Smuggler Joe's Brew Pub
- ⑫ Steamworks Brewing Company

Southwest

Crested Butte, Dolores, Durango, Montrose, Ouray, Pagosa Springs, Paonia, Ridgway, Silverton & Telluride

With the majority of Coloradoans living within an hour and a half of Denver, the breweries and brewpubs located in the towns of the far south and west of the state can seem like a lifetime away, especially for the occasional out-of-state visitor, most of whom enter and leave via Denver. But in these far-flung towns the adventerous and brave traveler can discover some of the finest beers brewed in America. Without the groundbreaking efforts of brewpubs in towns like Durango, it is doubtful whether the craft-beer movement in the state would have gained the momentum it has enjoyed since the early 1990s. It is here, in the far southwest part of the state, where trendsetters, like Ska, have thrived and become much in demand well beyond Colorado. Next time you are thinking of taking a road trip in Colorado, or indeed, if you're looking for off-the-beaten-path breweries to visit, you'd be wise to consider southwestern Colorado.

Breweries

DURANGO BREWING CO.

3000 Main Ave., Durango, CO 81301; (970) 247-3396; DurangoBrewing.com;
Twitter: @DurangoBrewing
Founded: 1990 **Founder:** Scott Bickert **Brewer:** Scott Bickert **Flagship Beer:** Durango Dark Lager **Year-round Beers:** Durango Dark Lager, Durango Wheat Beer, Durango Golden Ale, Durango Amber Ale, Durango Derail Ale **Seasonals/Special Releases:** Durango Pale Ale, Durango Blueberry Wheat Ale, Durango Colorfest, Durango Winter Ale, Hop Hugger IPA, Ghost Train Pumpkin Ale **Tours:** None **Taproom:** Mon 1 to 9 p.m., Tues through Thurs 10 a.m. to 10 p.m., Fri through Sat 11 a.m. to midnight, Sun 2 to 10 p.m. Growlers and bottles are available to go.

Durango Brewing Co. is one of the oldest breweries in Colorado. It opened in 1990 and pretty much kept to itself in the busy southwestern city of the same name until it came under new management in 2006 by Scott Bickert and the business was relaunched. A year after the relaunch, Durango beers began appearing on tap and in liquor stores as far north as Denver. A new taproom followed, and within two years production had doubled.

The core classics that have been with the brewery over the decades remain, alongside many new creations. **Durango Wheat Beer** is a 5.3 percent ABV American pale wheat beer, brewed with barley and wheat malts. The hazy soft yellow pour has a refreshing crispness, but it is not without a delicate weight as well. **Durango Golden Ale** is a 5.8 percent ABV American blonde ale, with a light quaffable body, a soft cereal aroma, and a soft fruit finish. Bitterness is very low. **Durango Amber Ale** is a 5.5 percent ABV classically built American red ale with a soft caramel and biscuit body and aroma. Sweetness is the focus, not bitterness.

Durango Dark Lager is that unusual beast, an American dark lager. The 5.8 percent ABV sooty pour is brewed with chocolate and crystal malts, and the malts speak the loudest in this beer. Hop profile and bitterness take a backseat to the pleasant smoky charcoal personality of the beer.

Durango Derail Ale ups the hop ante a touch. This 8.5 percent American strong ale has floral aroma, a moderate hop spiciness and bite and slightly chewy finish. The warmth of the higher alcohol is intentionally noticeable.

Durango Blueberry Wheat Ale

Style: Fruit Beer

ABV: 5.3 percent

Availability: Occasionally on tap and in bottles

Fruit wheat beers too often get an unnecessarily bad wrap, which is a shame because, done well, they are the perfect accompaniment to the long, hot, summer months. Durango Brewing's Durango Blueberry Wheat Ale is a great example of the style. It's a tweaked version of the brewery's popular year-round Durango Wheat Ale. The addition of blueberries to the brew is subtle but brings an added depth and soft sweetness to the beer that is the perfect complement to a blue-sky, 90-degree, summer day in Colorado.

Southwest

REVOLUTION BREWING

325 Grand Ave., Paonia, CO 81428; (970) 260-4869; Revolution-Brewing.com

Founded: 2008 **Founders:** Mike King and Gretchen King **Brewers:** Mike King and Gretchen King **Flagship Beer:** Colorado Red Ale **Year-round Beers:** Miner's Gold, Colorado Red Ale, Jessie's Garage, Rye Porter, Stout Ol' Friend **Seasonals/Special Releases:** Hefeweisen, Sticky Thickett, TJ 60/40 Wheat Lager, Gorgeous G.A.L. (Grand Avenue Lager), The "20 Can" Summer Ale, Cherry IPA, OAO, SEIPA **Tours:** None **Taproom:** Tues through Sun 4 p.m. to close. Closed Mon. Growlers are available to go.

The family-run Revolution Brewing has been serving the small Colorado Western Slope town of Paonia since 2008. Husband and wife owners Mike and Gretchen

King have an admirable ethos, believing firmly in local pride, and in locally growing or sourcing all of the ingredients they need to produce their beer. Mike and Gretchen also believe in limiting their carbon footprint and only delivering beer within a small radius of their brewing and busy taproom.

In the unlikely venue of a small former church, Mike and Gretchen brew a healthy assortment of beer styles on their trusty six-barrel brew system. **Miner's Gold** is a bright American blonde ale with strong cereal character and a lively, but restrained hop character. Bitterness is intentionally lower, with clean, pint-after-pint quaffability the objective. **Colorado Red Ale** is a 6.2 percent ABV American amber ale, with solid resinous kick and soft notes of brown sugar, caramel, and biscuit. **Jessie's Garage** is Revolution's entry into the popular American pale ale category. The sunshine-yellow pour bristles with the aroma of grapefruit and eucalyptus. Alongside **Rye Porter, Stout Ol' Friend** waves the dark-beer flag on a regular basis for Revolution. Stout is brewed with roasted barley and black-patent malts, giving the beer pitch-black hue and length-charred biscuit character. The finish has a note of dryness and hint of dark fruit.

Rye Porter
Style: Rye Beer
ABV: 6.3 percent
Availability: Year-round on tap
Rye Porters are a rare but interesting breed. Revolution Brewing clearly enjoys the combination of peppery rye malt and roasted barley, as this unusual style has the honor of pouring year-round at the brewery. The busy combination of spiced charcoal aroma and body and earthy espresso finish is winning and definitely deserves your attention.

SILVERTON BREWING COMPANY

1333 Greene St., Silverton, CO 81433; (970) 387-5033; SilvertonBrewing.com
Founded: 2005 **Founders:** Joel Harvie and Kate Harvie **Brewer:** Caroline Morris **Flagship Beer:** Bear-Ass Brown **Year-round Beers:** Bear-Ass Brown, Ice Pick Ale, Red Mountain Ale, Gold Digger Lager **Seasonals/Special Releases:** Snowmelt Sour, Greene Street Wheat, Ladder Truck Lager, Silverton Oktoberfest **Tours:** None **Taproom:** May through Oct Mon through Sat 11:30 a.m. to 9 p.m., Sun 11:30 a.m. to 7 p.m. Closed Nov through Apr. Growlers are available to go.

Silverton Brewing Company is located in the small, secluded, former mining town of Silverton. The brewery opened for business in 2005, under the ownership of Joel and Kate Harvie. Joel had more than 20 years of homebrewing experience and training at the highly regarded Siebel Institute of Technology and World Brewers Academy before he and Katie took the commercial plunge.

The town of Silverton is unable to sustain the brewery in the colder months, so it is closed November through May. Bear-Ass Brown is available in cans year-round in the local area and throughout the Western Slope.

Silverton brews a broad range of beers, from session friendly to more robust and stronger styles. **Ice Pick Ale** is a 6.4 percent, American-style IPA, brewed with Summit, Cascade, and Palisade hops. The beer has a thick orange-and-yellow citrus character, with a noticeable malt foundation. A touch lighter and more drinkable that many of the higher ABV IPAs in Colorado.

Red Mountain Ale is a nice example of that old amber-colored standard, the Irish-style red ale. This malt-forward 5.5 percent ABV pub ale has thick bread and a biscuit aroma and body. Some clean bitterness and brightness comes courtesy of noble Czech Saaz hops.

Gold Digger Lager is a German Munich-style helles lager beer, with a definite and immediate American-size hop bite. At 4.9 percent ABV the beer is moderately sessionable and the sweetness of the malt foundation and vibrant carbonation make it a one of the brewery's lighter options.

Silverton has brewed a lively selection of changing seasonal brews in the past, including a Berliner Weisse, American pale wheat, smoked lager, an Oktoberfest, and a barleywine.

Bear-Ass Brown
Style: English Brown Ale
ABV: 4 percent
Availability: Year-round on tap and in cans.
Silverton Brewing Company's Bear-Ass Brown is a Northern England–style brown ale, with a deep brunette hue and a nutty aroma. The beer has a long velvety chocolate texture and mocha finish. The beer is a delight and has been the recipient of numerous prestigous awards, including the gold medal at both the 2011 World Beer Championships and 2009 United States Open Beer Championships.

SKA BREWING COMPANY

225 Girard St., Durango, CO 81303; (970) 247-5792; SkaBrewing.com;
Twitter: @skabrewing
Founded: 1995 **Founders:** Bill Graham and Dave Thibodeau **Brewer:** Bill Graham
Flagship Beer: True Blonde Ale **Year-round Beers:** Modus Hoperandi, Pinestripe Red Ale, Buster Nut Brown Ale, Ten Pin Porter, ESB Special Ale, Steel Toe Stout, Nefarious Ten Pin, Decedent Imperial IPA, True Blonde Ale **Seasonals/Special Releases:** Mexican Logger, Euphoria Pale Ale **Tours:** None **Taproom:** Mon through Fri 9 a.m. to 8 p.m., Sat 11 a.m. to 6 p.m. Closed Sun. Growlers, bottles, and cans are available to go.

Ska Brewing Company is the largest brewery in southwestern Colorado, and its beers are found far beyond the state's borders. It cans, bottles, and kegs a wide variety of year-round and seasonal offerings and has an ongoing series of one-off experimental beers under the Local series label that it bottles and sends to its preferred accounts around Colorado.

Founded in 1995 by Bill Graham and Dave Thibodeau, Ska was named after the jaunty music of the same name that they love so much. There is an irreverent and sassy vibe about the beers brewed by Ska. This can be partly attributed to the colorful comic-book characters that are posed and emblazoned on every can and bottle released by the brewery. The characters are lifted from an unpublished comic book that Bill, Dave, and a friend created while at college. New characters appear with the release of new beers, and each character has an interrelated backstory.

Ska was the second craft brewery in the US to can its beer, trailing only slightly behind the pioneering Oskar Blues. Ska cans its best-selling year-rounds, **True Blonde Ale, ESB Special Ale,** and **Modus Hoperandi,** and seasonals, **Euphoria Pale Ale** (winter) and **Mexican Logger** (summer). The brewery's other year-round beers, **Ten Pin Porter, Steel Toe Stout, Pinstripe Red Ale,** and **Buster Nut Brown Ale,** are sold in 12-ounce bottles. Ska also sells a line of year-round imperial strength beers in colorful 22-ounce, wax-sealed bottles.

Ska is most well-known in beer-circles for it's 6.8 percent ABV canned IPA, Modus Hoperandi. The shining copper-colored ale is a complex hop bomb with a brilliant sappy green aroma and a bitter sticky body. Notes of sage, pine, lime peel, and basil are all present and accounted for. Bitterness is significant but not overwhelming.

Beer Lover's Pick

ESB Special Ale
Style: ESB
ABV: 5.7 percent
Availability: Year-round on tap
and in cans

Ska Brewing Company's ESB Special Ale was the second craft beer in the nation to be packaged in cans, the first being Oskar Blues Brewery's Dale's Pale Ale. The comparison, though, ends there. ESB Special Ale is a beer designed to highlight dark fruit and caramel aromatics and deliver a smooth flavor profile. It has a moderate-to-medium bitterness, but the malt backbone of the beer is the key to fully appreciating this 5.7 percent ABV, English-inspired pub ale.

TELLURIDE BREWING COMPANY

156 Def Society Dr., Telluride, CO 81435; (970) 728-5094; TellurideBrewingCo.com;
Twitter: @TellurideBrew
Founded: 2011 **Founders:** Chris Fish, Tommy Thacher, Brian Gavin, and John Lehman
Brewer: Chris Fish **Flagship Beer:** Bridal Veil Rye Pale Ale **Year-round Beers:** Bridal Veil
Rye Pale Ale, Smoke Shack Porter, Local's Lager, Ski-in-Ski-Stout, redFISH Ale, Face Down
Brown, Whacked Out Wheat, Tempter IPA **Seasonals/Special Releases:** Changes **Tours:**
None **Taproom:** Mon through Sat 9 a.m. to 5 p.m. Closed Sun. Growlers are available
to go.

Outdoor sports, the Grateful Dead, and good local beer are all popular in Colorado. So then it should come as no surprise that Telluride Brewing Company cofounders Chris Fish and Tommy Thacher, lovers of all those things, should one day meet and hatch a plan to open a brewery in the state. Fish was already a prized award-winning brewmaster; Thacher was a bartender. The pair seemed positively destined to make sweet beer together.

The pair joined forces with Brian Gavin, a real estate broker, and John Lehman, a local artist, to give their dream and business plan more viability, and the four opened Telluride Brewing Company in May 2011.

Telluride pours a well-rounded selection of core styles year-round. **Smoke Shack Porter** is 5.4 percent ABV black ale brewed with a peppery assortment of hops and beech wood–smoked malt. The result is a charred earthy brew with notes of bitter baker's chocolate, espresso, and black walnut. **Local's Lager** is a 5.3 ABV golden refresher, perfectly suited to accompany a broad range of savory meat and seafood dishes. The lager has low bitterness and a clean finish.

Tempter IPA is brewed with six varieties of hops and delivers a bold herbaceous aroma and a grassy green body. This 6.4 percent ABV American IPA has layers of earthy depth, a good amount of bitterness, and a robust finish. The malt foundation is present and brings a level of balance to the significant hop character. **Ski-in-Ski-Stout** is a 5.8 percent ABV, dessert-friendly, chocolate-forward American stout, with moderate bitterness and a full mouthfeel. The hearty black pour is an appropriate companion to all manner of foods, including forward and dairy-heavy desserts, full breakfast plates, and meat and potato dishes.

Beer Lover's Pick

Bridal Veil Rye Pale Ale
Style: Rye Beer
ABV: 5.5 percent
Availability: Year-round on tap and in cans
Telluride Brewing Company's Bridal Veil Rye Pale Ale, available on tap and in 12-ounce cans, is packed with bitter yellow citrus and green basil, tarragon, and sage herbal notes. This lively, bitter brew is a brilliant companion to Mexican and Asian dishes.

Southwest

Brewpubs

CARVER BREWING COMPANY

1022 Main Ave., Durango, CO 81301; (970) 259-2545; CarverBrewing.com;
Twitter: @CarverBrewing
Founded: 1988 **Founders:** Jim Wynne, Bill Wynne, and Barb Wynne **Brewer:** Eric Maxson
Flagship Beer: Jack Rabbit Pale Ale **Year-round Beers:** Jack Rabbit Pale Ale, Old Oak
Amber Ale, Lightner Creek Lager, Colorado Trail Nut Brown Ale, Rasberry Wheat Ale,
Cascade Canyon Cask IPA, Iron Horse Stout **Seasonals/Special Releases:** Changes

Carver Brewing Company in the southwestern Colorado town of Durango prides itself on local firsts. It was the town's first coffee shop, first nonsmoking bar, first restaurant to be green powered, first user of ecofriendly growlers and, of course, first brewery.

When Carver opened for business in 1988, it was the first brewery to open in the Four Corners region since the repeal of Prohibition and only the second brewpub in the state; the first being Wynkoop in Denver. Carver was the brainchild of Jim, Bill, and Barb Wynne, who had previously owned a bakery and a cafe under the Carver name in the city of Winter Park.

The first beer hop lovers should order when visiting Carver is the **Cascade Canyon Cask IPA.** The beer pops with spiky yellow grapefruit and full earthy pine bitterness before opening up to a long resinous herbal finish. **Jack Rabbit Pale Ale** is another hoppy Carver staple that hopheads should sample. The sunshine-colored pour is loaded with spritzy citrus and fresh grassy notes. Bitterness is even sip through swallow, with the finish medium dry. Served on nitrogen, **Iron Horse Stout** is a robust roast-forward American oatmeal stout, with a moderate-to-high hop-derived bitterness. The oatmeal makes for a requisitely smooth and even drink. Serving a beer on nitrogen lends it a smooth and creamy texture.

Carver's restaurant offers a host of all-American breakfast, lunch, and dinner staples. Enjoy the likes of eggs Benedict, all manner of pancakes and French toast, breakfast burritos, and frittatas; nachos, bread bowl soups, and stews; burgers, steaks, seafood, Mexican dishes, and classic desserts.

COLORADO BOY PUB & BREWERY

602 Clinton St., Ridgway, CO 81432; (970) 626-5333; ColoradoBoy.com
Founded: 2007 **Founder:** Tom Hennessy **Brewer:** Danny Wilson **Flagship Beer:** IPA
Year-round Beers: Colorado Boy IPA, Best Bitter, Blonde, Irish Ale, Pale Ale, Porter
Seasonals/Special Releases: Changes

There is no shortage of entrepreneurial spirit in American craft beer, but even in an industry of dreamers and executors, Tom Hennessy stands tall. Over the years Tom has opened, run, and sold five different breweries in New Mexico and Colorado. In 2007 he opened his sixth, Colorado Boy Pub & Brewery, which he hopes will be his last and most-remembered brewing venture. Colorado Boy is located in a 100-year-old building on a main street in the small town of Ridgway on Colorado's Western Slope. The small, 25-seat brewpub offers up a focused selection of core styles and a small menu of pizzas.

The beers take much influence from the styles and methods of the British Isles. **Irish Ale,** a GABF silver medal winner, is a bold Irish red ale with a rich toffee caramel character, low bitterness, and a biscuit finish. **Colorado Boy IPA** is a beer that carefully balances its malt foundation with its abundant hop bitterness, flavor, and aroma. The beer is more akin to modern British Indian pales, than the bold, hop-forward citrus and pine variety normally associated with Colorado and the western US.

Another British-inspired trait of Colorado Boy is the ongoing presentation of a beer that has been cask conditioned. The likes of the malt-forward house **Best Bitter** benefit greatly from this method of finishing, much more so than being forced carbonated.

DOLORES RIVER BREWERY

100 N. 4th St., Dolores, CO 81323; (970) 882-4677; DoloresRiverBrewery.com
Founded: 2002 **Founder:** Mark Youngquist **Brewer:** Mark Youngquist **Flagship Beer:** ESB
Year-round Beers: ESB, Dry Stout **Seasonals/Special Releases:** Sweet Jamaican Brown Ale, Liquid Sunshine

Many a beer geek might be surprised to learn that Mark Youngquist, the founder of Dolores River Brewery, was once a traveling craft beer go-getter who worked for well-known breweries like Rock Bottom and BridgePort of Portland, Oregon. But such is the beer industry, and surprises lurk behind every mash tun and bubbling fermentation vessel. Everyone has a unique story to tell, with a personal path to their desired place in the sprawling and often contradictory beer industry.

Southwest

Mark prides himself on not really brewing to style. Walk into his tiny, 40-odd seat taproom and you'll find beers of familiar styles, like an **English Extra Special Bitter** or an American pale ale, being poured alongside beers like **Liquid Sunshine,** an IPA-modeled beer.

Dolores River has a local, community-centric vibe quite different from the ever-changing crowds that frequent the locations of Mark's former employer, Rock Bottom. Mark eschews traveling with his beers or entering competitions. That said, the brewery did start small batch canning of some of its beers in 2011, and if you're lucky, you'll find four-packs of your favorite Dolores River beer for sale at the brewery or in a nearby liquor store.

ELDO BREWERY AND TAPROOM
215 Elk Ave., Crested Butte, CO 81224; (970) 349-6125; EldoBrewpub.com
Founded: 1998 **Founder:** Fred Orndorff **Brewer:** Fred Orndorff **Flagship Beer**: King's Kolsch **Year-round Beers:** King's Kolsch, Breakfast Ale, Northside Ale, Session Ale, Pivo Blond Ale, Wildfire ESB, Secret Trail Ale, Paradise Pale Ale, Hooligan IPA, Beckwith Brown Ale, Sock-it-to-me Scottish Ale, Abominable Strong Ale, Sledgehammer Porter, Stout **Seasonals/Special Releases:** Changes

Eldo Brewery and Taproom is located, like so many small brewpubs in Colorado, in the most unlikely of places. In this instance, Eldo found its home in the small ski town of Crested Butte. Eldo opened for business in 1998, a lifetime ago in craft-beer years. The taproom can be found in a second floor walk up, and once inside you'll find a decidedly malt-focused list of beers on tap. Eldo's head brewer took over brewing duties in 2007 and upped the diversity of the tap list considerably. No longer would the beers being poured be an afterthought.

The brewery offers well-excuted staple styles, like the nutty **Beckwith Brown Ale** (6.5 percent ABV); **Secret Trail Ale** (5.6 percent ABV), an orange pith and biscuit balanced amber ale; and **Paradise Pale Ale** (6.5 percent ABV), a yellow citrus and grassy pale ale. Alongside these offerings you can also find an ever-changing selection of more interesting and esoteric styles.

Wildfire ESB (6.5 percent) is brewed to the traditional English model with its bitter red fruit and thick toffee base. **Northside Ale** (5 percent ABV) is an archtypal English session bitter, with a fruit basket nose and toasted malt foundation. **Sledgehammer Porter** (5.6 percent ABV) is an American porter, matured on dark-roasted espresso beans and served Guinness style on nitrogen.

Eldo also serves a solid menu of bar fare, including the likes of bacon-cheese fries, nachos, burgers, veggie burgers, grilled cheese, BLTs, and salads.

HORSEFLY BREWING COMPANY

846 E. Main St., Montrose, CO 81401; (970) 249-6889; HorseflyBrewing.com
Founded: 2009 **Founders:** Nigel Askew and Phil Freismuth **Brewer:** Nigel Askew
Flagship Beer: Pub Pale Ale IPA (IPA) **Year-round Beers:** Tabano Red, Paso Fino Porter,
6 Shooter Pale Ale, Highland Scottish, Jazzy Razzy, Bug-Eyed Blonde, Pub Pale Ale (IPA)
Seasonals/Special Releases: Changes

Horsefly Brewing opened for business in Montrose in September 2009, or more precisely, the supposedly lucky day of 09/09/09. The brewery was the brainchild of homebrew friends Nigel Askew, a former London hotel managing magnate, and Phil Freismuth, a local police officer. Not the most likely of individuals to dedicate themselves to an upstart brewery but so goes the story of many breweries and brewpubs in Colorado.

Horsefly offers up a southwestern-centric menu of grilled appetizers, wings, sandwiches, soups, salads, and burgers. Spice and peppers are prominently featured. To complement the food menu, the brewery pours a range of recognizable classic beer styles.

Tabano Red is an American amber ale with warm biscuit, red fruit, and caramel notes. The body is less bitter than the average American red ale, and as such, pairs more confidently with many items on the pub's menu. **Bug-Eyed Blonde** is a hay-colored, American-blonde ale positioned by the brewery as a good alternative for customers more accustomed to ordering light lagers at less beer-savvy establishments. The beer is brewed with a mix of pale malts to lend depth and an earthy combination of European hops to give bitterness and a leafy aroma to the cereal foundation of the beer. **Paso Fino Porter** is an American take on the classic English dark-ale style and delivers thick black-coffee, toffee-caramel, and dark-chocolate notes. The finish is smooth, with a lingering black licorice flavor. A classic American pale ale, **6 Shooter Pale Ale** is abundantly hopped for a bright yellow-citrus aroma, bold medium-bitter body, and a clean, bitter, semiarid finish.

southwest

OURAY BREWERY

607 Main St., Ouray, CO 81427; (970) 325-7388; OurayBrewery.com;
Twitter: @OurayBrewery
Founded: 2010 **Founder:** Erin Eddy **Brewer:** Jeff Lockhart **Flagship Beer:** San Juan
IPA **Year-round Beers:** Alpine Amber, Autum Rye Ale, Box Canyon Brown Ale, Camp Bird
Blonde, San Juan IPA, Silvershield Stout **Seasonals/Special Releases:** Changes

Ouray is yet another of Colorado's seasonal, small towns that boasts its own brewpub. The aptly named Ouray Brewery opened in August 2010, serving up a recognizable list of foundation craft beer styles to complement its broadly American-Cajun bent.

Ouray's bright new taproom opened in spring 2012. The roomy space has plenty of seating and a pool table for the cue-happy. The three-level brewpub also has a rooftop patio with spectacular views of the surrounding mountainscape. Whether dining on southwest blackened salmon or a grilled avocado shrimp remoulade salad, the brewery has a handful of beers to match.

The core beers that Ouray's brewmaster, Jeff Lockhart, brews are complemented by changing seasonals and one-off brews. **Camp Bird Blonde** is like any good, hay-colored, American-blonde ale, an easy drinking affair. It is engineered to be the quicker-to-brew ale equivalent of an effervescent and bright lagered Pilsner style. **Box Canyon Brown Ale** has medium bitterness and soft residual biscuit sweetness. The nose has inviting notes of English toffee, mocha, and hazelnut. **Alpine Amber** is a low-bitterness, American amber ale with a malty caramel base and smooth, clean finish that doesn't weigh the palate down. Along with the house brown ale, this is the most food-friendly of the beers Ouray brews year-round. For hop lovers, **San Juan IPA** will be the no-brainer, go-to choice at Ouray. This American-style IPA has a big yellow citrus and tropical fruit profile. Pair this with spicier dishes on the menu. **Autum Rye Ale** is a gorgeous auburn pour, with a peppery nose, a deep-butter body, and a lively spicy finish. **Silvershield Stout** is a strong inky stout with a thick, dark-chocolate aroma, a bitter cocoa and espresso body, and a roasted cocoa nib and licorice finish.

PAGOSA BREWING COMPANY

118 N. Pagosa Blvd., Pagosa Springs, CO 81147; (970) 731-2739; PagosaBrewing.com;
Twitter: @PagosaBrewingCo
Founded: 2006 **Founder:** Tony Simmons **Brewer:** Tony Simmons **Flagship Beer:** Poor
Richard's Ale **Year-round Beers:** Poor Richard's Ale, Wolf Creek Wheat, Kayaker Cream Ale,
Pagosa Pale Ale, Powder Day IPA, Eagle ESB, Rodeo Rider Red, Soaker's Stout **Seasonals/
Special Releases:** Changes

Owner Tony Simmons of small brewpub Pagosa Brewing Company was vaulted into the craft-beer industry spotlight in 2006 when his entry in a beer competition beat entries from more than 100 other breweries, including many from much larger and more established breweries.

In honor of the 300th birthday of Benjamin Franklin, the Brewers Association held a competition to create the best beer that Franklin might have enjoyed. Tony's winning entry, called **Poor Richard's Ale,** was brewed with an abundance of fermentable corn and molasses, instead of grain. Grain might well have been in short supply 300 years ago because of the war with England, the colonies' early grain supplier. The recipe for this intriguing competition-winning beer can be found in the BYOB: Brew Your Own Beer chapter of this book.

Pagosa brews upwards of 50 different beers throughout the year with plenty of options to complement the pub menu of burgers, salmon, brats, hot dogs, pizzas, soups, and salads, all cooked with fresh, cage-free, organic, local, or humanely sourced ingredients.

Kayaker Cream Ale should be the first port of call for any self-respecting beer geek visiting Pagosa. Tony's incarnation of the style was inspired by the quaffable Bavarian helles lager style. Tony actually studied brewing in Bavaria, so perhaps the ale is not such a coincidence. Kayaker is a bright and inviting cereal-forward ale, with drinkability on its mind. It will come as no surprise that this beer medaled at the World Beer Championships in 2012.

Another of Pagosa's World Beer Championship winning beers is **Pagosa Pale Ale,** an approachable, but full-flavored American pale brewed with a small amount of rye malt. The beer is twice dry hopped, giving the beer a bold herbaceous aroma. Pagosa suggests pairing this beer with one of its lovingly prepared pizzas, and I couldn't agree more.

Southwest

SMUGGLER JOE'S BREW PUB

225 S. Pine St., #G, Telluride, CO 81435; (970) 728-0919; SmugglerJoesTelluride.com
Founded: 1996 **Founder:** Mike Metz **Brewer:** Mike Metz **Flagship Beer:** Rocky Mountain Rye **Year-round Beers:** Rocky Mountain Rye, Knuckledragger Extra Pale Ale, Wildcat Wheat, Shred Betty Raspberry Wheat, Road Rash Red, Ingram's IPA, San Juan SkyHop, Smugglers Strong Scottish Ale, Two Planker Porter, Powder Night Espresso Porter, 10:13 Oatmeal Stout, Imperial San Juan SkyHop **Seasonals/Special Releases:** Varies

Smuggler Joe's is located in a former warehouse in downtown Telluride, a ski mecca that was once a mining town. The brewpub has an extensive menu of appetizers, burgers, sandwiches, wings, burritos, pastas, baby back ribs, steaks, and fish-and-chips. The bar menu also offers up a long list of cocktails to supplement the 16 taps of house-brewed beer.

Some of the standouts include **Rocky Mountain Rye,** a 5.3 percent ABV GABF-winning rye beer with a nose of fresh-cracked pepper and a long, spicy, bitter body; **Knuckledragger Extra Pale Ale,** a 5 percent ABV American pale ale with a big floral aroma and citrus fruit body; **Wildcat Wheat,** a smooth, 5.2 percent ABV, American wheat ale with a soft fruity body and clean and slightly tart finish; **Ingram's IPA,** a big and bold 6.4 percent ABV American IPA, with a leafy green nose and substantial notes of menthol, fresh-cut grass, and lemon peel; and **Powder Night Espresso Porter,** a 5.5 percent ABV, coffee-infused, American porter with a thick, dark, chocolate aroma and a long, dry, molasses-flavored body.

STEAMWORKS BREWING COMPANY

801 E. Second Ave., Durango, CO 81301; (970) 259-9200; SteamworksBrewing.com;
Twitter: @Stmworks
Founded: 1996 **Founder:** Kris Oyler and Brian McEachron **Brewer:** Spencer Roper
Flagship Beer: Colorado Kolsch Ale **Year-round Beers:** Colorado Kolsch Ale, Third Eye Pale Ale, Steam Engine Lager, One Wit Wunder, Lizard Head Red, Weizenbock, Wanna Git Rye?, Powder Daze Porter, Backside Stout **Seasonals/Special Releases:** Quince Años Barleywine, Conductor, Elephant Rider Imperial IPA, Imperial Mole Stout

When Steamworks opened in 1996, it was the fourth brewery to open in Durango, a town of just 2,000 people. Founders Kris Oyler and Brian McEachron set up their brewpub in a 1920s-era car dealership. Only a year after opening, Steamworks won a gold medal at the GABF for its amber lager, **Steam Engine Lager** (see recipe, page 193). In subsequent years the beer went on to win an astounding six medals at the GABF. Showing a knack for full-flavored and characterful lighter styles, the award-winning **Colorado Kolsch** followed. Now canned and distributed statewide, Steam Engine, Colorado Kolsch, and the brewery's dry-hopped **Third Eye Pale Ale** have gone on to successfully spread the good name of Steamworks far beyond its local southwestern catchment area.

Much like a handful of other brewpubs in the state, Steamworks prides itself on sourcing the highest quality ingredients for its inventive and attention-grabbing menu. Appetizers include Kobe beef sliders, chorizo cheddar fritters, smoked salmon flatbread, and cajun-dusted popcorn shrimp. Beyond a mouthwatering menu of soups, salads, quiche, calzones, burgers, and sandwiches, entrees have included a full cajun boil with Alaskan dungeness crab, wild Texas shrimp, andouille sausage, new potatoes, and sweet corn. The full menu is detailed and exhaustive.

Beer Festivals

There simply isn't a better way to try a bunch of new beers at one time than going to a beer festival. Want to try a hard-to-find beer before buying it? Interested in sampling some quality craft brew that's not sold locally in your hometown? If you consider yourself a beer lover and you haven't been to a beer fest before, find the nearest event and go. Immediately.

January

BIG BEERS, BELGIANS AND BARLEYWINES FESTIVAL
Vail Cascade Resort & Spa, 1300 Westhaven Dr., Vail, Colorado 81657; bigbeersfestival .com; @BigBeersFest

Big Beers, Belgians and Barleywines Festival takes place each January in the snow-covered ski-resort town of Vail at the Cascade Resort & Spa. The emphasis, as you might have surmised from the name of the festival, is squarely on strong Belgian-inspired beer styles, warming barleywines, and American strong ales. The festival is one of the most well received and attended in the state. Head brewers from many of the best breweries in the nation attend, hosting seminars and epic beer dinners and sharing their creations. If your tastes lean more toward big sweet barleywines, strong dark Belgians, and generally beers that pack a punch in terms of aroma, flavor, and boozy heat, then attending this festival is a no brainer. Many breweries brew beers especially for this festival, so it is also great for those who go out of their way to taste the rarest and newest American craft-beer creations. Since it is a strong ale festival, pacing your intake is essential, even if you consider yourself a "seasoned" drinker. If there is a downside to the festival, it's cost. Vail isn't cheap off-season, and a high-end beer festival hosted at the spa during peak ski season is expensive. It's definitely worth attending once; just be prepared to save your pennies beforehand.

WINTER BREW FEST
Mile High Station, 2027 W. Colfax Ave., Denver, CO 80204; denverbrewfest.com; @DenverBrewFest

Winter Brew Fest, held at the Mile High Station special events venue each January, is one of Colorado's everyman, good-beer festivals. It isn't expensive and lacks some of the elitism of many of its counterparts. The focus is mainly on showcasing and sharing beers from Colorado-owned and -operated breweries, although there is plenty of beer pouring from out-of-state breweries as well. One of the nicest things about Winter Brew Fest is that it requires little advance planning to attend compared to many of the more in-demand beer festivals in the state. Tickets are plentiful, and the scope of the festival is more mainstream. This is a great beer fest to attend with less hard-core beer lovers, many of whom would surely be more than a little overwhelmed by the intensive and focused nature of many of Colorado's more geeky and expensive beer festivals. The festival has plenty of live music and food vendors. Tickets run $30 to $45, depending on options.

March

BOULDER STRONG ALE FESTIVAL

Avery Brewing Company, 5763 Arapahoe Ave., Unit E, Boulder, CO 80303; averybrewing .com; @AveryBrewingCo

One of three festivals run by and at Avery Brewing Company in Boulder, Strong Ale Festival is not a festival for unseasoned beer drinkers. The concept of the festival is a great fit for Avery, which consistently arguably produces the strongest ales of any brewery in America. This fest is not just about showcasing Avery creations, though; the organizers go to great lengths to source strong ales from breweries from across the country, including many that only distribute in their local area. In 2012 beers were sourced from the likes of Allagash, Cigar City, Cambridge, and Surly. Being located in Boulder and being quite easy to get to, this fest sells out very quickly indeed, so be ready to buy tickets as soon as they go on sale or risk having to purchase tickets on the secondary market at inflated prices. Another word of advice: Get a hotel in Boulder for the night. This is a strong ale fest, and you likely won't want to make a long journey at the end of the day.

May

ODELL SMALL BATCH REVIVAL

Odell Brewing Co., 800 E. Lincoln Ave., Fort Collins, CO 80524; odellbrewing.com; @OdellBrewing

Odell Small Batch Revival is held each May at Odell Brewing Company in Fort Collins. There is no entrance fee. Instead attendees simply pay as they go by purchasing beer tokens at $4 each. The festival is a chance to try many of the best small-batch pilot beers and barrel-aged ales and lager that Odell produces throughout the year. It takes places outside in the space surrounding the brewery, and beers are poured from kegs under tents. Small, focused festivals like the Odell Small Batch Revival are often a lot less stressful and, thus, more enjoyable than many of the oversubscribed large beer festivals. Food is available from some local vendors. In 2012 Uncle's Pizzeria, Nordy's BBQ, and Matador Mexican Grill offered food for sale. There's plenty of opportunity to soak up some of the great and often strong beer on offer.

June

BOULDER SOURFEST

Avery Brewing Company, 5763 Arapahoe Ave., Unit E, Boulder, CO 80303; averybrewing. com; @AveryBrewingCo

Boulder SourFest, held each June at and by Avery Brewing Company in Boulder, is the premiere sour beer festival in America. It brings together the best, rarest, and most-inventive sour beers from across America. The festival is extremely popular and well attended; tickets for the 2012 festival sold out in under a minute. If you are lucky enough to score tickets, they usually cost in the region of $50 per person. If you're a sour beer aficionado, there is absolutely no question that attending SourFest once in your life is a must. The popularity and interest in sour beers is rising year after year at an exponential rate, and because many of the best sour beer producers are based in Colorado, and because Avery is building a much larger campus and brewery to host such events in the future, Boulder SourFest is surely at the center of a perfect storm to become one of the largest and most-talked about beer festivals in America, possibly even the world. Sour beer is here to stay in America, and with it, the Boulder SourFest.

COLORADO BREWERS' FESTIVAL

Civic Center Park Area, Fort Collins, CO 80521; downtownfortcollins.com/dba.php/ brewfest; @COBrewersFest

Colorado Brewers' Festival takes place over one weekend each June in Fort Collins at the Civic Center Park Area, near Laporte Avenue and Mason Street. Held every year since 1989, it is one of the longest-running beer festivals in Colorado. Tickets usually run from $25 to as high as $100, and various options are available. At the 2012 festival almost 40 Colorado breweries poured more than 60 different beers. Food vendors are in attendance, and there are also two stages of live music. One of the more legendary festivals in the state, the Colorado Brewers' Festival attracts many of the brewers themselves and is a great event to actually meet and possibly pick the brains of the people behind the beers so many of us enjoy. Being held in Fort Collins, the festival has a warm, welcoming, and cozy vibe and is greatly supported by the many breweries that call the sleepy college town home. Many of the local breweries also brew up something special for the event, so those who seek out one-of-a kind regional creations have the opportunity to find something new and different. Along with the GABF and the Boulder SourFest, Colorado Brewers' Festival is one of Colorado's must-attend annual beer events.

GREAT DIVIDE ANNIVERSARY PARTY

Great Divide Brewing Company, 2201 Arapahoe St., Denver, CO 80205; greatdivide.com; @GreatDivideBrew

Great Divide Anniversary Party takes place block-party style on a closed-off street adjacent to the brewery and taproom of the Great Divide Brewing Company. Tickets usually run $25 each, and they include admission, all of your beer, and one food ticket. The beer is a wonderful mix of regular, seasonal, and very special one-off Great Divide brews. In years past these have included all manner of special, barrel-aged versions of Yeti Imperial Stout and barrel-aged treatments of other high ABV Great Divide beers. The brewery recently installed a dedicated pilot system, so expect the number of unique one-off beers to increase dramatically in the future. Food in the past has been provided by Basic Kneads Pizza, Stick It To Me Fine Cuisine On A Stick, Chef Driven Food Truck, and Bob's Blazin' BBQ.

July

SUMMER BREW FEST

Mile High Station, 2027 W. Colfax Ave., Denver, CO 80204; denverbrewfest.com; @DenverBrewFest

Summer Brew Fest, held at the Mile High Station special events venue each July, is the summer version of the Winter Brew Fest that is held each January. The focus is mainly on showcasing and sharing beers from Colorado breweries, although there is plenty of beer pouring from out-of-state breweries as well. As with Winter Brew Fest, which is run by the same organization, Summer Brew Fest requires little advance planning to attend in comparison to many of the more in-demand beer festivals in the state. Tickets are plentiful and the scope of the festival is more mainstream, so it is a great beer event to attend with less hard-core beer lovers, many of whom would surely be more than a little overwhelmed by the intensive and focused nature of many of Colorado's more geeky and expensive beer festivals. This festival has plenty of live music and food vendors. Tickets run $30 to $45, depending on options.

August

CRAFT LAGER & SMALL BATCH FESTIVAL
Memorial Park, 502 Manitou Ave., Manitou Springs, CO 80829; craftlagerfestival.com; @CraftLagerFest

Craft Lager & Small Batch Festival takes place each August at the Memorial Park in Manitou Springs. The one-day festival attracts about 20,000 attendees and lager beer producers from across the state and country. Craft distilleries are also in attendance, offering tastings of their spirits. There is food and live music. An all-day pass will set you back around $40 per person. The Craft Lager & Small Batch Festival is one of the more mainstream festivals in the state. Lager is the grand unifier among beer drinkers around the world in its most prevalent form, the ubiquitous and ever-popular Pilsner. Needless to say, if you're fan of any style of lager, then this unique fest needs to be on your list of Beer-Related Things To Do in Colorado. Not to mention, you also get to visit and take in the beauty of Manitou Springs while you do so.

FOAM FEST: AT THE COLORADO STATE FAIR
1001 Beulah Ave., Pueblo, CO 81004; coloradostatefair.com

Foam Fest is a component of the Colorado State Fair, which takes place late each August in Pueblo. It seeks to promote and celebrate beer brewed in Colorado. Some 20 Colorado breweries take part and pour beer during the festivities. Foam Fest tickets usually run $30 per person. Though a part of the State Fair, Foam Fest is its own ticketed event. Held every year since 2002, Foam Fest seems to only grow in popularity each year. If you plan well enough in advance, you can include a visit to the breweries located in the south and southwest of Colorado when you visit Foam Fest. With so much beer and brewery action taking place in and around Denver, Boulder, Fort Collins, and Colorado Springs, it is easy to forget that there are many breweries located farther afield to the south of those major metropolitan areas. The fact that Foam Fest takes place at the Colorade State Fair is great for any friends or family members in your group who are not all that interested in beer. There is an abundance of other events, attractions, and food available for the less beer inclined.

September

BOULDER IPA FESTIVAL

Avery Brewing Company, 5763 Arapahoe Ave., Unit E, Boulder, CO 80303; averybrewing .com; @AveryBrewingCo

O rganized by Avery Brewing Company, the Boulder IPA Festival was first held in fall 2012. IPAs are by some margin the most popular beer style in American craft beer. The well-run and -curated likes of the Boulder Strong Ale Festival and the Boulder SourFest, which are both hosted and organized by Avery, proved a great model for Boulder IPA Festival, an absolute must-attend for hopheads no matter how far away you live. Avery has a knack for sourcing the best and hardest to find examples of any beer style from breweries across the country. With IPAs showing no signs of waning in popularity, the Boulder IPA Festival came along at just the right time and, as such, has become one of the most talked about and well-attended beer fests in the region. Prepare your palate; this festival will wreck it.

TELLURIDE BLUES AND BREWS FESTIVAL

Telluride Town Park, 500 E. Colorado Ave., Telluride, CO 81435; tellurideblues.com; @TellurideBlues

H eld every year since 1993, the popular Telluride Blues and Brews Festival takes place each September in Telluride, a historic mining town located almost 9,000 feet above sea level. Ticket prices for this massive blues and beer event vary. There is plenty of beer to accompany the live music, with 12 booths pouring Colorado beer and selling local food. The best way to enjoy this festival is to camp or lodge locally. Telluride is a long drive from major gateway cities like Denver, Boulder, and Fort Collins.

October

DENVER RARE BEER TASTING

Wynkoop Brewing Co., 1634 18th St., Denver, CO 80202; pintsforprostates.org; @Pints4Prostates

T he Denver Rare Beer Tasting is a charity event run by Pints for Prostates. It is one of the many events that third-party organizers run alongside the GABF each year, shrewdly capitalizing on the 60,000 visiting beer lovers who descend on the city for the main event. The Denver Rare Beer Tasting takes place upstairs at the

Wynkoop Brewery in downtown Denver. Tickets usually cost around $80 per person and that covers all of your beer and food for the session. In years past the event has sold out very quickly, appealing as it does to the most hard-core beer aficionados. For those who want to try the rarest and most-limited barrel-aged and sour releases by some of the most prolific and respected breweries in America, this event is a must. The Denver Rare Beer Tasting is nice because many of the brewers who made the beers are in attendance and are often pouring their creations. So it's a great time to catch a few words with some of your brewing idols.

GREAT AMERICAN BEER FESTIVAL (GABF)
Denver Convention Center, 700 14th St., Denver; greatamericanbeerfestival.com; @GABF

The Great American Beer Festival (GABF) is the jewel in the crown of the Brewers Association. It is the largest festival of its kind in the world and one of the oldest. GABF takes place over three days at the massive Denver Convention Center, located downtown close to many of the city's hotels; and you will need a hotel. Over the course of the festival, some 2,200 different beers are poured by 500 American breweries. If those numbers are staggering, they pale in comparison to the 50,000 people who attend the festival each year. This is a festival of pilgrimage, a festival that people travel to from across America and the world to attend. It's something of a religious experience. A rite of passage for every self-respecting beer lover. Ticket prices vary greatly, and it is advisable to become a member of the American Homebrewers Association or the Brewers Association if you plan on buying tickets, as members get first pick before sales are opened up to the general public. There is also a Members Only session that is by far the best way to experience the festival as it has fewer people and fewer amateur drinkers simply looking to get drunk. Held every year since 1982, GABF is one of the best-managed beer festivals in the country, despite its size. In addition to the thousands of beers being poured, there are many satellite seminars, tastings, and specialist beer-related events, like the very popular Farm to Table showcase that sees some of the best breweries in America pairing and cooking special beers with very high-quality food. Admittance to events like Farm to Table can be very limited and require an additional fee, so plan accordingly. The best recommendation to newbies attending the GABF is to not rush, drink slowly, and take it all in. Even one session is plenty of time to get the lay of the land.

BYOB: Brew Your Own Beer

This chapter includes over a dozen clone beer recipes submitted by some of Colorado's finest brewers. From stouts to hoppy IPAs, there's enough in here to keep even the most avid homebrewers busy. **Note:** All of the following recipes have been scaled to yield five gallons of beer.

Beer Recipes

AVERY CZAR IMPERIAL STOUT

This high ABV creation holds lots of chocolate, toffee, and molasses notes, making it a perfect beer for pairing with desserts. Avery's The Czar is also great for cellaring, so don't fret if you can't drink the entire batch in one go!

OG: 1.104, FG: 1.025, IBU: 60, SRM: 35+

Malt:

17 pounds 2-row malt

11.5 ounces cara 45 malt

11.5 ounces honey malt

5.9 ounces cara 8 malt

4.6 ounces carafa III

3.8 ounces debittered black malt

3.8 ounces chocolate malt

Hops:

0.94 ounce Magnum (60 minutes)

0.89 ounce Magnum (30 minutes)

0.52 ounce Sterling (0 minutes)

0.52 ounce Hallertau (0 minutes)

Yeast:

California Ale Yeast (White Labs WLP001 or Wyeast 1056)

Mash at 152 degrees for 60 minutes. Boil for 60 minutes. Ferment at 66 degrees for the first half of fermentation, then allow the temperature to rise to 74 degrees until complete.

COURTESY OF AVERY BREWING COMPANY (P. 62)

BRECKENRIDGE LUCKY U IPA

Whether you're feeling lucky or just in the mood for a good, sturdy IPA, Breckenridge's Lucky U IPA will do the trick. This balanced ale satisfies both you hopheads and you malt lovers.

OG: 1.056, FG: 1.011, IBU: 68, SRM: 9.7

Malt:

7.7 pounds 2-row malt

10.7 ounces Munich 10-liter malt

9.1 ounces crystal 80-liter malt

6.1 ounces carapils malt

1.4 ounces torrified wheat

Hops:

0.32 ounce Magnum (90 minutes)

0.51 ounce Perle (30 minutes)

0.36 ounce Cascade (30 minutes)

0.28 ounce Apollo (15 minutes)

0.30 ounce Fuggle (15 minutes)

1.28 ounces Cascade (flame out)

0.56 ounce Goldings (flame out)

1.32 ounces Goldings (dry hop)

2.02 ounces Cascades (dry hop)

Yeast:

California Ale Yeast (White Labs WLP001 or Wyeast 1056)

Mash at 152 degrees for 45 minutes. Boil for 90 minutes. Ferment at 68 degrees until complete and then dry hop.

COURTESY OF BRECKENRIDGE BREWERY (P. 4)

COPPER KETTLE ENGLISH STYLE BLACK IPA

This rich and malty concoction boasts a bold, roasted flavor. English hops are abundant enough to balance out the intense malty backbone of this British-style black IPA.

OG: 1.072, FG: 1.018, IBU: 76, SRM: 29

Malt:

7.3 pounds Marris Otter

2.75 pounds light Munich

1.4 pounds CaraMunich II

11.2 ounces dextrine malt

7.3 ounces dehusked carafa II

3.6 ounces roasted barley

Hops:

1.25 ounces Magnum (60 minutes)

1 ounce East Kent Goldings (60 minutes)

1 ounce East Kent Goldings (5 minutes)

1 ounce UK Fuggle (5 minutes)

1.5 ounces East Kent Goldings (dry hopped, 5 days)

1.5 ounces UK Fuggle (dry hopped, 5 days)

Yeast:

British Ale Yeast (Wyeast 1098)

Mash at 152 degrees for 60 minutes, then add boiling water to increase mash temperature to between 165 and 170 degrees. Boil for 60 minutes. Cool to 66 degrees before pitching yeast, and ferment between 66 and 68 degrees for 6 to 9 days. Add dry hops and let rest for 4 to 6 days.

COURTESY OF JEREMY GOBIEN, COPPER KETTLE BREWING COMPANY (P. 8)

DENVER BEER CO. SMOKED LAGER

Bacon, bacon, bacon, and bacon! This clean and woody smoked lager drink is the perfect complement to summertime cookouts.

OG: 1.053, FG: 1.013, IBU: 17, SRM: 9

Malt:

5 pounds smoked malt (Bamberg)

2.5 pounds Pilsner malt

1.5 pounds Munich malt

8 ounces crystal 80-liter malt

Hops:

0.75 ounce Hallertauer Mittelfruh (60 minutes)

0.5 ounce Hallertauer Mittelfruh (10 minutes)

Yeast:

Southern German Lager Yeast (White Labs WLP838 or Wyeast 2308)

Mash at 152 degrees for 60 minutes. Boil for 60 minutes. Ferment at 54 degrees for 7 days, then allow the temperature to rise to 66 degrees for 36 hours. Lager at 36 degrees for 2 weeks.

COURTESY OF CHARLIE BERGER AND PATRICK CRAWFORD, DENVER BEER CO. (P. 11)

DRY DOCK DOUBLE IPA

If you're a fan of hop flavoring (grapefruit, pine, et cetera,) but not of the bitterness that often comes along with excessive hops, Double IPA will tickle your palate. Unlike most other double IPA recipes, this one does not use the dry-hopping method, leaving the hop flavoring without all that bitterness.

OG: 1.083, FG: 1.021, IBU: 110, SRM: 7

Malt:

14.8 pounds Golden Promise malt

Hops:

0.6 ounce Chinook (First Wort Hop)

0.3 ounce Citra (70 minutes)

0.3 ounce Columbus (50 minutes)

0.7 ounce Crystal (50 minutes)

0.5 ounce Challenger (45 minutes)

0.4 ounce Centennial (30 minutes)

0.3 ounce Cascade (20 minutes)

0.3 ounce Chinook (10 minutes)

0.8 ounce Challenger (5 minutes)

0.8 ounce Cascade (2 minutes)

0.5 ounce Columbus (flame out)

Yeast:

American Ale II Yeast (Wyeast 1272)

Mash at 152 degrees for 60 minutes. Boil for 90 minutes. Ferment at about 69 degrees until complete.

COURTESY OF KEVIN DELANGE, DRY DOCK BREWING COMPANY (P. 46)

EQUINOX ECLIPSE BROWN

The crisp, clean malty Eclipse Brown is bready, nutty, and sweet, like toffee. A very versatile style, brown ales are good complements to appetizers, entrees, and desserts.

OG: 1.053, FG: 1.013, IBU: 23, SRM: 20

Malt:

6.75 pounds pale malt

0.9 pound amber malt

0.9 pound Munich malt

10.4 ounces crystal 80-liter malt

7.2 ounces pale chocolate malt

4 ounces crystal 120-liter malt

Hops:

0.7 ounce Perle (60 minutes)

0.6 ounce Golding (10 minutes)

Yeast:

British Ale Yeast (Wyeast 1098)

Mash at 154 degrees for 60 minutes. Boil for 60 minutes. Ferment at 68 degrees until complete.

COURTESY OF EQUINOX BREWING COMPANY (P. 86)

FUNKWERKS SAISON

Saison (French for "season") is the name originally given to pale ales brewed season-ally in farmhouses in the French-speaking region of Belgium. These ales were brewed for the farm workers during harvest season. Funkwerks Saison is a celebration of the modern saison style with citrus and pepper tastes and a dry finish.

OG: 1.056, FG: 1.005, IBU: 25, SRM: 5

Malt:

4.7 pounds Pilsner malt

3.6 pounds 2-row malt

1.1 pounds Munich malt

1 pound pale wheat malt

Hops:

0.75 ounce Opal (60 minutes)

0.5 ounce Opal (15 minutes)

1 ounce Opal (flame out)

0.5 ounce Opal (dry hop, 7 days)

Yeast:

French Saison Yeast (Wyeast 3711)

Mash at 152 degrees for 60 minutes. Boil for 60 minutes. Pitch yeast at 68 degrees and allow the temperature to free rise to 73 degrees. Hold at this temperature until fermentation is complete, then dry hop with 0.5 ounces of Opal for 7 days.

COURTESY OF GORDON SCHUCK AND BRAD LINCOLN, FUNKWERKS (P. 91)

GRIMM BROTHERS SNOW DROP

When the *Reinheitsgebot* declared that German beer was only pure if it consisted solely of water, barley, hops, and yeast, kottbusser ale became all but extinct, as it contains oats, molasses, and honey. Snow Drop is Grimm Brothers' delicious homage to resurrect the style.

OG: 1.054, FG: 1.013, IBU: 16, SRM: 4

Malt:

6.8 pounds Pilsner

3.8 pounds wheat malt

0.8 pound flaked oats

Hops:

0.5 ounce Hallertauer (first wort hop)

0.5 ounce Hallertauer (75 minutes)

0.5 ounce Hallertauer (30 minutes)

0.5 ounce Hallertauer (flame out)

1 ounce Saaz (flame out)

Adjuncts:

0.6 ounce molasses

1.3 ounces clover honey

Yeast:

German Ale/Kölsch Yeast (White Labs WLP029)

Mash at 152 degrees for 60 minutes. Boil for 90 minutes, adding the molasses and clover honey in the last 5 minutes of the boil. Ferment at 70 degrees until complete, then condition for 1 week at 35 degrees.

COURTESY OF GRIMM BROTHERS BREWHOUSE (P. 109)

PAGOSA POOR RICHARD'S ALE

Poor Richard's Ale is an all-American, colonial-style ale brewed to commemorate Ben Franklin's 300th birthday. This modern-day interpretation of the colonists' brown ale is brewed with corn and spiced with molasses (a common sweetener back in the day!).

OG: 1.068, FG: 1.018, IBU: 27, SRM: 17

Malt:

7.4 pounds pale malt

2.4 pounds flaked corn

1.6 pounds biscuit malt

14 ounces special roast

2.1 ounces black patent

Hops:

0.7 ounce Kent Goldings (60 minutes)

0.7 ounce Kent Goldings (45 minutes)

0.7 ounce Kent Goldings (30 minutes)

Adjuncts:

3 ounces molasses

Yeast:

English Ale Yeast (White Labs WLP002 or Wyeast 1968)

or

Scottish Ale Yeast (White Labs WLP028 or Wyeast 1728)

Mash at 154 degrees for at least 45 minutes. Boil for 60 minutes, adding the molasses in the last 5 minutes of the boil. Ferment at 68 degrees until complete.

COURTESY OF TONY SIMMONS, PAGOSA BREWING COMPANY (P. 173)

PATEROS CREEK CACHE LA PORTER

Cache la Porter is categorized by Pateros Creek Brewing Company as a brown porter, differentiating it from other porters due to its lighter-chocolate and less-roasted coffee taste. Toasty, but not overly roasted, this 5 percent ABV brew is very quaffable.

OG: 1.051, FG: 1.013, IBU: 27, SRM: 27

Malt:
7.7 pounds 2-row malt
13.3 ounces biscuit malt
13.3 ounces special B malt
3.3 ounces chocolate malt
1.7 ounces black malt
1.7 ounces dark chocolate malt

Hops:
0.4 ounce Magnum (50 minutes)
0.4 ounce Goldings (15 minutes)
0.4 ounce Fuggle (15 minutes)
0.4 ounce Fuggle (flame out)

Yeast:
English Ale Yeast (White Labs WLP005)

Mash at 155 degrees for 60 minutes. Boil for 60 minutes. Ferment at 68 degrees for 2 weeks.

COURTESY OF STEVE JONES, PATEROS CREEK BREWING COMPANY (P. 97)

STEAMWORKS STEAM ENGINE LAGER

Refreshing, clean, and malty, Steam Engine Lager is beautiful, clear, and amber in color. Another super versatile brew, this recipe has won awards at many festivals including the GABF and the World Beer Cup.

OG: 1.050, FG: 1.010, IBU: 22, SRM: 11

Malt:

6.7 pounds pale malt
12 ounces crystal 15-liter malt
12 ounces crystal 60-liter malt
12 ounces light Munich malt
6 ounces crystal 75-liter malt

Hops:

0.4 ounce Chinook (90 minutes)
0.2 ounce Cascade (30 minutes)
1 ounce Cascade (flame out)

Yeast:

California Lager (Wyeast 2112)

Mash at 152 degrees for 60 minutes. Boil for 90 minutes. Ferment at 59 degrees until 75 percent attenuated and then let the beer rise to 64 degrees for a diacetyl rest.

COURTESY OF STEAMWORKS BREWING COMPANY (P. 174)

UPSLOPE BELGO

Belgian pale ale has become one of the more popular "experimental" styles in the US, and Upslope's Belgo is a clear example of this emerging style. Funky on the nose, the esters from the yeast give a fruity edge to this brew.

OG: 1.068, FG: 1.010, IBU: 45, SRM: 5

Malt:

7.2 pounds Marris Otter

2.5 pounds American Pilsner malt

1.3 pounds American white wheat

Hops:

2.5 ounces Fuggle, 42 IBUs total (60 minutes)

1 ounce East Kent Goldings (5 minutes)

Adjuncts:

0.5 ounce crushed organic coriander (added to mash)

1.3 pounds organic turbonado sugar

1 ounce crushed organic coriander (added to boil, 5 minutes)

Yeast:

Trappist Ale Yeast (White Labs WLP500)

Mash at 148 degrees for 60 minutes, making sure to add 0.5 ounce crushed organic coriander to the mash. Boil for 75 minutes, adding the organic turbonado sugar and 1 ounce crushed organic coriander in the last 5 minutes. Ferment between 70 and 72 degrees for 16 days, rack to secondary and condition for 7 to 14 days.

COURTESY OF UPSLOPE BREWING COMPANY (P. 70)

WIT'S END SLAM DUNKELWEIZEN

Slam Dunkelweizen combines roasted wheat with Hefeweizen yeast strains, creating a taste that mimics chocolate-chip banana bread. The Dunkelweizen style works well in any season due to its light body, fruity notes, and sweet, roasted base.

OG: 1.055, FG: 1.012, IBU: 15, SRM: 22

Malt:

4 pounds white wheat malt

2.6 pounds Pilsner malt

14 ounces honey malt

7 ounces dextrine malt

6.1 ounces Munich malt

4.7 ounces rye malt

4.7 ounces biscuit malt

4.7 ounces special B malt

4.7 ounces crystal 80-liter malt

4.7 ounces caramel wheat malt

4.7 ounces chocolate wheat malt

Hops:

0.15 ounce Columbus (60 minutes)

0.5 ounce Tettnag (30 minutes)

0.2 ounce Tettnag (15 minutes)

Yeast:

Hefeweizen Ale Yeast (Wyeast 3068 or White Labs 300)

Mash at 151 degrees for 75 minutes. Boil for 75 minutes. Pitch 1 package of yeast (a starter is NOT recommended) and ferment between 72 and 75 degrees for 5 to 7 days or until complete.

COURTESY OF SCOTT WITSOE, WIT'S END BREWING COMPANY (P. 20)

In the Kitchen

There are a lot of recipes that call for wine to be used as an ingredient, but more and more restaurants are using beer in their food. It just makes sense—beer adds a wider range of flavors than wine can. Depending on the style of beer you add to your recipe, you can get sweet, fruity, or bitter flavors; notes of chocolate or coffee; and anything and everything in between. Beer offers up more diversity than wine ever could.

This chapter offers up a handful of food recipes that feature beer as an ingredient as well as some refreshing beer cocktails that you can make at home.

Food Recipes

AGAVE WHEAT CHEESE SOUP

A spicy take on the classic beer cheese soup, this recipe will certainly warm you up! Just make sure to save some Agave Wheat to cool you down.

> $^1/_4$ cup butter or margarine
> $^1/_4$ cup all-purpose flour
> 2$^1/_2$ cups milk
> 1 cup Breckenridge Agave Wheat beer
> 2 teaspoons Worcestershire sauce
> 1½ teaspoons dry mustard
> $^1/_2$ teaspoon salt
> $^1/_4$ teaspoon (cayenne) pepper
> 2 cups shredded sharp cheddar cheese

Melt butter in large saucepan over medium heat. Stir in flour until smooth; cook 1 minute, stirring constantly. Stir in milk, Agave Wheat, Worcestershire sauce, mustard, salt, and pepper. Heat to a boil, stirring frequently. Reduce heat and simmer for 10 minutes, still stirring frequently.

Stir in cheese until melted.

COURTESY OF BRECKENRIDGE BREWERY (P. 4)

BEER-CRUSTED CHEESE DIPPERS

A gourmet twist on mozzarella sticks, these cheese dippers up the ante on everyday appetizers. The process may be a bit time-consuming, but the results are well worth the effort.

1 cup cornstarch
2 cups pale ale (Odell Brewing Company 5 Barrel Pale Ale)
4 medium eggs
1 box cheese crackers
2 cups panko
4 cups of your favorite melting cheese in ¾-inch cubes

Whisk together the cornstarch, ale, and eggs. Add the cheese crackers and the panko to a food processor and fully combine. Divide the cheese into four portions. Use your hands to mix each cheese portion individually into the slurry of ale, then strain lightly. Add this to the cracker mixture in a large bowl. Repeat this process two more times for each cheese portion. In the end, this should be a total of 3 "breadings" per portion. Let sit for at least an hour before frying at 350 degrees.

Freshcraft serves the cheese dippers topped with crumbled Gorgonzola and with house-made smoked onion ketchup and cashew-spinach pesto for dipping.

COURTESY OF LUCAS FORGY, FRESHCRAFT (P. 34)

STONEHENGE STOUT BBQ SAUCE

Can it get simpler than the instructions for this unique and delicious barbecue sauce recipe? Doubtful, but don't take my word for it. Give it a go for yourself!

¼ cup apple cider
½ teaspoon tabasco
½ tablespoon liquid smoke
⅓ cup brown sugar
1 pint (16 ounces) Stonehenge Stout beer
1½ tablespoons granulated garlic
1½ tablespoons celery seeds
1 cup Worcestershire sauce
¼ cup molasses
¼ cup chile powder
4 cups ketchup

Heat all ingredients on stove and let simmer for 20 minutes. Cool and enjoy!

COURTESY OF BULL & BUSH PUB & BREWERY (P. 22)

BLACKBERRY SAISON GLAZE

Tart meets funk in this far from boring blackberry glaze. Freshcraft suggests using the glaze on fish, but it can also double as a delicious salad dressing.

½ cup yellow onion
2 teaspoons minced garlic
1 pint blackberries, washed
½ cup sherry vinegar
1 cup water
1 cup white sugar
½ cup Funkwerks Saison, reserved at room temperature

Place all ingredients except the saison into a saucepot, adding the sugar last to prevent burning.

Bring the mixture to a boil, then reduce to a simmer. When the mixture reaches 235 degrees, remove from the heat and whisk in the saison. Allow the glaze to cool before serving.

Freshcraft uses this glaze on mahimahi served with cornbread and jalapeño corn sauté.

COURTESY OF LUCAS FORGY, FRESHCRAFT (P. 34)

HOPS & PIE IPA MAC & CHEESE

It is impossible to live in Colorado without hearing about the Hops & Pie IPA Mac & Cheese (see photo, page 36), and, honestly, this dish is even better than can be described with words. Hops & Pie spices this recipe to a perfection only achieved by years of working to find the utopian ratio of cream to pepper to fennel.

3 cups cream
1 teaspoon fennel seeds, whole
1 teaspoon coriander seeds, whole
1 teaspoon black peppercorns, whole
2 each fresh bay leaves
1 cup sharp cheddar, shredded
To taste: cracked black pepper
To taste: tapatio
3 cups elbow macaroni, cooked
1 cup peas, cooked
¼ cup braised smoked ham hock, shredded
¼ cup Hops & Pie IPA from Strange Brewing or other West Coast–style IPA
1 tablespoon bacon, chopped
¼ cup bread crumbs

In a sauce pan, add cream, fennel seeds, coriander seeds, peppercorns, and bay leaves. Turn heat up to high and bring to a boil. Once a boil is reached, reduce heat to medium and stir constantly to prevent burning.

Once cream is reduced, strain through a fine mesh strainer into another saucepan. Return pan with strained cream to a medium flame and stir in the sharp cheddar. Add cracked black pepper and tapatio to taste.

Add macaroni, peas, and ham hock to the pan and stir well. Add IPA and continue stirring until hot. Add salt and pepper to taste and place in a large ramekin. Top with chopped bacon and bread crumbs

Bake in oven at 400 degrees until bread crumbs become golden brown and crispy.

COURTESY OF LEAH AND DREW WATSON, HOPS & PIE (P. 36)

VANILLA PORTER BEERAMISU

Anyone who has told you that beer cannot be classy is wrong, and here is your proof. Also, "beeramisu" is just fun to say. Impress and entertain your friends with this fantastic recipe!

1 cup heavy whipping cream
8 ounces mascarpone cheese—Italian cream cheese
1 cup powdered sugar
1 tablespoon vanilla
2 eggs
48 lady finger cookies
12 ounces Breckenridge Vanilla Porter
½ cup cocoa powder

Whip heavy cream to soft peaks and set aside. Combine mascarpone, sugar, vanilla, and eggs by whipping them together. Fold the whipped cream into the cheese mixture. Quickly dip the lady fingers (one at a time) into the vanilla porter. Place these in a glass, 8-inch by 8-inch casserole dish, making a single layer of dipped cookies. Cover the cookies with the cheese and cream mixture (1/2-inch thick). Dust with cocoa powder and repeat the process. Finish with dusted cocoa. Refrigerate for at least 2 hours before serving.

COURTESY OF BRECKENRIDGE BREWERY (P. 4)

STOUT CREME BRÛLÉE

This rich dessert is truly a mouthful to behold. It's decadent, creamy, and lavish—your tastebuds will thank you, over and over again.

15 ounces cream
14 ounces milk
2 whole eggs
7 egg yolks
1¾ cups sugar
7 ounces Denver Beer Co. or Upslope Stout brewed with cherries
1 ounce candied orange peel
1 blood orange cut into six segments

Warm the cream and milk together, then whisk together the whole eggs, yolks, and sugar; temper the egg mixture into the milk and cream mix. Return the mixture to the heat while whisking until nape (the mixture should coat your finger). Remove from heat and add the stout.

Pour into brûlé ramekins and bake at 300 degrees for 45 minutes in a water bath.

Finish with fresh blood orange segments and candied peel.

COURTESY OF KEVIN BURKE, COLT & GRAY (P. 31)

Beer Cocktails

THE BELGIAN SUNSET

Who needs dessert when you can have this cocktail? While there are many stout and fruit beer combinations being made out there these days, this combination of creamy milk stout and tart raspberry is truly mind-blowing.

6 ounces Left Hand Milk Stout Nitro
4 ounces framboise (Freshcraft typically uses Timmerman's)
Cocoa sugar*

Rim** a tulip glass with cocoa sugar, then fill the glass with the stout and framboise; no premixing needed.

*Cocoa Sugar: 1 part cocoa powder to 2 parts super-fine sugar. Super-fine sugar can be purchased or made by putting table sugar in a blender/food processor and pulsing in 2- to 4-second bursts until granules are very fine.

**Rimming a glass: Coat a flat surface, such as the lid from a plastic food storage container, with a small layer of simple syrup. Spread a fine layer of cocoa sugar on a second lid. Lightly press the rim of the glass in the syrup. Lift straight up, keeping the glass upside down for a moment to allow any excess syrup to drip off. At a 45-degree angle press the rim of the glass in the cocoa sugar and roll until the entire rim is coated.

COURTESY OF AARON FORGY, FRESHCRAFT (P. 34)

EUCLIDIAN 75

This concoction is a controlled explosion of bitter, sweet, and sour on your tongue. Mix it up and let the fireworks fly!

1.5 ounces Leopold Bros. Gin
0.5 ounce fresh lemon juice
0.5 ounce simple syrup
7 ounces of Crabtree Berliner Weiss

Mix together the gin, lemon juice, and syrup. Top with Berliner Weiss.

COURTESY OF RYAN CONKLIN, EUCLID HALL BAR & KITCHEN (P. 32)

FRONT-RANGE SHANDY

Originally made from beer and lemon soda, a shandy is a glass of light and fizzy fun. Colt & Gray adds some adult to their shandy by upping the ante with some campari and imperial IPA.

> 1.5 ounces campari
> 0.75 ounce ginger syrup*
> 0.75 ounce lemon Juice
> 6 to 7 ounces imperial IPA**

Combine campari, syrup, and lemon in a mixing tin with plenty of ice. Shake firmly and deliberately for 15 seconds. Strain contents into tall Pilsner glass and top with IPA.

*To make ginger syrup: Bring 1 cup of sugar and 1 cup of water to a boil, then take the mixture off the heat and add ¼ cup of finely diced ginger root. Let steep for 20 minutes, strain, and refrigerate before use.

**Make sure to use an imperial IPA to stand up to the character of the campari. We have been most successful using Avery DuganA, Great Divide Hercules, and Upslope 2xIPA.

COURTESY OF KEVIN BURKE, COLT & GRAY (P. 31)

RUSTY BUS

A thicker variation of the Belgian Sunset cocktail (page 203), the Rusty Bus mixes chocolate with cherry into a malty sweet, brown-ale dream. A dangerous concoction, this drinkable dessert cocktail is best enjoyed in slow sips.

> 1 ounce Van Gogh Dutch Chocolate Vodka
> ½ ounce Luxardo Cherry Liqueur
> 8½ ounces Avery Ellie's Brown Ale

Add vodka and cherry liqueur in a glass. Top off with ale.

COURTESY OF THE WEST END TAVERN (P. 78)

Pub Crawls

While Colorado has more breweries than any state except California, it can be quite a trek to visit some of them when traveling from gateway cities like Denver, Boulder, and Fort Collins. In truth Colorado probably isn't the first state you think of as an easy place to do a bar and brewery crawl. Outside of Denver, Boulder, and Fort Collins, bar crawls aren't really viable in Colorado due to distances between venues and lack of public transportation. That said, those three urban hubs are fantastic places to explore the great beer on offer.

Downtown Denver

Denver is the easiest of Colorado's larger cities to do a bar crawl because you can easily walk between every venue. There are 11 best bars and taprooms that can be strung together in downtown to fit a crawl of whatever size or duration you and your party desire.

If you want to hit all 11 stops, begin on the west side of downtown at **Euclid Hall Bar & Kitchen,** 1317 14th St., Denver, CO 80202; (303) 534-4255. Euclid serves some of the finest beer-centric food in the city and offers up a fresh and carefully curated selection of craft taps and a long list of craft beer in bottles and cans. There are few better places to begin a bar crawl in Denver.

Walk 2 blocks east and catch the free 16th Street mall ride bus (it runs every few minutes) 4 blocks south to:

Rock Bottom Restaurant & Brewery, 1001 16th St., #100, Denver, CO 80265; (303) 534-7616. This is another great place to eat a little more food and the only place to try some of the most creative small-batch beers brewed anywhere in the nationwide Rock Bottom empire. It's the original Rock Bottom and is one of the only locations that bottles many of its beers to go. Ask your server to show you the to-go cooler.

Return to the 16th Street mall ride bus and ride it 5 blocks north to Blake Street to:

Freshcraft, 1530 Blake St., Denver, CO 80202; (303) 758-9608 (between 15th and 16th Streets). Freshcraft has 20 taps of the best-selected craft beer in the city and a bottle list that numbers more than 100. **Tip:** Ask your server if you can see the extra-special, rare-bottle list. Freshcraft serves a seasonal menu of beer-inspired American comfort food. It's some of the best beer food in Denver.

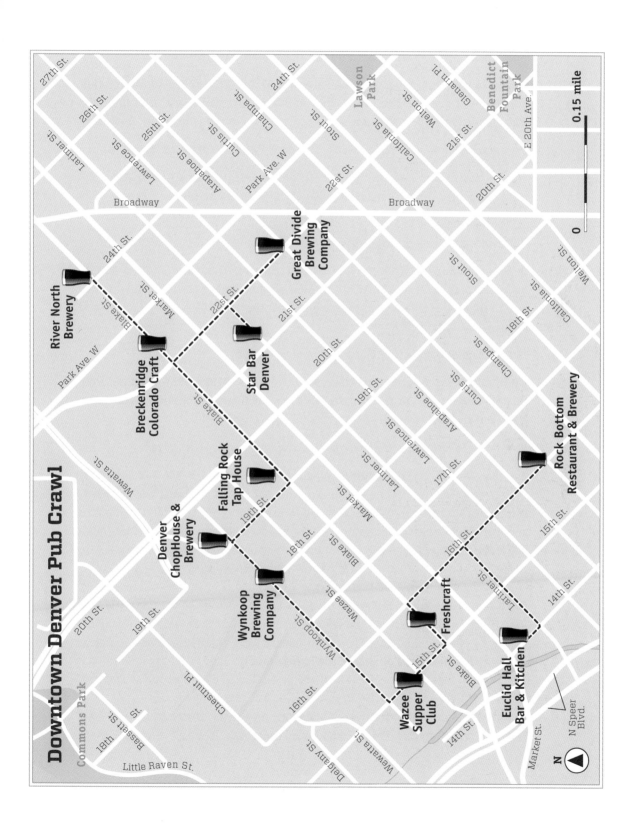

Downtown Denver Pub Crawl

Walk 1 block north to the corner of Wazee Street and 15th Street to:

Wazee Supper Club, 1600 15th St., Denver, CO 80202; (303) 623-9518. Wazee offers up 20 taps of great beer to choose from and if you're still hungry, or in need of a midcrawl pick-me-up, then it also serves some of the best pizza in downtown Denver.

Onward to the fifth stop. Walk 1 block north to Wynkoop Street and 3 blocks east to:

Wynkoop Brewing Company, 1634 18th St., Denver, CO 80202; (303) 297-2700. More great beer-centric food and some 20 taps of house-brewed beer of every imaginable style and strength. No bar crawl is complete without a pint here.

The sixth stop is 1 block east of Wynkoop Brewing Company:

Denver ChopHouse & Brewery, 1735 19th St., Denver, CO 80202; (303) 296-0800. A high-end steak house and brewery, ChopHouse pours some of the best house-brewed beer in the state. Find a seat at the bar and order the Wild Turkey Barrel Conditioned Stout. You will not be sorry.

Two blocks south of the ChopHouse is stop number seven:

Falling Rock Tap House, 1919 Blake St., Denver, CO 80202; (303) 293-8338. More than 70 taps of some of the best beer in the world await you at Falling Rock. Also check out the extensive bottle list.

Walk 3 blocks east on Blake Street and 2 blocks south on 22nd Street to:

Star Bar Denver, 2137 Larimer St., Denver, CO 80205; (720) 328-2420. Star Bar is one of my favorite bars in Denver. No other bar has its dark and moody charm. Fourteen of the best curated beer taps and an excellent selection of local craft spirits and canned craft beer await you here. Star Bar does not serve food, allowing for a quick visit to Biker Jim's across the street for one of his exotic meat sausages.

Located 2 blocks south of Star Bar Denver is:

Great Divide Brewing Company, 2201 Arapahoe St., Denver, CO 80205; (303) 296-9460. Great Divide pours all of its familiar year-round and seasonals and some one-off special beers as well. There is a to-go cooler by the entrance and now is a great chance to buy one of the brewery's comfy hoodies.

Located just 5 blocks north of Great Divide is:

Breckenridge Colorado Craft, 2220 Blake St., Denver, CO 80205; (303) 297-3644. Thirty-two taps of Breckenridge and beers from other Colorado breweries await you here, as well as a menu of all-American bar food should you need a snack or something more substantial.

Located 2 blocks east of Breckenridge is the 11th and final stop:

River North Brewery, 22401 Blake St., Denver, CO 80205; (303) 296-2617. Specializing in beers brewed with Belgian yeast, River North is one of Denver's newest breweries and is the perfect bookend to any tour of the city's vibrant craft-beer scene.

Denver: Highland–Berkeley

Located a very short distance northwest of downtown Denver is the city's Highland and Berkeley neighborhoods, which between them make for a nice little bar crawl.

We begin at **Denver Beer Co.,** 1695 Platte St., Denver, CO 80202; (303) 433-2739. One of Denver's newer breweries, Denver Beer Co. has a lovely outdoor beer garden and an ever-changing selection of beers. The brewery prides itself on brewing new beers every week. Food trucks are usually parked just outside in the evening, making for a good bar crawl pit stop.

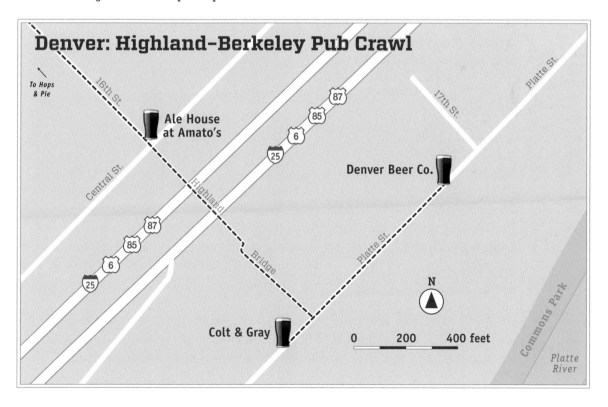

Located just 1 block west of the Denver Beer Co. is our second stop:

Colt & Gray, 1553 Platte St., Denver, CO 80202; (303) 477-1447. Colt & Gray is an excellent craft-beer and spirit-focused restaurant that always has carefully selected taps of craft beer and a nice bottle and can list. The food here is outstanding. Highlights include fried oysters, snails with garlic herb butter, bacon and cashew caramel corn, and crispy pig trotter. A wide selection of house-made charcuterie and cheese is offered a la carte. Larger plates are also available.

A quick walk across the bridge that goes over I-25 leads to the third stop:

Ale House at Amato's, 2501 16th St., Denver, CO 80211; (303) 433-9734. This bar and restaurant has 40 taps, 15 dedicated to the beers of Breckenridge Brewery and Wynkoop Brewing Company, and 25 dedicated to beers from Colorado and out-of-state craft breweries. The food menu is extensive and designed to pair well with beer.

Our fourth and final Highland-Berkeley neighborhood crawl stop requires a quick 5-minute cab ride to:

Hops & Pie, 3920 Tennyson St., Denver, CO 80212; (303) 477-7000. Hops & Pie is one of the best beer bars and restaurants in Denver. Its high-quality menu of pizzas and beer comfort food is outstanding and is the perfect complement to its carefully curated 10 taps of American craft beer. Hops & Pie also maintains a nice bottle list, so be sure to ask to see it.

Uptown Denver

This crawl requires a little more walking than the downtown crawl but is easily walkable on one of Denver's more than 300 sunny days.

Our crawl begins at **Pint's Pub Brewery & Freehouse,** 221 W. 13th Ave., Denver, CO 80204; (303) 534-7543. Pint's Pub is a British-themed brewpub that brews a nice selection of English, Scottish, American, and German ales and lagers, including two that are only available cask conditioned. The cask-conditioned English IPA is an absolute must try for hopheads and a perfect pairing to some vinegar-doused fish-and-chips.

Located 8 blocks east and 2 blocks north of Pint's Pub is:

Cheeky Monk Belgian Beer Cafe, 534 E. Colfax Ave., Denver, CO 80203; (303) 861-0347. The Cheeky Monk is heaven for Belgian beer lovers, pouring a comprehensive selection of classic and modern imported Belgian beers and American Belgian styles.

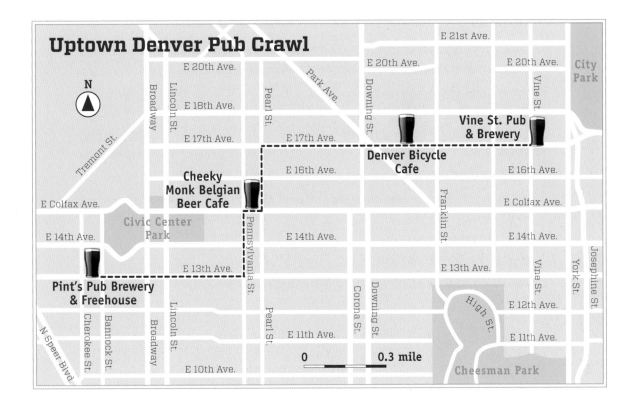

The food menu is Flemish inspired and includes a hearty selection of mussels, frites, stews, and waffles. Don't forget to browse the bottle list as well.

Located 2 blocks north and 14 short blocks east of Cheeky Monk is the third stop at:

Denver Bicycle Cafe, 1308 E. 17th Ave., Denver, CO 80218; (720) 446-8029. This coffee shop meets craft beer bar meets bicycle repair shop is one of the best places in Denver to taste beers from some of the area's smaller and newer breweries. The cafe has six taps and stocks virtually every canned craft beer brewed in Colorado. In short, the list is long.

Twelve short blocks east is the fourth and final stop on the uptown bar crawl:

Vine St. Pub & Brewery, 1700 Vine St., Denver, CO 80206; (303) 388-2337. This relaxed bar and restaurant offers fresh and seasonal food, a vast selection of house-brewed beer, and six or seven guest taps. The perfect finish to a good beer tour of Uptown Denver.

South Denver

Depending on how you want to approach this bar crawl, you will need to either rent bikes or take a couple of short cab rides from bar to bar.

Our South Denver bar crawl begins just southwest of downtown in an industrial area at the taproom of **Strange Brewing Company**, 1330 Zuni St., Denver, CO 80204; (720) 985-2337. Strange brews all manner of American, British, and Belgian beer styles and is a great place to kick off a tour of some of Denver's lesser-known beer spots.

A 10-minute ride just east along 13th Avenue and south on Kalamath Avenue will land you at:

Renegade Brewing Company, 925 W. 9th Ave., Denver, CO 80204; (720) 401-4089. Renegade is one of Denver's class of 2011 of new breweries and has built a solid reputation for itself as a neighborhood brewery. Renegade's Rye IPA is a must sample.

Located 4 blocks south of Renegade is the taproom and restaurant of:

Breckenridge Brewery, 471 Kalamath St., Denver, CO 80204; (303) 573-0431. In addition to a full tap list of Breckenridge year-round, seasonal, and special one-off beers, the kitchen cooks up a full menu of top-quality barbecue.

A 6-block cab or bike ride south of Breckenridge Brewery will get you to:

Rackhouse Pub, 208 S. Kalamath St., Denver, CO 80223; (720) 570-7824. The Rackhouse has one of the best beer- and whiskey-friendly menus of food in Denver. A good thing as it pours 40 taps of Colorado brewed beer and has a list of some 60 world-class whiskeys. The Rackhouse is located in the same building as Stranahan's Colorado Whiskey, a famous whiskey distillery.

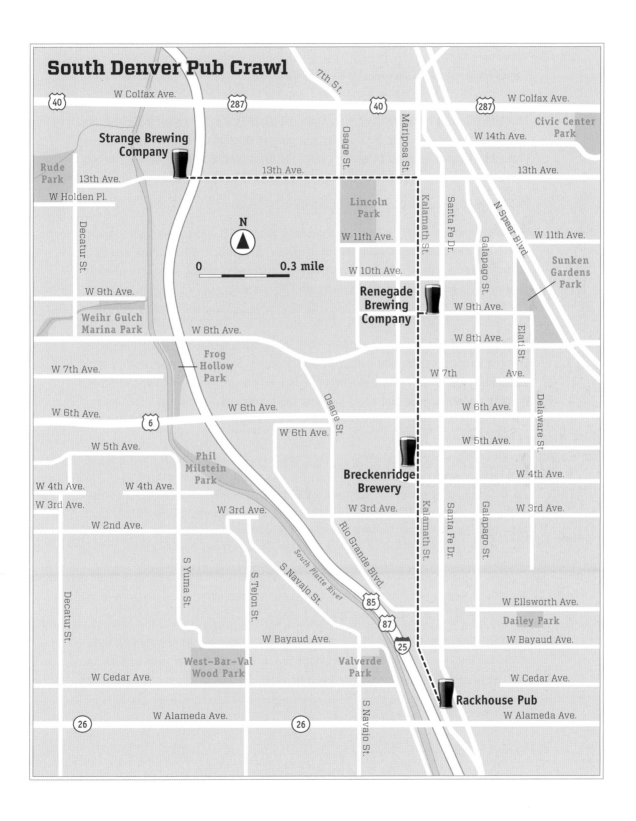

South Denver Pub Crawl

7th St.

W Colfax Ave.

Strange Brewing Company

Rude Park

13th Ave.

13th Ave.

W Holden Pl.

Osage St.

Mariposa St.

Civic Center Park

W 14th Ave.

13th Ave.

Lincoln Park

Kalamath St.

Santa Fe Dr.

W 11th Ave.

N Speer Blvd.

W 11th Ave.

Sunken Gardens Park

Decatur St.

W 9th Ave.

N

0   0.3 mile

W 10th Ave.

Galapago St.

Renegade Brewing Company

W 9th Ave.

W 8th Ave.

Elati St.

Weihr Gulch Marina Park

W 8th Ave.

Frog Hollow Park

W 7th Ave.

W 7th   Ave.

W 6th Ave.

Osage St.

W 6th Ave.

W 6th Ave.

Delaware St.

W 5th Ave.

Phil Milstein Park

W 5th Ave.

W 4th Ave.   W 4th Ave.

Breckenridge Brewery

W 4th Ave.

W 3rd Ave.

W 3rd Ave.

W 3rd Ave.

W 3rd Ave.

W 2nd Ave.

S Yuma St.

S Tejon St.

S Navajo St.

South Platte River

Rio Grande Blvd.

Kalamath St.

Santa Fe Dr.

Galapago St.

Decatur St.

W Ellsworth Ave.

Dailey Park

W Bayaud Ave.

W Bayaud Ave.

West-Bar-Val Wood Park

W Cedar Ave.

Valverde Park

W Cedar Ave.

Rackhouse Pub

W Alameda Ave.

S Navajo St.

W Alameda Ave.

Boulder

Our Boulder bar crawl begins at The West End Tavern, one of the best beer bars in the US.

The West End Tavern, 926 Pearl St., Boulder, CO 80302; (303) 444-3535. With its superbly curated tap and bottle list, warming atmosphere, exclusive house beer brewed by Victory Brewing Company of Pennsylvania, and a menu of to die for food, the West End Tavern is the best place to begin a good beer tour of Boulder.

Two blocks south and 3 blocks east of the West End Tavern is:

Walnut Brewery, 1123 Walnut St., Boulder, CO 80302; (303) 447-1345. Walnut Brewery is the brewpub that spawned a thousand others in the form of the Rock Bottom empire. The Walnut location, however, has always retained its own identity, personality, and beers. A fitting second stop in our tour.

The third stop is 3 blocks east and 2 blocks north of Walnut Brewery:

Mountain Sun Pub & Brewery, 1535 Pearl St., Boulder, CO 80302; (303) 546-0886. Few places sum up Boulder beer culture better than the happy-go-lucky, hippie vibe of Mountain Sun on Pearl Street. The house beers are outstanding, the service friendly and educated, and the food fresh and seasonal. It's always a struggle to leave a Mountain Sun brewpub, but this is a bar crawl after all, so onward to stop number four.

A 10-minute walk 4 blocks south on 16th Street and 7 blocks east along Arapahoe Avenue will lead you to:

Backcountry Pizza & Tap House, 2319 Arapahoe Ave., Boulder, CO 80302; (303) 449-4285. Few bars in Colorado besides Falling Rock Tap House in Denver rival Backcountry's globe-spanning selection of American craft and imported beer. Food is well represented too with a wide selection of pizzas and sandwiches.

Another 10-minute walk east along Arapahoe Avenue and north along 33rd Street will land you at the fifth stop on this crawl:

Twisted Pine Brewing Company, 3201 Walnut St., Boulder, CO 80301; (303) 786-9270. Twisted Pine pours a lot of special beers in addition to its year-rounds and seasonals. Be sure to sample its famous chili beers, Billy's Chilies, and the extra-hot Ghost Face Killah.

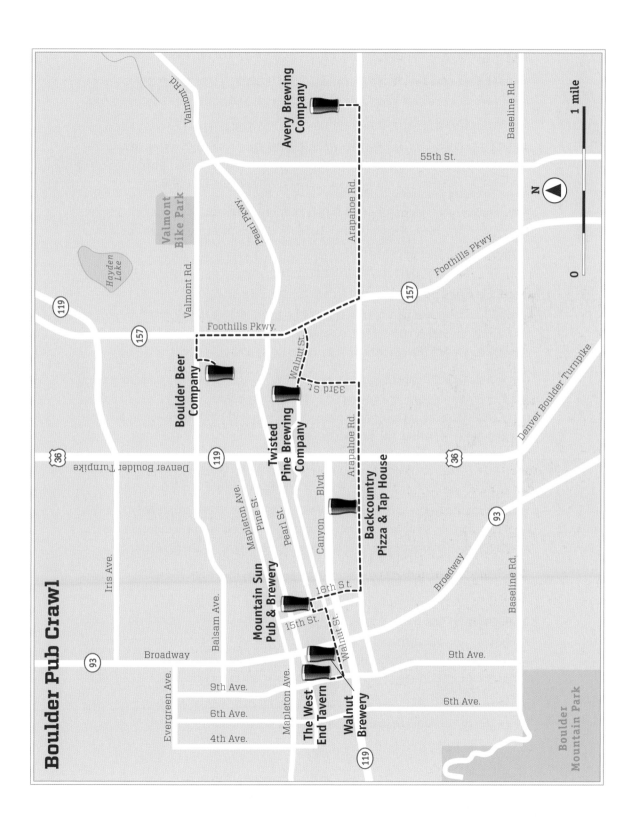

Boulder Pub Crawl

Avery Brewing Company

Boulder Beer Company

Twisted Pine Brewing Company

Backcountry Pizza & Tap House

Mountain Sun Pub & Brewery

The West End Tavern

Walnut Brewery

Valmont Bike Park

Hayden Lake

Boulder Mountain Park

N

0   1 mile

Valmont Rd.

Pearl Pkwy.

Foothills Pkwy.

Walnut St.

33rd St.

Arapahoe Rd.

55th St.

Baseline Rd.

Denver Boulder Turnpike

Broadway

Arapahoe Rd.

Canyon Blvd.

Pearl St.

Pine St.

Mapleton Ave.

16th St.

15th St.

Walnut St.

Iris Ave.

Balsam Ave.

Broadway

9th Ave.

6th Ave.

4th Ave.

Evergreen Ave.

Mapleton Ave.

9th Ave.

6th Ave.

Baseline Rd.

Foothills Pkwy

Denver Boulder Turnpike

119

157

119

157

36

93

93

119

36

A 1.25-mile walk or cab ride will get you to the brewery and taproom of:

Boulder Beer Company, 2880 Wilderness Place, Boulder, CO 80301; (303) 444-8448. This is one of the oldest craft breweries in America, and a trip here to enjoy a fresh pint of Hazed and Infused is an absolute rite of passage.

A quick 10-minute cab or bike ride from Boulder Beer Company will get you to the seventh and final stop on this Boulder beer tour:

Avery Brewing Company, 5763 Arapahoe Ave., Boulder, CO 80303; (303) 440-4324. This taproom pours upwards of 20 different Avery beers and is open until 11 p.m. every day of the week. Keep an eye on the ABV of beers at Avery, though, more than a few are as strong as wine. Cheers.

Fort Collins

A good bar crawl through the pretty college town of Fort Collins takes in no less than seven breweries and three bars and with a little planning can be undertaken entirely on foot in the space of an afternoon and evening.

Our Fort Collins bar crawl begins on the far east of the city at the home of saison and farmhouse ale brewers **Funkwerks,** 1900 E. Lincoln Ave., Fort Collins, CO 80524; (970) 482-3865. The taproom here pours every color and shade of saison or Belgian-inspired table beer that the brewery creates, including many small-batch, one-off affairs.

Just under a mile west along East Lincoln Avenue from Funkwerks is:

Fort Collins Brewery, 1020 E. Lincoln Ave., Fort Collins, CO 80524; (970) 472-1499. Both the taproom and the restaurant are worth checking out here. Keep an eye out for special one-off brews. The beer-centric menu at Gravity 1020 is outstanding.

Less than 100 yards farther west along East Lincoln Avenue from Fort Collins Brewery is:

Odell Brewing Company, 800 E. Lincoln Ave., Fort Collins, CO 80524; (970) 498-9070. The taproom here pours a dizzying number of year-rounds, seasonals, and special releases and dedicates quite a few taps to limited pilot beers. This is one of the best taprooms in the state. Be sure to browse the to-go cooler before you leave.

A 5-minute walk farther west along East Lincoln Avenue and north along First Street brings you to the fourth stop on our Fort Collins crawl:

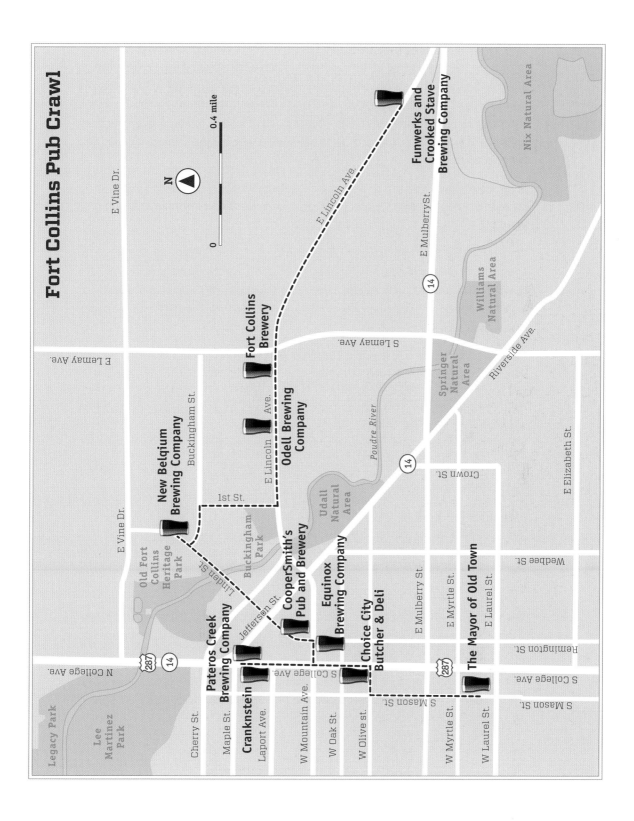

Fort Collins Pub Crawl

N

0   0.4 mile

E Vine Dr.

E Lemay Ave.

E Lincoln Ave.

Funwerks and
Crooked Stave
Brewing Company

E Mulberry St.

Nix Natural Area

Williams
Natural Area

14

S Lemay Ave.

Riverside Ave.

Fort Collins
Brewery

Odell Brewing
Company

E Lincoln Ave.

Springer
Natural
Area

Poudre River

New Belgium
Brewing Company

Buckingham St.

1st St.

Buckingham
Park

Udall
Natural
Area

14

Crown St.

E Elizabeth St.

E Vine Dr.

Old Fort
Collins
Heritage
Park

Linden St.

CooperSmith's
Pub and Brewery

Equinox
Brewing Company

Choice City
Butcher & Deli

Wedbee St.

The Mayor of Old Town

Legacy Park

Lee
Martinez
Park

Cherry St.

Maple St.

N College Ave.

287

14

Pateros Creek
Brewing Company

Cranknstein

Laport Ave.

Jefferson St.

S College Ave.

E Mulberry St.

E Myrtle St.

Remington St.

E Laurel St.

S College Ave.

W Mountain Ave.

W Oak St.

W Olive st.

S Mason St.

S Mason St.

W Myrtle St.

W Laurel St.

287

New Belgium Brewing Company, 500 Linden St., Fort Collins, CO 80524; (970) 221-0524. New Belgium is one of the largest craft breweries in America. Tours need to be booked in advance on New Belgium's website. Tours are free but in high demand year-round, so book your tour well in advance. The tour is extensive and informative and takes about 90 minutes. In lieu of a tour, the brewery taproom will more than suffice. Many one-off and special beers are poured here alongside more familiar New Belgium offerings.

Upon leaving the beer mecca that is New Belgium, walk south down Linden Street toward the center of Fort Collins. Our first stop in the downtown area and fifth stop overall is:

CooperSmith's Pub and Brewery, 5 Old Town Sq., Fort Collins, CO 80524; (970) 498-0483. CooperSmith's is one of the oldest and best brewpubs in Colorado. The number of different house-brewed beers that CooperSmith's brews in a given year is jaw-dropping, and the quality is consistent. The food menu here is wide-ranging, hearty, and satisfying.

Our sixth destination is just across the street from CooperSmith's:

Equinox Brewing Company, 133 Remington St., Fort Collins, CO 80524; (970) 484-1368. Opened in 2010, Equinox offers beer that is creative and of extremely high standard. The taproom has a cozy and friendly neighborhood feel, especially compared to the more industrial scale of the bigger breweries along Lincoln Avenue.

A quick 2-minute walk west on East Mountain Avenue and north along North College Avenue brings you to:

Cranknstein, 215 N. College Ave., Unit A, Fort Collins, CO 80524; (970) 818-7008. The seventh stop on our tour is this hybrid craft beer bar, coffee shop, and bike repair shop. Simply put, it's one of the more unique places to grab a good beer in Fort Collins. The well-curated taps are a mix of the best and most-experimental beers brewed in the state.

You won't have to walk far to the eighth stop on this crawl. It's just across the street:

Pateros Creek Brewing Company, 242 N. College Ave., Unit B, Fort Collins, CO 80524; (970) 484-7222. This new brewery opened for business in 2011 and specializes in more sessionable lower ABV beers. In addition to full-bodied year-round and seasonal beers, make sure you try whatever is pouring on the Outlaw small-batch tap handle.

A short walk south along North College Avenue (which turns into South College Avenue) will lead you to:

Choice City Butcher & Deli, 104 W. Olive St., Fort Collins, CO 80524; (970) 490-2489. Choice City is a meat- and beer-lover's delight. The 40 taps behind the bar pour some of the rarest beers you'll find in the state, and there is a nice list of bottles to supplement the taps. There's also no better place to get a hearty end-of-the-day meal. The selection of high-quality meat sandwiches here is a wonderful, wonderful thing.

Our final stop in Fort Collins is short 10-minute walk along South Mason Street to:

The Mayor of Old Town, 632 S. Mason St., Fort Collins, CO 80524; (970) 682-2410. Here you will find 100 carefully sourced taps of beer from Colorado, from across the country, and from around the world. There is also an extensive all-day breakfast sandwich and pizza menu.

Appendix

Beer Lover's Pick List

Amber Ale, Crazy Mountain Brewing Company, American Amber Ale, 148

Barley Wine, Estes Park Brewery, American Barleywine, 108

Barrel Aged Yeti, Great Divide Brewing Company, Whiskey Barrel-Aged Imperial Stout, 15

Bear-Ass Brown, Silverton Brewing Company, English Brown Ale, 164

Beaver Stubble Stout, Big Beaver Brewing Company, Foreign Extra Stout, 105

Berliner Weisse Ale, Crabtree Brewing Company, Berliner Weisse, 107

Bligh's Barleywine Ale, Dry Dock Brewing Company, English Barleywine, 48

Blue Moon Belgian White Ale, Blue Moon Brewing Company at the Sandlot, Witbier, 4

Bridal Veil Rye Pale Ale, Telluride Brewing Company, Rye Beer, 167

Butt Head Bock Lager, Tommyknocker Brewery, Bock, 116

Centurion Barleywine, Golden City Brewery, American Barleywine, 51

Cherry Kriek, Strange Brewing Company, Fruit Lambic, 19

Coors Banquet, Coors Brewing Company (MillerCoors), American Adjunct Lager, 46

Deviant Dale's, Oskar Blues Brewery, American IPA, 114

Doc's American Porter, Crystal Springs Brewing Company, American Porter, 67

Don't Call Me Wit, Black Fox Brewing Company, Witbier, 126

Double Chocolate, Fort Collins Brewery, American Double Stout, 90

Durango Blueberry Wheat Ale, Durango Brewing Co., Fruit Beer, 161

Eclipse Brown, Equinox Brewing Company, American Brown Ale, 87

ESB Special Ale, Ska Brewing Company, ESB, 165

Foreign Style Stout, Upslope Brewing Company, Foreign Extra Stout, 72

Friek, Odell Brewing Company, Fruit Lambic, 96

Ghost Face Killah, Twisted Pine Brewing Company, Chili Beer, 69

Graham Cracker Porter, Denver Beer Co., American Porter, 13

Greenade Organic Double IPA, Asher Brewing Company, Double IPA, 61

The Griffin, Grimm Brothers Brewhouse, Hefeweizen, 109

Hypothesis, River North Brewery, American Double IPA, 18

Independence Pass IPA, Aspen Brewing Company, American IPA, 145

Key Lime Cheesecake, Rocky Mountain Brewery, Fruit Beer, 129

Killer Penguin, Boulder Beer Company, American Barleywine, 66

Kitchen Sink Porter, Wit's End Brewing Company, American Porter, 21

La Folie, New Belgium Brewing Company, Flanders Red Ale, 94

Lao Wang Lager, CAUTION: Brewery Company, Happoshu, 8

Latzenbier, BierWerks Brewery, Latzenbier, 125

Mañana, Del Norte Brewing Company, American Amber Lager, 11

Mexican Chocolate Stout, Copper Kettle Brewing Company, American Stout, 9

Michelob AmberBock, Anheuser-Busch, Fort Collins, Bock, 83

Old Jubilation Ale, Avery Brewing Company, Old Ale, 64

Olde Town Brown, Arvada Beer Company, American Brown Ale, 45

Peche Belgian-Style Ale Aged in Oak Wine Barrels with Peaches Added, AC Golden Brewing Company (MillerCoors), American Wild Ale, 43

Puddle Jumper Pale Ale, Lone Tree Brewing Company, American Pale Ale, 53

Rye Porter, Revolution Brewing, Rye Beer, 162

Ryeteous Rye IPA, Renegade Brewing Company, Rye Beer, 16

Snowy River Vanilla Porter, Pateros Creek Brewing Company, American Porter, 98

Stranahan's Breckenridge Well Built ESB, Breckenridge Brewery, ESB, 6

Stranger Blonde, Bonfire Brewing, American Blonde Ale, 146

Super Chicken, Grand Lake Brewing Company, American Barleywine, 150

Surette, Crooked Stave Brewing Company, Saison, 85

Tropic King, Funkwerks, Saison, 92

Vanilla Caramel Porter, Elk Mountain Brewing, American Porter, 50

Wake Up Dead Stout, Left Hand Brewing Company, Russian Imperial Stout, 112

Winter Warlock Oatmeal Stout, Bristol Brewing Company, Oatmeal Stout, 128

Photo Credits

Photos on pp. vi, 3, 5, 6, 12, 13, 19, 21, 24, 27, 28, 48, 69, 74, 76, 85, 125, 150, and 155 by Lee Williams.

Photos on pp. 7, 9, 11, 14, 16, 18, 34, 51, 52, 60, 61, 63, 68, 77, 82, 93, 106, 107, 117, 119, and 148 by Sean Buchan.

Photos on pp. 49, 53, 54, 56, 57, 67, 87, 89, 95, 104, 111, 126, 127, 131, 133, 135, 136, 139, and 141 by Stevie Caldarola.

p. iv, licensed by Shutterstock.com; p. 23, Bull & Bush; p. 33, Euclid Hall; p. 35, Freshcraft; p. 36, Hops & Pie; p. 47, Dry Dock; p. 64, Avery Brewing Co.; pp. 65, 66, Boulder Beer Co.; pp. 71, 72, Upslope; p. 79, West End Tavern; p. 94, New Belgium; p. 97, Pateros Creek; pp. 113, 114, 121, Oskar Blues; p. 165, Ska Brewing.

Index

A

AC Golden Brewing Company
   (MillerCoors), 42
Agave Wheat Cheese Soup, 196
Ale House at Amato's, 30, 208
Amicas Pizza & Microbrewery, 130
Anheuser-Busch, Fort Collins, 82
Arvada Beer Company, 44
Asher Brewing Company, 60
Aspen Brewing Company, 144
Avery Brewing Company, 62, 214
Avery Czar Imperial Stout, 183

B

Backcountry Brewery, 151
Backcountry Pizza & Tap House,
   77, 212
Beer-Crusted Cheese Dippers, 197
Belgian Sunset, The, 202
Bierwerks Brewery, 124
Big Beaver Brewing Company, 104
Big Beers, Belgians and Barleywines
   Festival, 176
Blackberry Saison Glaze, 198
Black Fox Brewing Company, 125
Blue Moon Brewing Company at the
   Sandlot, 2
Bonfire Brewing, 145
Boulder Beer Company, 64, 214
Boulder IPA Festival, 181
Boulder pub crawl, 212
Boulder SourFest, 178
Boulder Strong Ale Festival, 177

Breckenridge Brewery, 4, 210
Breckenridge Colorado Craft,
   30, 206
Breckenridge Lucky U IPA, 184
Bristol Brewing Company, 127
Bull & Bush Pub & Brewery, 22

C

Carbondale Beer Works, 152
Carver Brewing Company, 168
CAUTION: Brewing Company, 6
Cheeky Monk Belgian Beer Cafe,
   31, 208
Choice City Butcher & Deli,
   100, 217
Colorado Boy Pub & Brewery, 169
Colorado Brewers' Festival, 178
Colorado Mountain Brewery, 131
Colt & Gray, 31, 208
CooperSmith's Pub and Brewery,
   99, 216
Coors Brewing Company
   (MillerCoors), 45
Copper Kettle Brewing Company, 8
Copper Kettle English Style Black
   IPA, 185
Crabtree Brewing Company, 105
Craft Lager & Small Batch
   Festival, 180
Cranknstein, 100, 216
Crazy Mountain Brewing Company, 147
Crooked Stave Brewing Company, 84
Crystal Springs Brewing Company, 66

D

Dad & Dude's Breweria, 54
Del Norte Brewing Company, 10
Denver: Highland-Berkeley pub
   crawl, 207
Denver Beer Co., 11, 207
Denver Beer Co. Smoked
   Lager, 186
Denver Bicycle Cafe, 32, 209
Denver ChopHouse & Brewery,
   24, 206
Denver Rare Beer Tasting, 181
Dillon Dam Brewery, 152
Dolores River Brewery, 169
downtown Denver pub crawl, 204
Dry Dock Brewing Company, 46
Dry Dock Double IPA, 187
Durango Brewing Co., 160

E

Eddyline Restaurant & Brewery, 132
Eldo Brewery and Taproom, 170
Elk Mountain Brewing, 48
Equinox Brewing Company, 86, 216
Equinox Eclipse Brown, 188
Estes Park Brewery, 107
Euclidean 75, 202
Euclid Hall Bar & Kitchen, 32, 204

F

Falling Rock Tap House, 33, 206
Foam Fest: At the Colorado State
   Fair, 180
Fort Collins Brewery, 88, 214
Fort Collins pub crawl, 214
Freshcraft, 34, 204
Front-Range Shandy, 203

Funkwerks, 91, 214
Funkwerks Saison, 189

G

Glenwood Canyon Brewing
   Company, 153
Golden City Brewery, 50
Grand Lake Brewing Company, 149
Great American Beer Festival
   (GABF), 182
Great Divide Anniversary Party, 179
Great Divide Brewing Company,
   13, 206
Grimm Brothers Brewhouse, 109
Grimm Brothers Snow Drop, 190

H

Hops & Pie, 36, 208
Hops & Pie IPA Mac & Cheese, 199
Horsefly Brewing Company, 171

K

Kannah Creek Brewing Company, 154

L

Left Hand Brewing Company, 110
Lone Tree Brewing Company, 52

M

Mayor of Old Town, The, 101, 217
Mountain Sun Pub & Brewery,
   73, 212

N

New Belgium Brewing Company,
   92, 216

O

Odell Brewing Company, 94, 214
Odell Small Batch Revival, 177
Oskar Blues Brewery, 113
Oskar Blues Home Made Liquids
   & Solids, 120
Ouray Brewery, 172

P

Pagosa Brewing Company, 173
Pagosa Poor Richard's Ale, 191
Pateros Creek Brewing Company,
   97, 216
Pateros Creek Cache la Porter, 192
Phantom Canyon Brewing
   Company, 134
Pikes Peak Brewing Co., 136
Pint's Pub Brewery & Freehouse,
   25, 208
Pitcher's Brewery & Sports
   Shack, 117
Pug Ryan's Steakhouse &
   Brewery, 155
Pumphouse Brewery &
   Restaurant, 118

R

Rackhouse Pub, 37, 210
Renegade Brewing Company,
   15, 210
Revolution Brewing, 161
River North Brewery, 17, 207
Rock Bottom Restaurant &
   Brewery, 26, 204
Rockslide Restaurant & Brewery, 156
Rockyard American Grill & Brewing
   Company, 55

Rocky Mountain Brewery, 128
Rusty Bus, 203

S

San Luis Valley Brewing
   Company, 137
Shamrock Brewing Company, 138
Silverton Brewing Company, 163
Ska Brewing Company, 164
Smuggler Joe's Brew Pub, 174
South Denver pub crawl, 210
Southern Sun Pub & Brewery, 73
Star Bar Denver, 38, 206
Steamworks Brewing Company, 174
Steamworks Steam Engine
   Lager, 193
Stonehenge Stout BBQ Sauce, 197
Stout Creme Brûlée, 201
Strange Brewing Company, 18, 210
Summer Brew Fest, 179

T

Telluride Blues and Brews
   Festival, 181
Telluride Brewing Company, 166
Tommyknocker Brewery, 115
Trinity Brewing Company, 139, 141
Twisted Pine Brewing Company,
   68, 212

U

Upslope Belgo, 194
Upslope Brewing Company, 70
uptown Denver pub crawl, 208

V

Vanilla Porter Beeramisu, 200

Vine St. Pub & Brewery, 38, 73, 209

W
Walnut Brewery, 75, 212
Wazee Supper Club, 39, 206
West End Tavern, The, 78, 212
Winter Brew Fest, 176

Wit's End Brewing Company, 20
Wit's End Slam Dunkelweizen, 195
Wynkoop Brewing Company,
  28, 206

Y
Yak & Yeti Restaurant & Brewpub, 56